Language to go

INTERMEDIATE

TEACHER'S RESOURCE BOOK

Araminta Crace and Robin Wileman

with Rolf Donald, Robert Armitage and Kenna Bourke

Series Editor: Simon Greenall

Longman

www.longman.com

Pearson Education Limited
Edinburgh Gate, Harlow
Essex CM20 2JE, England
and Associated Companies throughout the world.

www.language-to-go.com

Language to go is a trademark of Pearson Education Limited.

© Pearson Education Limited 2002

First published in 2002
Second impression 2003
Set in 10pt Univers Light

Printed in Spain by Mateu Cromo, S. A. Pinto (Madrid)

ISBN 0 582 40415 0

Publishing Acknowledgements

Development Editors: Caroline Mapus-Smith, Bernie Hayden.
Editors: Caroline Mapus-Smith, Catriona Watson-Brown,
Shona Rodger.

We are grateful to the author's agent for permission to
reproduce extracts from *Harry Potter and the Philosopher's
Stone* by J K Rowling, © J K Rowling 1997 and to Bloomsbury
for permission to reproduce the cover illustration of
Harry Potter and the Philosopher's Stone by J K Rowling from
original artwork by Thomas Taylor.

Designed by Gemini Design.
Cover design by Juice Creative.
Series design by Steve Pitcher.
Photographs of the authors on page 10 by: Trevor Clifford (top)
and James Walker (bottom).

Illustrated by: Gary Andrews, David Cuzik (Pennant Inc.),
Kes Hankin and Mark Vallance (Gemini Design) and Ian West.

We are grateful to the following for their permission to
reproduce copyright photographs:
The Image Bank / Ghislain & Marie David de Lossy for 111 (right).
Stone / Charles Gupton for 111 (left).

Front cover photographs left to right:
Telegraph Colour Library; Photo Disc; Corbis Stock Market;
Superstock.

Contents

Contents map of Students' Book

The past

The present

The future

Vocabulary

Modals

Connecting

The perfect

Functions

Conditionals

Verb patterns

5

Introduction

About *Language to go*

Many adult students of English have a limited amount of time for their studies. They may require English for both professional and social reasons, and are also aware that they're likely to use it in a number of international situations. They need to ensure that the time they spend on their English learning is highly focused and goal oriented. They need to be able to achieve certain tasks and to leave a language class, sometimes after a busy and tiring day of working or studying, with a bite-sized chunk of *Language to go* and a sense of 'Yes, I can do that – anywhere in the world, in English!'

Language to go is a short course for this kind of adult student. Our underlying principle is that students start the class with an objective defined in terms of a realistic outcome, and finish with the language they need to achieve it. So here's a quick overview of what the course contains:

- Four levels: Elementary, Pre-Intermediate, Intermediate and Upper Intermediate. Each level has 40 teaching lessons, and each lesson has been carefully written so that it takes around 60 minutes in the classroom.
- A Practice section, a Grammar reference and the recording scripts at the back of the Students' Book.
- A detachable Phrasebook in the Students' Book.
- A class cassette or CD with the listening material.
- This Teacher's Resource Book, containing a step-by-step guide to every lesson (including answer keys), photocopiable activities, photocopiable tests and a writing bank.
- The *Language to go* website (www.language-to-go.com).

Language to go – a closer look

Students' Book

Content
Each teaching lesson is designed to last 60 minutes and is contained on two facing pages, which reinforces visually the relationship between the Students' Book lesson and the classroom lesson. It focuses on a final activity, by presenting and practising the language required and then inviting students to perform the activity at the end of the lesson. The lesson begins with a presentation of the vocabulary needed for the final activity, then continues with reading or listening material which presents the target structure(s) in a meaningful context. This is followed by some inductive grammar work, focusing on the meaning and the form of the structure, and by some practice exercises. Students should now be equipped to do the final activity in the *Get talking* section at the end of the lesson, which is sometimes accompanied by a *Get writing* section. The *Language to go* is exemplified in an easily memorised dialogue in the bottom corner of each right-hand page and acts as the focus and goal of the lesson.

Motivation is at the core of successful learning in general, and language learning in particular; we have therefore taken great care to choose topics and texts which will stimulate the student intellectually as well as linguistically. Much of the material has been chosen so that it reflects the international community of English users, as native or non-native speakers.

We have tried to use as many international contexts as possible, since we're aware that our students will use their newly acquired linguistic competence not just in their own country or in an English-speaking one, but all around the world.

Cyclical syllabus
The course design of Pre-Intermediate, Intermediate and Upper Intermediate is based on a **cyclical syllabus**, in which different aspects of language, such as tenses, modals, vocabulary or functions, are presented several times in the same level. The advantage of this approach is that the structures can be naturally revised, recycled and consolidated on a regular and frequent basis. It also allows schools and institutes with a system of continuous enrolment to ensure that students who arrive later in the course are not disadvantaged by missing out on lessons which have already dealt with key structures.

At Elementary level, we have not used a cyclical syllabus, as it does not meet the needs of Elementary students, for whom a specific sequence of acquiring language is more useful. It is also true that this level lends itself less well to courses with continuous enrolment.

The principal **syllabuses** in the course are Grammar and Vocabulary. The approach to grammar is largely one of guided discovery in which the students are presented with examples of the target structure and then invited to work out the rules relating to form and meaning. Much of the vocabulary is presented in chunks as well as individual words, to reflect the way we use English in real life.

Skills

The **skills** of reading, listening, writing and speaking are all practised. Speaking is at the core of the philosophy of *Language to go*, and is the skill most often practised, both in the *Get talking* sections and in the pair and group work activities. The reading and listening material includes examples of English which may be beyond the immediate level of students, but is treated in a way which prepares them for dealing with it in a real-life context. Writing is deliberately not practised extensively, since we feel that it is a skill which can be more usefully developed outside the classroom, allowing the interactive opportunities of the classroom to be exploited to their maximum on a short course. However, several lessons also include a *Get writing* activity, and further guidance is given in the Writing bank in this book.

Pronunciation is dealt with wherever it is appropriate to the grammar or the vocabulary syllabus strands, focusing on stress in words, stress in sentences and intonation patterns rather than individual phonemes.

Additional material

The **Practice section** provides further exercises to consolidate the language taught in the main lesson. For teachers who have classes lasting longer than 60 minutes, it can be used in class, either after the *Practice* exercises or at the end of the main lesson. The exercises in the Practice section can also be set for homework and have been written so that students can work on them alone.

The **Grammar reference** is designed to be a more descriptive explanation of the grammar points covered in the main teaching lesson.

Phrasebook

This is a reformulation of some of the language taught in the course, as well as a reminder of other relevant words and expressions which are appropriate to the level, and presented in a familiar phrasebook style. A traditional phrasebook, with its list of useful words and expressions, is at the core of the concept of *Language to go*; in other words, language which is organised and can be readily accessed when required in real-life situations.

Teacher's Resource Book

This book contains:
- a lesson-by-lesson contents map;
- this introduction, with an overview of the course;
- some tips on how to make the most of the material;
- a personal statement from the authors;
- how *Language to go* links with external examinations;
- a phonemic chart;
- step-by-step Teaching notes for each lesson including answer keys;
- photocopiable activities;
- photocopiable Tests with answer key;
- photocopiable Writing bank.

Photocopiable activities

Teachers who have more than 60 minutes' class time available may wish to provide further skills practice, so we have provided some extra material. There are 40 extra activities, each one corresponding to a Students' Book lesson, which are designed to be photocopied and distributed to the students. Each activity will provide a further twenty to 30 minutes' practice of the language taught in the lesson. The teaching notes opposite each photocopiable activity are for your reference, providing a guide to how the activity should be organised and answer keys where relevant.

Photocopiable tests and answer keys

These are to be used to check on the students' progress at regular intervals during the course. There are four for each level, and they focus on the vocabulary and grammar covered in every ten lessons. So the ideal time to do these tests will be when you have finished Lessons 10, 20, 30 and 40.

Photocopiable writing bank

This can be used at any point in the course when you think it appropriate for students' needs, or to help guide them with a particular *Get writing* activity.

The *Language to go* website

By clicking onto www.language-to-go.com, you will find material of interest to both students and teachers, including further interactive practice exercises for each lesson.

Language to go is an exciting and innovative course of international English. It combines the basic requirements of a tightly focused and minimalist short course with the wealth of materials appropriate to the learning potential of adults in the 21st century. It contains topics and texts designed to motivate adult students with social and professional reasons for learning English. It has been written with a mixture of enthusiasm, passion and pedagogical rigour by a team of talented authors, and produced by editors, designers, researchers and many others with much love and care. So, now it's over to you with *Language to go*. We hope you and your students enjoy it.

Simon Greenall
Series Editor

A few ideas for classroom procedures

Personalisation

Most adult students of English are willing to trust their teachers because they believe everything they do is in their best interests. But now and then, they must ask themselves, 'Why am I doing this? How is this relevant to me?' When this happens, both student and teacher are faced with a potential challenge to their motivation.

Personalisation allows students to relate material to their own world. It is therefore a key factor in maintaining their motivation, especially during challenging activities like roleplays. The teacher has to make sure the student understands how an activity relates to their language-learning needs. Every activity in *Language to go* is designed to allow maximum personalisation for students. The lessons are all constructed around a final activity, and these activities will usually provide an opportunity for them to adapt the language being used to their own circumstances. For example, during the presentation of a new topic, there is usually an appeal to the student to think about how much they might know about it. On other occasions, there may be an invitation to use the target vocabulary or grammar in sentences which are relevant to the student.

If you feel that personalisation might be lacking at any stage, for example, after a vocabulary exercise, you could suggest that students choose four or five words which they think might be useful to them, or which look like words in their language, or which sound nice, or which they can place in categories of their own choice. After a grammar activity, encourage students to write a couple of sentences about themselves using the target structure.

You don't need to correct these extra activities, although you may want to ask them to share their answers with the rest of the class. In this way, personalisation can have two purposes: to consolidate the learning process and to make what they're doing relevant to themselves.

Vocabulary

The words and expressions which form the focus of the Vocabulary sections are those which we think are important at this level. Most lessons only contain between eight and ten items for productive learning (that is, words which the student should be able to use in spoken or written work, and not words which they are able to recognise).

Many of the vocabulary items are grouped in topics; others are grouped according to some of the rules behind word formation or collocation in English.

Encourage students to keep a vocabulary list containing all the items which they have learnt. Try to ensure that the list categorises the words in different ways, in order to consolidate the learning process.

When students ask for help in understanding words, try not to explain too many immediately, but ask them to help each other, or to use dictionaries if they're available in the classroom. Remember also that explaining new words may build their vocabulary, but it may not develop their ability to work out the meaning of words in reading and listening activities.

Speaking

There are many opportunities for speaking practice in *Language to go*. Firstly, there are many pair and group work activities based on a reading, listening, grammar or vocabulary task. Secondly, there are some lessons which focus on functional language where there is a clear model of the language to be used. Thirdly, most of the final activities in the lesson (*Get talking*) are opportunities to practise speaking. Remember to aim for a balance between accuracy and fluency; not every activity needs your close and careful correction of errors.

Listening

The listening material contains examples of everyday, natural spoken English. Students may be worried by the speed of delivery, thinking that it's too fast, so reassure them that this is also quite normal in real life, and that the classroom is the best place to be exposed to this type of natural language. They don't need to speak as fast themselves, but they do need practice in understanding authentic spoken English. The following guidelines should help them:

- Encourage students to focus on the main ideas of the listening passage and not get distracted by words they don't understand. The main activity will usually help them to do this.
- Help them to interpret clues from the context (situation, tone of voice etc.). This will usually enable them to understand a great deal more than the words will convey.
- Play the recording a couple of times (more than this will start to compromise their motivation), even if the instructions only suggest once.
- Try not to play the recording and stop after every phrase, as this will not give them the important practice in listening to the discourse of spoken English.

Writing

Writing is usually suggested in the *Get writing* sections as a way of showing that students have mastered the language which has been focused on in the lesson. They are all meant to be classroom versions of situations they may encounter outside the classroom – letters, e-mails, exam-style essays etc. The *Writing bank* in this Teacher's Resource Book provides photocopiable models of these writing genres with accompanying suggestions on how to exploit them in class.

Encourage students to practise a form of *process writing*: ask them to write down as much as they can without worrying too much about being accurate. Then ask them to reread what they have written, or maybe even show it to a partner. Encourage them to be critical and to revise their work if necessary. Then ask them to write a final version which incorporates extra ideas and all their corrections. Remember that writing can be an exercise in fluency as well as accuracy.

Reading

Much of the reading material involves words which students may not have come across, just like in real life. Many of the accompanying activities are designed both to support their general understanding of the passage as they read it, and to check their comprehension afterwards.

Try not to answer questions about difficult words, but instead, encourage students to work out the meaning for themselves.

Make sure that students read the passage once, perhaps at the end of the lesson, just to enjoy it, to respond with natural interest to it and without having to answer difficult questions!

Roleplays

The roleplays are presented as a further opportunity for students to practise speaking. Some students enjoy roleplays, especially in a foreign language. Others find they make enormous demands on their imagination. For this reason, we have tried to provide suitable support into the roleplays, so that less imaginative or creative students don't feel under pressure to come up with all the ideas themselves. Go round the pairs or groups as they are doing the roleplays, listening but not interrupting, unless they want help in what they need to do.

Try to avoid correcting students as they are doing their roleplays, but make a note of major mistakes, if you wish, and discuss them with the whole class at the end of the lesson.

Error correction

It's a good idea to think about what and when you correct before the lesson begins. Make this decision part of your lesson plan.

It's best to avoid correction during an activity which focuses on fluency until after it's over; on the other hand, it may be best to correct students in an activity which focuses on accuracy as they do it. Look at each activity in turn, decide what its aim is and choose the best strategy.

Remember that less-confident students will need more encouragement than others, and your correction may compromise their motivation. You may also decide you only want to indicate the student has made an error rather than correct it yourself. Think carefully about your attitude to error correction, and share your opinions with the whole class.

Jigsaw reading

Some activities involve a technique known as *jigsaw reading*. This involves students working in pairs. The first instruction will be to work separately on a reading passage, with separate but complementary tasks to perform. This usually involves them turning to a specified text or activity in the *Information for pair and group work* section at the back of the Students' Book. The second instruction will be to work together and to share the information they have gathered from the separate tasks.

This technique is at the very heart of communicative language teaching, as it involves an information gap (Student A knows something that Student B doesn't, and vice versa) and a meaningful exchange of information during the second stage of the activity, where the students tell each other what they have learnt.

As long as the students understand the instructions, it's best for the teacher simply to signal the start of the two stages of the activity, and listen as the pairs/groups perform it. You can finish the activity sequence with group feedback to check the answers are correct.

Pronunciation

Pronunciation work in *Language to go* focuses more on word and sentence stress and intonation patterns than on individual phonemes. There are several techniques you can use:

- *Drilling* can be individual or choral repetition of a word or a sentence. Choral repetition with the whole class is a way of building up students' confidence in pronouncing strange words or new sentences.
- *Backchaining* involves the repetition of different parts of a sentence, often starting at the end, and gradually adding parts until you have reconstituted the whole sentence.
- *Word linking* focuses on the fact that when you say words in connected speech, the individual phonemes which make up the word may change. Say the words separately, then say them in connected speech and emphasise the way in which they sound different.

The *Language to go* authors

Araminta Crace

Robin Wileman

Araminta Crace and Robin Wileman

Araminta (Minty) and Robin live in North London with their two young daughters, Petra and Lola. Robin's grown-up children (Matilda and triplets Joe, Tim and Georgia) live nearby.

Minty works full time from home as a freelance writer of English-teaching materials. She has taught in Brazil, Egypt, Portugal and Spain. She also worked for many years as a teacher trainer at International House, London. Robin is based at International House, London, as a teacher trainer. His professional experience has taken him to Argentina, Brazil, Ecuador, Georgia, Indonesia, Italy, Poland, Russia, Ukraine, Vietnam and many other countries! He frequently travels abroad as an assessor of schools and training courses.

We believe that *Language to go* is …

fast: Our aim is that students get useable language fast. The clear contexts and realistic practice mean that language can be learnt quickly. At the end of each lesson, we hope students will feel confident about using the language they have learnt both *inside* and *outside* the classroom.

stimulating: We believe that both teachers and students will be genuinely interested in the material. The book is divided into 40 separate lessons, each with a different and (hopefully) engaging topic. Across the four levels, this means there are 160 different angles. There is a range of real-life scenarios which are original, up-to-date and international.

user-friendly: We have structured each lesson very carefully to aid both new and more experienced teachers. There should be little need to 'cut and paste' – each stage flows logically to the next. Lessons which can almost teach themselves should save valuable planning time and give both teachers and students confidence in the classroom.

flexible: The idea of the course is that it is both compact *and* expandable. Compact because each lesson is teachable in one hour. Expandable because of the Practice section, the Photocopiable activities, the extra ideas in the Teaching Notes, as well as the website. This 'shrink-stretch' feature means the book is suitable for a wide variety of course types and will cater for a wide range of student needs.

balanced: Within each lesson, there is vocabulary, grammar, receptive and productive skills. There are controlled and freer practice activities and lots of opportunities for students to speak.

international: We think the lessons have a broad appeal to students from many backgrounds and with varied interests. They provide the basis for communicating confidently in many situations internationally.

We very much enjoyed having the opportunity to write this book as part of the series and we really appreciate the care and hard work of all those involved in the process. We hope you enjoy using it.

Language to go and EFL exams

The table below shows *general* equivalences between the four levels of *Language to go* and two well-known international examination boards, UCLES (University of Cambridge Local Examinations Syndicate) and Trinity College, in terms of the language taught and the topics covered in the four books.

While *Language to go* is not an examination preparation course, a student who has, for example, completed the Elementary level would have sufficient language to attempt UCLES KET, and start a preparation course for UCLES PET. Examination training is required for all EFL examinations, and we would strongly advise students to follow an examination preparation course. But you will find that some of the exercises in the Students' Book lessons, the Practice section and the photocopiable Tests are similar in format to those found in EFL public examinations.

Note that higher-level exams, such as UCLES CPE and ESOL Grades 11–12, are not covered in this table.

For further information, contact:

UCLES
English as a Foreign Language
1 Hills Road
Cambridge
CB1 2EU
United Kingdom
Tel: +44 (0) 1223 553355
Fax: +44 (0) 1223 460278
E-mail: eflhelpdesk@ucles.org.uk
www.ucles.org.uk

Trinity College
89 Albert Embankment
London
SE1 7TP
United Kingdom
Tel: +44 (0)20 7820 6100
Fax: +44 (0)20 7820 6161
E-mail: info@trinitycollege.co.uk
www.trinitycollege.co.uk

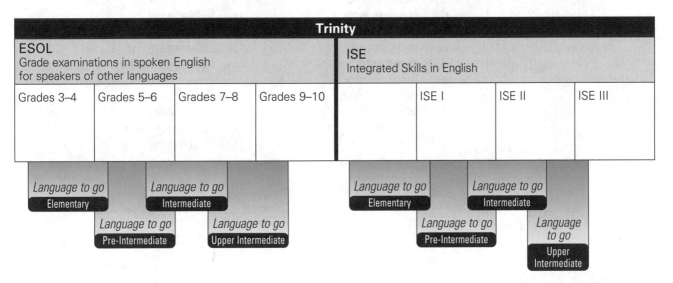

Phonemic symbols

The symbols in this chart represent the sounds used in standard British English and some of the most common variations in American English. We have used the symbols in the Teaching notes to help clarify pronunciation points dealt with in the lesson. We have not included them in the Students' Book, because we feel it is not always easy or practical to teach them on a short course or a course involving continuous enrolment.

However, you may find it useful to introduce certain symbols to students to help them with their individual pronunciation needs. If you do, we would recommend that you:
• only teach a few symbols at a time – little and often;
• get students to practise the sounds, but do not aim for perfection – a comprehensible approximation is good enough;
• relate the symbols to words which students already know.

The example words here are all taken from the Longman defining vocabulary of 2,000 words used in *The Longman Active Study Dictionary* and *The Longman Dictionary of Contemporary English*.

Consonants

p	pen; paper
b	boy; table
t	to; sit
d	do; made
k	car; make
g	go; big
f	four; wife
v	very; live
θ	think; tooth
ð	this; other
s	say; bus
z	zero; has
ʃ	shop; wash
ʒ	television; pleasure
h	have; ahead
tʃ	cheese; watch
dʒ	job; bridge
m	man; come
n	name; ten
ŋ	thing; singer
w	water; flower
l	late; yellow
r	run; carry
j	yes; you

Vowels

ɪ	it; sister
e	egg; said
æ	at; have
ɒ	on; dog (UK)
ɒː	on; dog (US)
ʌ	up; mother
ʊ	put; book
ə	address; brother
iː	easy; she
ɑː	art; father
ɔː	all; door
uː	boot; shoe
ɜː	early; work

Diphthongs

eɪ	able; wait
aɪ	I; buy
ɔɪ	toy; noise
əʊ	over; go (UK)
oʊ	over; go (US)
aʊ	out; town
ɪə	ear; here
eə	air; there (UK)
ʊə	sure; poor

Teaching notes

by Araminta Crace and Robin Wileman

Vocabulary Adjectives and intensifiers
Grammar Past simple and continuous
Language to go Telling stories and exaggerating events

It's absolutely true!

Language notes
- The vocabulary highlighted in Exercise 2 looks at ordinary and extreme adjectives. Problem areas are likely to be with the use of the intensifiers *very*, *really* and *absolutely*. *I'm absolutely tired*, [very] *He's very exhausted*. [absolutely]
- The lesson also reviews the past simple and the past continuous. The past continuous is especially useful for setting the context of a story (whereas the past simple is used for describing the events of a story). It can also describe longer actions, interrupted by shorter actions in the past simple, e.g. *It was raining when she arrived*.

Way in
- If this is your first lesson with the class, introduce yourself and write your name on the board. If students don't know each other, you may want to do further introductions or 'getting to know you' activities.

Vocabulary and speaking
1 Ask students to discuss in pairs what festival or public holiday in their country they like the best, and how they celebrate it. Do not spend too long on this warm-up activity.
   - Ask students to look at the photos and discuss the questions in pairs. Prompt them as necessary using further questions or information, e.g. *When is it? Why do they celebrate it?*

   Background information
   Carnival attracts thousands of local people and tourists. It was originally a celebration of indulgence lasting for four days before the Christian festival of Lent.
   In Rio, there is a lot of music, dancing and drinking in the streets during Carnival. The most important event, however, is in a special 'stadium' called the *Sambodromo* (in English: *Sambadrome*), where there is a big competition of all the samba schools in the city.

2 Tell students to match the easy adjectives first, then ask each other for help with the more difficult ones.
   - Check their answers. Focus also on correct pronunciation.

   interesting – fa̲scinating;   good – fan<u>tas</u>tic;
   crowded – packed;   tired – ex<u>haus</u>ted;
   big – e̲normous;   bad – awful.

3 Get students to describe the photos of Carnival using adjectives from Exercise 2, e.g. *It looks really packed*.
4 ▭▭ Students work individually to try to fill the gaps before they listen.
   - Play the recording (more than once, if necessary) and get students to check their answers.

   1 very; boiling   2 tired; absolutely   3 very; packed
   4 very; enormous   5 good; absolutely

   - Students work in pairs to discover the rules about intensifiers.

   very cannot be used in front of extreme adjectives like *boiling*
   absolutely cannot be used in front of ordinary adjectives like *hot*
   really can be used in front of both.

- If time, students repeat the dialogues in pairs, focusing on correct intonation.

Listening
5 ▭▭ Focus attention on the photo. Ask students to think of an adjective Sara might use to describe Carnival.
   - Play the recording and ask students to answer the question.

   She had a fantastic time.

6 Allow time for students to read the sentences before listening again.
   - Students check their answers in pairs.
   - Go through the answers.

   1 T   2 T   3 T   4 T   5 F

7 Refer students to the sentences in Exercise 6 and ask: *What tense is 'was staying'?* (past continuous). Ask students to circle the verb.
   - Students work in pairs to identify the other tenses.

   Past simple: *arrived, stopped, started*
   Past continuous: *was staying, was raining, were planning, was waiting*

Grammar focus
8 Students work individually to make the rules.

   1 b   2 c   3 a

Practice
9 Tell students to look at the example. Check understanding by asking: *Which verb is in the past continuous? Why?* (*was waiting*. It is a long action interrupted by meeting Tom).
   - Students do the activity and check with a partner.
   - Go through the answers.

   1 went   2 was driving; saw   3 was listening; didn't hear   4 Did you see; was wearing
   5 made; didn't eat   6 was enjoying; didn't realise

Get talking
10 Ask students to look at the ideas and decide what story to tell. You may want to give an example of something that happened to you.
   - Students write notes to prepare the outline story. Walk round the class, giving help as needed.
   - Students use their notes to tell their story to a partner. Encourage them to ask each other questions about their stories.

... and writing
11 Remind students how to start an informal letter and also to exaggerate the events in their story.
   - Encourage students to edit their own writing and to check their partner's.
   - For an example of a story, see **Writing Bank 1** page 146.

LESSON 2
The present

Vocabulary Sleep
Grammar Subject and object questions
Language to go Asking about and describing routines

Are you a morning person?

Language notes

- Some of the phrases in Exercise 1 have similar but different meanings, e.g. *have a lie-in* is intended, while *oversleep* is not intended. Other phrases are fixed and are best learned as chunks, e.g. *He got out of bed on the wrong side! I can't keep my eyes open. I need an early night.*
- Auxiliary verbs are only necessary for object questions. Students may try to use auxiliary verbs with subject questions e.g. *Who did wake you up this morning?* [woke]. Concept questions like *Is 'who' the subject of the question?* (Yes), and *Is an auxiliary verb necessary?* (No), can help clarify this for students.

Vocabulary and speaking

1   Ask students to work in pairs and to give reasons for their answers.

2   Tell students the phrases in the box are all to do with sleep. Do an example with the whole class, to check they understand what to do.
- Students match the phrases and definitions.
- Check their answers and point out the differences in meaning. See also **Language notes** above.

> 1 b   2 f   3 a   4 h   5 j   6 g   7 c   8 d   9 e
> 10 i

3   Ask students how they could describe the man in picture A using phrases from Exercise 2.
- In pairs, students describe the pictures. Make sure they are using the new vocabulary accurately.

> Picture A: He's not a morning person. He can't keep his eyes open. He got out of bed on the wrong side.
> Picture B: She's a morning person. She didn't oversleep. She's an early riser.
> Picture C: He overslept today. He's having a lie-in. He stayed up late last night.

Reading

4   Tell students that they are going to read about two of the people in the pictures.
- Encourage students to read quickly and not to worry about unknown words at this stage.

> Picture A is of Vic. Picture C could be of Gary or Raymond.

5   Ask students to look at the questions before reading the text again.
- Allow a few minutes for students to discuss the questions in pairs.
- Go through the answers

> 1 Tea and toast.   2 She doesn't like it.   3 Vic.
> 4 Sandra and Gary.   5 Raymond.   6 Their children.

Grammar focus

6   Ask students to discuss the questions in pairs before doing feedback.(See **Language notes**.)

> 1 the subject   2 the object   3 object questions
> 4 the same

7   Do an example with the class by telling students to look at question 1 in Exercise 5. Ask which auxiliary verb is used (did), and if it is a subject or object question (object).
- Students do the activity and check with a partner.
- Go through the answers.

> **Auxiliary verbs:** did, does, should and do
> **Subject questions:** Questions 3, 4 and 5
> **Object questions:** Questions 1, 2 and 6

Practice

8   Go through the example with students then ask them to do the exercise individually.
- Students check their answers in pairs.
- Go through the answers.

> 1 What does Marjorie wear for breakfast?
> 2 Who does Vic speak to first?
> 3 Who likes having a lie-in?
> 4 What does Vic glance at?
> 5 Who is taking Sandra to the doctor's?
> 6 What does Marjorie plan to do after the doctor's?
> 7 What does Marjorie say about the teachers?

Point out that answers are in the 'dramatic' present simple although it would be correct to use the past simple for questions 1, 2, 4, 6 and 7.

Get talking

9   Recheck the meaning of *a morning person* by asking students if it is a) *someone who gets up early* or b) *someone who is in a good mood in the mornings* (✓).
Tell students they are now going to do a survey to find the morning people in the class.
- In pairs, students make questions from the prompts to complete the questionnaire. Walk round the class as they prepare, giving help as needed.
- When students are ready, get someone to ask you (or another student) the first question.

> 2 What time do you get up?   3 What day do you have a lie-in?   4 Do you fall asleep in front of the TV?
> 5 Do you find it difficult to get up?   6 When do you have your best ideas?   7 Do you sometimes oversleep?
> 8 Do you find it hard to keep your eyes open?

They then ask and answer the questions in groups, making notes of the answers.
- At the end ask: *Who is (isn't) a morning person?* Write their names on the board. Encourage them to give reasons why they like or dislike mornings.

LESSON **3**

The future

Vocabulary Associations
Grammar Future with *will* and *going to*
Language to go Making decisions and giving reasons for decisions

What's in a name?

Language notes

- Exercise 1 focuses on words to do with associations. Encourage students to notice the words that come before and after the gaps: *remind* (somebody) *of* (something); *suggest* is followed by a noun or a pronoun; *make* (somebody) *think of* (something); *go + with* is followed by a noun or a pronoun; *image* is a noun and is often preceded by an adjective (e.g. *strong*); *sound + like* is followed by a noun or a pronoun; *suit* is followed by a noun or a pronoun; *associations* is a noun and is often preceded by an adjective (e.g. *happy*).
- Problem areas are likely to be the contrast between the use of *will* and *going to* based on the concept of *when* we make a decision, i.e. *before* or *at* the time of speaking.

Way in

- With the books closed, write or say: *Elvis, Flora, India, Augustus, Jorge, Lorna.*
- Ask students if they like these names. What do they make them think of?

Vocabulary and speaking

1 Check that students know which words in the box are nouns and which are verbs (see **Language notes**).
   - Do the first sentence as an example: read it to students and ask them which word from the box is correct. Suggest they look at the words before and after the gaps to help them decide.
   - Students read the gapped sentences. Allow time for them to focus on meaning.
   - Go through the answers. Check also for correct pronunciation: *image* /ˈɪmɪdʒ/, *associations*, *reminds*, *suggests*, *suits* /suːts/.

1 reminds	2 suggests	3 makes	4 go with
5 image	6 sounds	7 suits	8 associations

2 Perhaps talk about your name as an example. Students discuss the questions in pairs.
   - At the end, ask a few students to report an interesting fact about their partner.

Listening

3 Focus attention on the pictures. Ask students to describe what is happening.

   The mother and father want to name their new baby after someone they admire.
   Parents are choosing a name for their baby by using a name book.

   - Ask students to think of other ways of choosing a name.

4 ▭ Before playing the recording, read the names: Dawn, Lola and Matilda are girls' names. Stanley, George and Kevin are boys' names.
   - Play the recording and ask students to match the speaker with the correct child's name.

   See table in Exercise 5 for answers.

5 Tell students to look at the *Top 10 reasons* and find any reasons they hadn't thought of before.
   - Play the recording (more than once, if necessary).
   - Students listen to complete the table, then compare their answers with a partner.

Name	Speaker	Reason
Dawn	2	refers to the time of birth
Lola	3	creates a strong image
Kevin	5	famous person's name
George	4	name of a grandparent
Stanley	1	from a name book
Matilda	4	name of a grandparent

Grammar focus

6 Ask students to read the example sentences and decide which tense is being used in each example. (A *will*, B *going to*, C *will*). Draw attention to the negative *I don't think I'll call her …* instead of *I won't call her …* .
   - Students work individually to match the rules to the examples. Ask concept questions to check students understand the rules, e.g. *When did she make the decision? Before speaking?* (No) *At the moment of speaking?* (Yes) *So does she use* **will** *or* **going to**? (Will).

1 B	2 A	3 C

7 ▭ Stop the recording after each sentence for students to repeat. After sentence 1, ask students if they heard *I will* or *I'll*? (I'll). After sentence 3, ask students if they heard *going to* or *gonna?* (gonna).

Practice

8 Check students understand why we use *going to* in the example (because the decision was made before the time of speaking).
   - Students do the activity and check with a partner.
   - Go through the answers.

1 we're going to	2 I'll	3 are you going to
4 's going to; I'll	5 I'll	6 I will	7 aren't going to

Get talking

9 Ask students what the products are (watch, fashion magazine, toothpaste, ice lolly, can of dog food). Tell students to work individually to choose a name. Remind them that they can make up other names.
   - Divide students into groups to decide on the best names, and reasons for their choices. Encourage them to use language from the lesson, e.g. *We're **going to call** our watch Accurate because it **sounds** reliable.*
   - If time, have a 'pyramid discussion' to allow more speaking. After students have decided individually, they then decide in pairs. Then two pairs become a group of four, then two groups of four become a group of eight. At each stage, they have a short time limit and must come to a group decision for each product, with reasons.

Vocabulary Education
Grammar Comparatives and superlatives
Language to go Comparing careers

Career paths

Language notes

- The vocabulary in Exercise 1 is about education. Check students are clear about the difference between an *exam* (public and formal with national/international standards) and *a test* (usually at school – not public or formal). Also *qualifications* (proof that you have passed exams), *a degree* (a qualification you get when you pass your university course) and *good (or bad) grades* (to show how well, or badly, you do at school).
- This lesson reviews comparative and superlative structures. Students may need extra practice to say the constructions fluently and accurately. Draw students' attention to weak forms (reduced stress on grammatical words and some modal verbs) e.g. *than* /ðæn/ (strong) and *than* /ðən/ (weak). Also elision (the leaving out of sounds) of final consonants e.g. the final 't' of most in *the mos(t) successful*.

Way in

- Tell students they are going to read and talk about careers. Write the words *My ideal job is ...* on the board. Students complete the sentence in their own words. Ask them to read out their sentences. Is anyone doing their ideal job? How can students make their career 'dream' come true?

Vocabulary and speaking

1 Explain (or get a student to tell you) the meaning of the title *Career paths* (the history or different stages of someone's career).
- Focus students on the example and ask which other nouns collocate (or go with) the verb *get*.
- Students work in pairs to complete the exercise.
- Go through the answers checking the difference between words with similar meanings. See also **Language notes** above.

get a job / degree / good grades; go to / leave school / university / college; take / pass / fail a test / an exam

2 Ask students to work in pairs. At the end ask a few students to report back their ideas.

Reading

3 Focus attention on the photos of Carl and Gavin and ask students to predict what jobs they do.
- Students read the text to find the answers. Encourage them to read quickly and not to worry about any unknown words at this stage.

Gavin is unemployed. Carl is a Managing Director of a software company.

4 Ask students to look at the questions before reading the article for a second time.
- Students do the activity and check with a partner.
- Go through the answers.

1 T   2 F   3 F   4 T   5 F   6 F   7 T   8 F

Grammar focus

5 Focus attention on the comparative and superlative adjectives in the example sentences and use these to elicit rules from the class. (See **Grammar Reference** in the *Students' Book* pages 108–9.) Remind students about irregular forms (*good – better – the best* etc.) and constructions with *less...than* (comparatives) and *the least...*(superlatives). If necessary, write this on the board to check understanding:

Film A	Film B	Film C	Film D
not at all interesting	not very interesting	interesting	very interesting

the least   less than...   more than...   the most

2 *than* is a weak form /ðən/
3 *the* is a weak form /ðə/.

You may want to focus on other weak forms at this point.
-er /ə/ ; -est /əst/
Draw students' attention to the fact that some final consonants disappear before another consonant.
See also **Language notes** above.

6 ▭ Play the sentences one at a time allowing time for students to repeat accurately. (See page 9 for ways to deal with pronunciation.)

Practice

7 Go through the example with the class. Remind students to think about opposite adjectives, e.g. *old / new*.
- Students do the activity and check with a partner.
- Go through the answers.

Suggested answers
1 Gavin had a better education than Carl.
2 Yale University is newer than / isn't as old as Cambridge University.
3 Gavin's career path was safer / less risky than Carl's.
4 Gavin was the most expensive lecturer.
5 Carl was (probably) the least interested student in his school.
6 Last week's test was easier than today's test.

Get talking

8 Check that students understand the meaning of all the words in the box. They may not know *satisfied* (pleased), *stressed* (worried), *benefits* (advantages). Ask concept questions to check understanding, e.g. *What's another word for 'satisfied'?, Which things make people feel stressed and why?, What are the benefits of working for yourself?*
- Divide students into small groups to think of ways to compare the three people on page 84. Draw attention to the example on page 11 and encourage them to be creative.
- Walk round the class listening to the discussions. At the end write three or four mistakes you noted during the discussion on the board, and ask students to correct them. See page 9 for ways to deal with error correction:

Vocabulary Levels of difficulty
Grammar Modal verbs for ability
Language to go Describing abilities and difficulties

On the other hand

Language notes

- The title *On the other hand* is a play on words, rather than the usual meaning of the phrase (to offer an alternative idea or suggestion, e.g. *We could go to the beach. On the other hand, we could go shopping.*).
- In Exercise 1 students may have problems with *manageable* (able to succeed although it was difficult) and *complicated* (difficult to understand). Point out that *tough* /tʌf/ and *a piece of cake* are quite informal expressions.
- *Could* is used to talk about *general* ability in the past and *was/were able to* and *managed to* for ability on a *specific* occasion. Typical student errors may include sentences like *My memory is not good but I ~~could~~ learn all those irregular verbs last night.* [*was able to* or *managed to*]

Vocabulary and speaking

1　📖 Tell students that the highlighted vocabulary is to do with describing how difficult (or easy) we find things. Ask students to look at the examples then work in pairs to do the activity.
　　• Play the recording so students can check their answers. Allow time for students to repeat the words. See also **Language notes** above.

EASY	OK	DIFFICULT
a piece of cake	manageable	tough
straightforward	possible	complicated
simple		impossible
no trouble		hard

2　Focus attention on the photos and ask students to describe what is happening and how the children might be feeling.
　　• Talk about your experiences, e.g. *When I first rode a bicycle, I found it hard. It was impossible to balance.*
　　• In pairs, students talk about their own experiences. Encourage students to use the new vocabulary accurately.

3　Give students a time limit (five minutes) to discuss the questions. After they have checked the answers, ask them if anything was surprising.

Listening

4　📖 Ask if anyone in the class is left-handed. If so, do they use their 'other' hand (i.e. their right hand) for anything, e.g. can openers, scissors?
　　• Refer students to the list of topics and ask them to tick any that are mentioned on the recording.
　　• Play the recording.

tennis ✓　writing ✓　drawing ✓
being ambidextrous ✓

5　📖 Focus attention on the pictures and table and ask which test they think will be the hardest/easiest.
　　• Play the recording (more than once, if necessary) for students to listen and make notes.
　　• Students check with a partner. Go through the answers and play the recording again for a final check.

	Mike	Joanna
1 Throw a ball	quite easy with either hand	a piece of cake
2 Write a message	hard at first – then OK	couldn't write well
3 Cut with scissors	straightforward – easier with right hand	easier with right hand than left
4 Draw a face	very good!	wasn't able to hold pencil properly

Grammar focus

6　Refer students to the recording script and ask them to find the first example (*I managed to throw...*).
　　• Go through the answers, drawing attention to the verbs *can, could, managed to* and *was able to*. You may wish to write the answers on the board:

*I managed to throw the ball OK
I couldn't do that at all
I can read it OK
I found I could use them better with my right hand than I could with my left.
I wasn't able to hold my pencil properly!
Hmm, I can see that.*

7　Ask students to use the examples from the recording script to complete the rules. Remind students, if necessary, that *can* and *could* are followed by an infinitive, without *to*. *I can't ~~to~~ swim.*

1 can　2 could　3 was/were able to; managed to
4 couldn't; wasn't/weren't able to; didn't manage to

See also **Language notes** above.

Practice

8　Read the example and ask: *Is any other form possible and what is the rule?* (*was able to* is also possible; rule 3 – ability on a *specific* occasion in the *past*.)
　　• Students do the activity and check with a partner.
　　• Go over the answers referring back to the rules if necessary.

1 couldn't (*or* wasn't able to; *or* didn't manage to)
2 can't
3 could; could
4 can't
5 could
6 not able to
7 managed to (*or* was able to)
8 couldn't (*or* wasn't able to *or* didn't manage to)

Get talking

9　Put students into small groups.
　　• Remind them of the four ability tests that Mike and Joanna did.
　　• Ask students to predict their levels of ability but not to do the tests yet.
　　• Give each group a pair of scissors, a tennis ball (or ball of paper) a waste bin (or other kind of 'target') and some paper. Tell them to take notes and discuss their progress. Remind them to use the vocabulary and grammar of the lesson.
　　• If time, you may want to do a quick round-up and compare results of the ability tests around the class.

Vocabulary	Crime
Vocabulary	Adverbs of purpose
Language to go	Describing reasons for actions

Corporate spying

Language notes

- The grammar focus deals with adverbs of purpose. Point out that *in order to* and *so as (not) to* are more formal than *to,* although the meaning is the same. *So that* also has the same meaning but the form is different. Students may confuse *in order to* (describes the purpose of an action and answers the question *why?*) with *in case* (more specific and means *as a way of preparing for and being safe from something that might happen*).

Vocabulary and speaking

1   Read the example with the class. Ask: *Which is correct, 'looking at' or 'spying on'?* (*looking at*). Don't clarify *why* answers are correct at this stage. *CCTV = closed circuit television.*
    - Students do the activity and check in pairs.

    1 looking at   2 Thieves; stole   3 evidence; suspect
    4 accused   5 dishonest   6 deny

2   Explain (or get a student to tell you) the difference between *look at* and *spy on* (*look at* is not done secretly. *Spy on* means to watch secretly.) Ask for an example sentence to show they understand *spy on.*
    - Students work in pairs to find the difference between the pairs of words. If possible provide students with monolingual dictionaries.

    2 *Mugger(s):* someone who attacks people and robs them in a public place. *Thieves* (singular: *thief*) steal anywhere. *Borrow* means it will be returned and you have the person's permission. *Steal* means it will not be returned and you don't have permission.
    3 *Evidence* is information about a crime. A *sentence* is the time a criminal spends in prison. A *suspect* is someone who is thought to be guilty of a crime. A *prisoner* is someone who is kept in prison as a punishment for a crime.
    4 Criminals *commit* crimes. Other people *accuse* criminals *of* committing crimes.
    5 A person can be *dishonest*, not *illegal*. An action can be both.
    6 *Admit a crime* is to agree that you did it. *Deny* is to say that you did not do it.

3   Check the meaning of *employee* and *employer* then get students to discuss the questions in pairs.
    - Encourage students to give reasons for their answers, but do not spend too long on this activity.

Reading

4   Focus attention on the photo. Remind students to think about Exercises 1–3 when describing it.

    1 They are looking at the CCTV / spying on a couple kissing.
    2 Any illegal activities, e.g. people stealing office equipment, robbery etc.

5   Ask students to read the headings. Set a time limit for this activity to encourage students to read for gist.
    - Students read the article and match the headings.

    Paragraph 1: B   Paragraph 2: A   Paragraph 3: C

6   Allow time for students to look at the questions before reading the text again and answering the questions.

    1 Recording movements and voices of employees to check that they are not doing anything illegal.
    2 To check that employees aren't claiming expenses illegally for personal use of their car.
    3 What employees do on their computers, e.g. websites they visit and e-mails they send.

    - Ask if students think employers are within their rights to take security measures like this.

Grammar focus

7   Tell students to look back at the article and underline the different ways of expressing purpose, then use the examples to complete the rules.
    - Go through the answers checking meaning and pointing out register and form as necessary. See **Language notes** above.

    | 1 *to* + <u>verb</u> | *to watch employees' virtual movements* (para. 3) |
    | 2 *in order to* + <u>verb</u> | *in order to spy on staff* (para. 1) |
    | 3 *so as (not) to* + <u>verb</u> | *so as to check on* (para. 2) |
    | 4 *so that* + <u>subject</u> + <u>verb</u> | *so that they can record* (para. 3) |
    | 5 *in case* + <u>subject</u> + <u>verb</u> | *in case workers are tempted* (para 2) |
    | 6 *for* + <u>verb</u> /-ing | *for watching* (para. 2) |

Practice

8   Check that students understand the phrase *to spy on my boyfriend* explains the reason for the action (*I'm getting a private detective*). Ask students another way of saying the same thing (*in order to spy*).
    - Students do the activity and check in pairs.
    - Go through the answers.

    1 ... for recording ...
    2 ... in case there's an emergency.
    3 ... to / in order to / so as to find evidence ...
    4 ... to / in order to / so as to catch ...
    5 ... in case anyone breaks ...
    6 ... so that nobody can open ...

Get talking ...

9   Divide the class into As and Bs and ask them to read their role card and prepare in small groups.
    - Walk round the class giving help as necessary. Remind As they only have £10,000 to spend.
    - In new groups (A+B), students do the roleplay.
    - At the end ask a few students to report back.

... and writing

10
    - Students write an e-mail to their company about the meeting. Group A write to the Managing Director of *Sweets'R'Us*. Group B write to the Sales Director of *Safe & Sound*.
    - For an example of an e-mail, see **Writing Bank 2** page 147.

Vocabulary Work
Grammar Present perfect simple
Language to go Talking about your experience

Teamwork

Language notes

- This is the first lesson on the present perfect. (See also Lessons 17, 27 and 37.) The present perfect is often used to open a topic of conversation. As soon as the context becomes clear (e.g. the time reference is made definite), we use the past simple to describe the events. Students often confuse these tenses and use the present perfect with a specific time: *I've applied for a job* ~~yesterday~~.

Way in

- Ask students to think of the advantages and disadvantages of working (or studying) in a team and on your own. Write ideas on the board, e.g. *share ideas, more fun, get more done, easier to concentrate.*
- Ask students to briefly discuss which they prefer and why.

Vocabulary and speaking

1 Focus attention on the picture and ask for words to describe the man, e.g. *He's overworked / disorganised.*
   - In pairs, students help each other to name as many things in the picture as possible.

   phone, fax machine, computer, pen, paper, filing cabinet, desk, chair, keyboard, mouse, mousepad, pencil, stapler, noticeboard

2 Students do the activity and check answers in pairs.

   use a computer   send a fax / an e-mail   work in a team   organise an event / a team   apply for a job / a promotion   go for an interview / a promotion / a job   write a report / an e-mail / a fax   get a promotion / a job   receive an e-mail / a fax

   - Point out that *go for a job / go for promotion* are informal.
   - Students discuss their experiences. The aim here is to practise vocabulary, so no need to correct grammatical mistakes.

Listening

3 Focus attention on the photo and ask: *What is the situation? (A job interview.) Who has applied for the Team Leader job? (Dan Gray.) What experience do you think is needed? (e.g. working in a team).*
   - Ask students to predict the answers to the two questions.
   - Play the recording, then go through the answers.

   1 No, he wasn't.
   2 He sounds badly prepared and too casual. He doesn't have any relevant experience.

4 Play the recording again for students to listen and make notes about his experience.
   - Students check in pairs. Go through the answers and play the recording again for a final check.

   He has worked in a team.
   He hasn't had a similar job before / used a computer / organised an event.

Grammar focus

5 Ask students to read the examples and work in pairs to complete the sentences.

   1 present perfect simple
   2 *has / have* + past participle
   3 past simple

6 Students work together to underline the correct alternatives.
   - Go through the answers checking students understand the time / experience distinction between the tenses. See also **Language notes**.

   1 present perfect simple / don't need
   2 past simple / need

7 Refer students to the recording script on page 119 to find other examples of the present perfect.

   Have you had a job like this before?
   Have you worked in an office?
   … have you ever used a computer?
   … no, I haven't.
   Have you organised an event?
   … you've applied for this job.
   … have you ever worked in a team? Yes, I have.

   Play the recording. Students listen and repeat. Point out that the auxiliary verb *have* is not stressed in questions: *Have you had a job like this before?* However, it is stressed in short answers: *Yes, I have, No, I haven't.*

Practice

8 Go through the example with the class.
   - Students do the activity and check their answers with a partner.
   - Go through the answers.

   1 Have you (ever) organised an event? No, I haven't.
   2 Have you (ever) worked in a team? Yes, I have.
     When did you work in a team? In March.
   3 Have you (ever) sent a fax? No, I haven't
   4 Have you (ever) applied for a job? Yes, I have.
     When did you apply for it? I applied last year.
   5 Have you (ever) gone for promotion? Yes, I have.
     Were you successful? Yes, I was.

9 Students work in pairs and answer with facts that are true for them.

Get talking

10 Check students understand the job advert. If you prefer, choose one that is more relevant to their interests.
   - Divide the class into two groups: tell the *interviewers* to prepare together and tell the *applicants* to prepare together. Set a time limit of about five minutes.
   - If possible, arrange the chairs into an interview situation. Encourage the applicant in each pair to start the interview by physically walking into the 'interview area'. Remind them to ask about experience.
   - At the end, ask a few students if the interviews were successful and why.

LESSON 8
Functions

Vocabulary Topics of conversation
Function Managing a conversation
Language to go What to say in social situations

Nice to meet you

Language notes

- Students may confuse the function of *complimenting* (which expresses admiration of someone or something, e.g. *I love your shoes*) and *congratulating* (to tell someone you are happy for what they have achieved).
- Although intonation is difficult to teach, it is important to draw attention to intonation patterns. Encourage students to copy the patterns they hear and provide extra practice as needed.

Vocabulary and speaking

1   Focus attention on the vocabulary box and ask if students think it is appropriate to talk about the football results when you meet someone for the first time. Point out that it is in the UK/US, because it's a neutral topic.
   - Students work in pairs and discuss the other topics. Ask students which they think are appropriate in the UK/US (*last night's TV programmes, the weather, his/her good taste in clothes*).

Listening

2   Focus attention on the photo and ask students to describe what is happening.
   - Students discuss the questions in pairs.
   - Ask a few students for their ideas, but don't give the answers yet.

3   ▭ Play the recording (more than once, if necessary) and encourage students to give reasons for their answers.

> 1 Susie and Tom know each other well (they are a couple), and Susie knows Barry (they are friends).
> 2 Tom and Barry are meeting for the first time.

4   ▭ Read the sentences with the students and check understanding.
   - Play the recording (more than once, if necessary).
   - Students check their answers with a partner.
   - Go through the answers.

> 1 F   2 F   3 F   4 T   5 T   6 T

Language focus

5   Focus attention on the table and read the example. Ask why Barry says: *That's brilliant! Well done.* (He is *congratulating* Susie on her college course).
   - Refer students to the recording script to find examples of the other functions.
   - Go through the answers and ask students to choose three or four phrases they like and would use.

Functions	Examples
1 opening a conversation	Hi! What a nice surprise! / It's great to see you. How are you getting on?
2 congratulating	That's brilliant! Well done.
3 introducing	Can I introduce you? Barry, this is my boyfriend, Tom...Tom this is Barry. Pleased to meet you, Tom. Nice to meet you, too, Barry.
4 complimenting	You look very well, and I love the new hair style. It really suits you! You look better every time I see you.
5 'making conversation'	How do you like the States? I just love the weather here. I'm really enjoying the sunshine.
6 criticising	Better than your awful British summers.
7 closing a conversation	Oh, is that the time!? / Look, I'm real sorry...we've gotta go, I'm afraid. Good to see you again. / It was good to meet you. / Why don't you give me a call sometime? / Right...OK then...See you. / Bye now. Have a nice day! / Speak to you soon.

Practice

6   Look at the example with the class and ask students what the function of this sentence is (*opening a conversation*).
   - Students do the activity, but don't give the answers at this stage (see Exercise 7).

7   ▭ Play the recording once so students can check their answers.
   - Play the recording again, this time pausing after each sentence to give students time to repeat with the correct stress and intonation. See **Language notes**.

> 1   I really <u>love</u> the colour of your <u>hair</u>!
> 2   You're the most <u>beau</u>tiful woman at the <u>party</u>!
> 3   You haven't <u>phoned</u> me for <u>ages</u>!
> 4   Congratu<u>la</u>tions on the <u>birth</u> of your <u>baby</u>!
> 5   Can I intro<u>duce</u> you to my <u>wife</u>?
> 6   Did you hear the <u>news</u> this <u>morning</u>?
> 7   How are you <u>getting</u> <u>on</u> at the <u>moment</u>?
> 8   Please send my <u>love</u> to your <u>family</u>.
> 9   Your ex<u>am</u> results are fan<u>tas</u>tic! <u>Well done</u>!
> 10 It's a <u>love</u>ly day, <u>isn't it</u>?

Get talking ...

8   Divide the class into groups of two or three.
   - Students write a conversation which includes at least three of the functions in the lesson.
   - Students practise the conversation with notes briefly, but spend more time without notes. This will help them to use natural intonation.

... and writing

9   Ask students to write short conversations like the ones they did in Exercise 8. Hand out different situations, e.g. at a party, in the street, in a hotel lounge etc.

Vocabulary   Travel items
Grammar   First conditional
Language to go   Making suggestions to visitors to your area

Australia

Language notes

- Point out that the stress in compound nouns goes on the first part of the compound, e.g. <u>wa</u>ter bottle.
- The first conditional is used to give suggestions, advice or warnings about future possibilities.
  A typical error is the use of modal verbs in both clauses:
  If I <s>will</s> have time, I'll go shopping.

Way in

Ask students to write down one thing they never travel without (not including passport and money). Students then tell their partner what they have chosen and why.

Vocabulary and speaking

1   Focus attention on the photos of the travel items. Were any of these things on their list?
- Students work together to label the items by making compound nouns, e.g. *water + bottle = <u>wa</u>ter bottle.*
- Remind students that if they can understand each word then the meaning is usually clear, e.g. *walking boots* are boots for walking.
- Go through the answers focusing on correct pronunciation. See also **Language notes** above.

> 1 <u>rain</u> clothes   2 mos<u>qui</u>to repellent   3 <u>slee</u>ping bag
> 4 <u>guide</u> book   5 <u>sun</u> cream   6 <u>walk</u>ing boots
> 7 first-<u>aid</u> kit   8 <u>wa</u>ter bottle   9 <u>mon</u>ey belt

2   Allow a few minutes for students to discuss the questions with a partner.
- Ask some students to tell the rest of the class their answers.
- Ask how many students would choose the holiday to the middle of Australia? Has anyone ever been there?

Reading

3   Focus attention on the photo and elicit where it is. (Ayers Rock (Uluru) in the Australian Outback.)
- Give students time to read and predict answers to the questions but don't give the correct answers at this stage.

4   Divide the class into As and Bs for parts 1 and 2. (As and Bs work separately at this stage.)
- Walk round the class giving help and checking answers.

> 1 Group A   A 4   B 1   C 3
>   Group B   D 2   E 6   F 5
> 2 Group A   A 4 flying and hiring a car   B 1 April to June and October to November
>   C 3 crocodile, kangaroos, dingoes
>   Group B   D 2 canoeing, riding camels, walking, camping
>   E 6 cinema, theatre, opera, galleries, aboriginal art
>   F 5 dangerous snakes, very strong sun

- When students are ready to answer part 3, ask them to talk to a student from the other group. Encourage them to use their own words and not just read their answers. At the end, ask students to read the text they haven't read and say what they found most interesting or surprising about the article.

Grammar focus

5   Focus attention on the box and read the examples to the class. Ask students to find where they come from in the text.
- In pairs, students look at both texts to find other examples of the first conditional with *if* and *unless.*

> unless you have... (para. A)   *It'll be cheaper...* (para. B)
> *If you visit...* (para. C)   *If you want to see...* (para. C)
> *You may even...* (para. C)   *If you like outdoor...* (para. D)
> *If you want to go...* (para. D)   *If you prefer...* (para. E)

- Ask students to use these examples of the first conditional to work out the rules.
- Students do the activity and check with a partner.
- Go through the answers. You may want to point out the different functions of the first conditional. See **Language notes**.

> 1 present simple   2 will / may / can   3 if not
> 4 *avoid* is in the imperative. We use the imperative to make advice stronger.

6   🔊 Play the first sentence and ask students if they heard *It will* or *It'll.* Remind them that *will* and *will not* are usually contracted to *'ll* and *won't.*
- If students find the sentences are difficult to pronounce, try a back-chaining drill (see page 9).

Practice

7   Students do the activity and check with a partner.
- Go through the answers.

> Suggested answers
> 1e You may see fantastic sunrises if you get up early.
> 2f You'll need to wear walking boots if you visit the mountains.
> 3d Take a water bottle if you want to stay healthy.
> 4h You won't need rain clothes if you go in the dry season.
> 5c If you want to do canoeing, find tour companies offering adventure sports.
> 6g You'll need to use sun cream if you don't want to get sunburn.
> 7a Unless you book in advance, you won't get a ticket for the flights.
> 8b You won't have so much to carry if you travel light.

Get talking ...

8   Ask students to make notes about their chosen area. If students choose the same area they can work in pairs.
- Encourage students to start the roleplay with the *visitor* entering the travel agent's and the *travel agent* asking *Can I help you?.*
- When they have finished, students should change roles.

... and writing

9   Students write a short article (e.g. 200 words) about their area, using the Australian text as a guide.
- For an example of an article, see **Writing Bank 3** page 148.

Vocabulary Expressions with *take*
Grammar Verb constructions for likes and dislikes
Language to go Discussing sport

Take it easy

Language notes

* The grammar of phrasal verbs is complex (see also Lessons 13 and 34), and students often have trouble using them correctly due to their colloquial feel. Three of the expressions with *take* in Exercise 1 are phrasal verbs: *take something off*, *take something on* and *take something up*. They are transitive (i.e. they need a direct object), e.g. *She's taken up **tennis** She's taken up* and separable (i.e. the two parts of the verb must be separated when they are used with an object pronoun), e.g. *She's taken **it** up She's taken up it*.
* Point out that some of the expressions for likes and dislikes are idiomatic, e.g. *can't stand*, *sick of*.
* The form of the constructions in the Grammar focus may cause problems (e.g. the choice between infinitive and the *-ing* form), as there is no 'rule'. The pronunciation practice in Exercise 6 can therefore be exploited in order to help students to remember.

Way in

* Ask students: *What do you like to do to relax?* Give an example of what you do (*I go running in the park*).
* Students mingle (i.e. walk round the room) and ask each other what they do to relax in order to try and find someone who does the same.
* Ask one or two students to report back to the whole class.

Vocabulary

1 Focus attention on the speech bubbles and read the first one out. Ask who might say this (e.g. a student). Point out the expressions with *take* and ask students to write them next to the correct definitions in the table.
 * Students work together to complete the table.
 * Go through the answers (see also **Language notes**) but do not focus on the expressions for likes and dislikes at this stage (see Exercise 4).
 * You may want to remind students of the common transitive phrasal verb *take something off* (e.g. *I took off my coat and sat down*) and the intransitive *take off* (e.g. *The plane took off on time*).

> 1 take part in   2 take on   3 take it easy   4 take up
> 5 take (a day) off   6 take a break

 * If time, ask the students to choose two or three of the new expressions they like and write their own sentences using the phrases.

Listening and speaking

2 Focus attention on the photo and ask students to describe the people and what they are doing.
 * In pairs, students suggest answers to question 2, but don't confirm or reject at this stage.
3 📖 Read through the questions with the students and make sure they understand them.
 * Play the recording (more than once, if necessary) for students to do the activity.
 * Allow time for students to discuss their answers with a partner before going through the answers.

> 1 He says he's taken on too much, he's sick of running round the gym and he needs a break.
> 2 She is confused and surprised.
> 3 He wants to watch the football on TV.

 * Ask if students know anyone like Ian.

Grammar focus

4a Students work individually to name the parts of speech in italics. Go through the answers together.

> A 2   B 4   C 3   D 1

4b Write two columns on the board for likes and dislikes. Elicit ways of expressing likes and dislikes from students (e.g. *like*, *love*, *enjoy*, *hate*).
 * Ask students to look back at Exercise 1 and at the recording script on page 119 to find other expressions.

Ways of expressing likes	Ways of expressing dislikes
I'm really into getting fit	I can't stand studying
You said you were into getting fit	I'm sick of this report / running round the gym
I'm really keen on it.	I can't stand it
But I thought you liked going?	
I don't mind helping / staying in	
You'll enjoy it	

Practice

5 Students do the activity then check their answers with a partner. Do not go through the answers at this stage. (See Exercise 6.)
6 📖 Play the recording for students to check their answers. Play the recording again, this time stopping after each sentence to let students repeat.

> 1 I was sick of being unfit so I took up aerobics.
> 2 We enjoy taking exercise, but we like taking it easy at other times.
> 3 It's quiet at 6.00, so I don't mind getting up early to go running.
> 4 Are you keen on getting fit?
> 5 After I've done two hours' exercise, I need to take a break.
> 6 They love watching baseball on television.

Get talking

7 Check students understand the questions. Ask them to make notes about their own views first.
 * Students work in small groups to discuss the questions. Encourage them to use the new language from the lesson.
 * At the end write three or four mistakes you noted during the discussion on the board and ask students to correct them. See page 9 for ways to deal with error correction.

Vocabulary Determination
Grammar *Used to* and *would*
Language to go Comparing past and present habits

Determination

Language notes

- Encourage students to notice what is around the new word and to store new vocabulary in full sentences to show this, e.g. *He is dependent <u>on</u> coffee. I'm addicted <u>to</u> drinking coffee.*
- Draw attention to the word-building aspect of *addict* (noun), *addiction* (noun), *addicted* (adjective) and *addictive* (adjective).
- Both *used to* and *would* can be used to describe repeated actions and events in the past. However, *would* is **not** used to describe past states, *I ~~would~~ live in Portugal.* [*used to*]

Way in

- Explain (or get a student to tell you) the meaning of determination /dɪtɜːmˈneɪʃən/. Ask students to describe a time when they had to use a lot of determination, e.g. *to pass an exam / stop smoking.*

Vocabulary and speaking

1 Focus attention on the picture and elicit words to describe the man. Ask: *What kind of job do you think he has? Is he stressed?*
- In pairs, students discuss the questions.
- Ask a few students to report their ideas, but do not confirm or reject suggestions at this stage.

2 Students read the text quickly to see if their predictions were correct. Tell students not to worry about filling the gaps at this stage.
- Go through the example with students before asking them to read the text again and complete the text.
- Students check their answers with a partner.
- Go through the answers. See also **Language notes**.

> 1 quit   2 willpower   3 gave up   4 dependent
> 5 addiction   6 cut down   7 addicted   8 addict

3 Read out the questions and check students understand the meaning of *addictive*. Ask if students know anyone who is addicted to the Internet. Is this a serious addiction? Why / Why not?
- In pairs, students discuss the questions.
- Ask a few students for their opinions.

> 2 possible answers: smoking; alcohol; drugs; eating; coffee; chocolate; television; gambling; shopping.

Listening

4 🔲 Refer students to the table. Ask for a synonym for *give up* (*stop, quit*).
- Play the recording for students to complete the table.
- Allow time for students to discuss their answers before playing the recording again.
- Go through the answers.

Speaker	Addiction	Have they given up?	Details
1	chocolate	yes	willpower because she was getting fat
2	the Internet	no	he loves it – it's like having a best friend
3	exercise	no	she loves it and she wants to look good
4	smoking	yes	hypnotherapy – because his wife hated it

Grammar focus

5 Refer students to the recording script and ask them to find the words to complete sentences A–D.
- Students work in pairs to answer the questions.
- Go through the answers.
- Point out that although the spelling changes for the question and negative forms of *used to*, the pronunciation of *used to* and *use to* is exactly the same:

> A I *used to* live alone.
> B I didn't *use to* do much sport.
> C I'd have some chocolate before meals.
> D Did you *use* to smoke?
>
> 1 *I would*
> 2 Example A is talking about a past state, B, C and D are all talking about a repeated action in the past.
> 3

> | | used to | would |
> |---|---|---|
> | Single past action | ✗ | ✗ |
> | Repeated past action | ✓ | ✓ |
> | Past state | ✓ | ✗ |

Practice

6a Read out the instructions and check students know what to do.
- Students complete the activity and check their answers with a partner.
- Go through the answers.

> 1 I used to hate sport.
> 2 He used to go to Italy every year when he was a child.
> 3 Did she use to go skiing?
> 4 He didn't use to like computers.
> 5 Did she use to bite her nails (as a child)?
> 6 I used to walk our dog every afternoon when I was younger.

6b Ask students if we use *would* for past states or repeated actions. (Answer: repeated actions only – often when we are telling a story.) Get them to look again at the sentences and decide which are OK with *would*. (Sentences 2 and 6.)

7 🔲 Stop the recording after each sentence for students to repeat.

Get talking

8 Allow a few minutes for students to write their sentences. They then hand them to you. Distribute these around the class.
- Students mingle to try and find the person whose 'naughty' habit is described on the paper.
- At the end ask a few students to report back on what people used to do.

LESSON 12
The present

Vocabulary Money and banks
Grammar Verbs with two objects
Language to go Talking about money

Money matters

Language notes
- The lesson title may need explaining: *matters* (as a verb), meaning money is important, and *matters* (as a noun) meaning the subject of money.
- Indirect objects usually tell us who (or what) receives something. We only use them when we also use a direct object, e.g. *The bank lent me the money.* If the indirect object comes **after** the direct object, we need to use *to* or *for*, e.g. *The bank lent the money to me.* It is not possible to use an indirect object with *borrow. Can I borrow ~~you~~ some money?*

Way in
- Write: *Neither a borrower, nor a lender be;* – William Shakespeare, (*Hamlet*, I, iii, l.73) on the board. Check students are clear on the meanings of *borrower / to borrow* and *lender / to lend* (see Exercise 2).
- Students discuss if they agree or disagree with the quotation and give reasons.

Vocabulary and speaking
1 Focus attention on the photos and elicit the three different ways of banking: traditional banking (going to the bank and dealing with someone face to face); telephone banking (all transactions done by phone) and e-banking (all transactions done over the Internet).
- Read out the questions and ask students to discuss them.
- Ask a few students for their opinions and elicit some advantages and disadvantages of each kind of banking.

Possible answers

Traditional banking	Telephone banking	e-banking
+ personal service	+ convenient, quick	+ convenient, quick
– inconvenient, time-consuming, queues, restricted opening hours	– impersonal, may be difficult to get through	- impersonal, possible security risk (other people may access your details)

2 If you did the **Way in**, get a student to remind the class of the difference between *lend* and *borrow*. (You *borrow* money from a bank (or someone), and the bank (or someone) *lends* it to you.)
- Students work with a partner to explain the other word-pairs. If possible, provide monolingual dictionaries to help.
- Go through the answers.

1 *invest* – use money to make a profit (e.g. buy shares in a company); *save* – keep money to use later.
2 *a bank account* – the arrangement you have with a bank; *a bank statement* – a list from the bank showing all transactions (payments, withdrawals etc.) over a period of time.
3 *a current account* – a kind of account with a cheque book, cash-machine card and instant access to your money; *a savings account* – an account to encourage you to save money, often no cash-machine card or cheque book. This account pays interest on your money.

4 *deposit* – pay money into an account; *withdraw* – take money out of an account.
5 *receive interest* – get money from a bank when you keep money in an account there; *pay interest* – pay a charge for borrowing money (e.g. on a bank loan).
6 *be in the black* – have a positive amount of money in your bank account; *be in the red* – have a negative amount of money in your bank account.

3 Students use the new vocabulary to help them answer the questions about the bank statement.

1 a current account   2 £150 (cheque)
3 £61 (£17.50 + £43.50)   4 receive interest (£14.52)
5 in the black (£2,416.30)

Reading
4 Check that students understand where the text comes from (a website for an Internet bank).
- Students read the text and answer the questions.

1 T   2 F   3 T   4 F

Grammar focus
5 Focus attention on the example sentences from the text. Check students know which parts of speech are being used, by eliciting the correct terms:

We	offer	you	a first-class service.
Subject +	Verb +	Indirect Object	Object

- Students work in pairs to answer the questions.

1 two   2 (*a first-class*) *service; money*
3 *you* (both sentences)   4 indirect object   5 after

6 Ask students to look back at the text and find other verbs which take two objects.
- Go through the answers. Check what the direct and indirect objects are in each case. See also **Language notes**.

owe   send   tell   deliver   give   bring   promises

Practice
7 Check that students understand what is wrong with the first sentence, (we don't need *to* when the indirect object comes *before* the direct object).
- Students do the activity and check with a partner.
- Go through the answers.

1 We promise you more choice.
2 Would you like to tell me (him etc.) anything?
3 He gave me a fantastic birthday present.
4 I can lend you the money.
5 When will you send me the products?
6 You don't owe me any money.
7 We will deliver your shopping direct to your home.

Get talking
8 You may want to specify how much the first prize is (either in local currency or £s or $s).
- Check students understand the questions and allow time for them to make individual notes before the group stage.
- At the end, ask a few students to report back.

Vocabulary   Phrasal verbs about tourism
Grammar   Present simple and continuous for future
Language to go   Describing plans for a trip

The river

Language notes

- Phrasal verbs can be divided into four types:
  Type 1 Intransitive (no direct object needed), e.g. *We set off at 9 p.m.*
  Type 2 Transitive (direct object needed) and inseparable, e.g. *I've got over my cold.*/*I've got my cold over.*
  (Some verbs e.g. *get off* can be type 1 or type 2.)
  Type 3 Transitive (direct object needed) and separable. e.g. *She put Ewa up for the night.* / *She put up Ewa for the night.*
  Type 4 Transitive (direct object needed) and inseparable, with two particles, e.g. *Students usually look up to their teachers.* (No Type 4 phrasal verbs appear in this lesson.)
- Students may be interested to note that phrasal verbs often have two meanings; a literal, and a non-literal one. To try and help students remember the non-literal phrasal verbs, it is a good idea to introduce them in groups within a context, as here for 'travel'. (See also Lessons 10, 24 and 34.)

Way in

- Make a statement about the traffic in your city, e.g. *It took me ages to get into work today – the traffic was terrible!* Get reactions to this from students, then ask: *What's the fastest way to get across town at rush hour? What's the most scenic / beautiful way to travel around town?*
- Students brainstorm ideas.
- At the end, ask each group to report their ideas to the class.

Vocabulary and speaking

1 Tell the students that the phrasal verbs in Exercise 1 are all to do with travel. (See **Language notes** for an explanation of the four types of phrasal verbs.)
- Read out the first sentence and ask: *Which is the correct definition for 'set off'?* (*d – to begin a journey*).
- Students do the activity and check their answers with a partner.
- When going through the answers you may wish to highlight the different types of phrasal verbs.

1 d	2 c	3 g	4 a	5 f	6 b	7 e

2 Read the instructions and ask students to think of a journey.
- Walk round the room helping students as required. Make sure students use the phrasal verbs from Exercise 1 accurately.

Listening

3 Refer students to the map of the River Thames /temz/.
- Encourage students who have been to London to share their knowledge with the rest of the class.
- If students are interested, tell them more details about the places that are mentioned on the recording. (See below.)

Background information
Kingston: busy, attractive shopping and residential area. *Richmond*: an area of SW London that includes *Hampton Court*, a 16th-century palace and gardens, *Kew /*kju:/ *Gardens*, famous gardens, and *Richmond*

Park, a very large park. *The Houses of Parliament*: home to the British government and adjacent to *Big Ben*, the famous clock. *Tate /*teɪt/ *Modern*: a modern-art gallery. *Shakespeare's Globe Theatre*: replica of Shakespeare's original theatre. *The Tower of London*: fortress dating from 11th century and former home to kings and queens of England. Now a museum and tourist attraction.

4 ▭▭ Play the recording for students to tick the places on the map which are mentioned. (Some places are mentioned which are not shown.)
- Go through the answers.

Hampton Court, Richmond, Kew Gardens, The Houses of Parliament, Tate Modern, Shakespeare's Globe Theatre, Tower Bridge

5 Allow time for students to read the questions before playing the recording again (more than once, if necessary).
- Students check their answers with a partner.
- Go through the answers.

1 At 9.00 Monday morning.
2 At 5.30 Monday afternoon.
3 He's meeting a friend for dinner.
4 He's going to the theatre.

Grammar focus

6a Refer students to the grammar box and ask volunteers to identify each tense.

A present simple	B present continuous
C present simple	D present continuous

6b Students complete the rules then check their answers in pairs.
- Go through the answers.
- Check that they understand that the verb tenses are *present* but the meaning is *future*.

1 *present simple:*   Sentences A and C
2 *present continuous:*   Sentences B and D

Practice

7 Ask students to look at the example. Elicit why the present simple is correct (*because it is a timetabled event at the cinema or on TV*).
- Students do the activity and check with a partner.
- Go through the answers.

1 finish   2 'm meeting   3 are you doing
4 starts   5 finishes   6 is coming
7 does your college course begin

Get talking

8 Make sure groups include students who are able to talk about the same river or city.
- If time, you could ask each group to make a poster advertising their trip.

Vocabulary 1   Weddings
Vocabulary 2   Uses of *get*
Language to go   Talking about relationships

Radio wedding

Language notes

- Students may have problems with the meaning of phrasal verbs and expressions with *get* because they are usually context-specific and difficult to guess from the separate words. After Exercise 6, you could ask students to choose three or four of the expressions and write sentences which are meaningful to them as an aid to memory.
- For information about the four types of phrasal verbs, see Lesson 13.

Vocabulary and speaking

1 Focus attention on the picture and elicit the situation (*a wedding*). Ask if anyone knows the word for a woman who is getting married (*a bride*).
- Refer students to the first pair of words and elicit the difference between *bride* and *bridesmaid* (see below).
- Students work in small groups to explain the differences in meaning. If possible, provide monolingual dictionaries.
- Go through the answers. If students are from different countries, encourage them to talk about similarities and differences.

1 On the wedding day, the *bride* (the woman) is helped by *bridesmaids*.
2 The *groom* (or *bridegroom*) is helped by the *best man*.
3 A *fiancé* /fɪˈɒnseɪ/ is a man and a *fiancée* /fɪˈɒnseɪ/ is a woman, who are engaged to be married.
4 Weddings usually take place either in a church – *a religious ceremony* – or in a registry office – *a civil ceremony*.
5 The *reception* is a formal party to celebrate the wedding. It usually takes place immediately after the wedding ceremony. A *honeymoon* is a holiday for the newly married couple.

2 Check students understand the questions. Stress they do not have to talk about any issues they may feel uncomfortable with.

Reading

3a Read the instruction and check students understand the three words by asking concept questions e.g. *What's your favourite radio station? What kind of things can you win in a competition?* and *What's another way of saying 'the press'?* (The media.)
- Students work in pairs to guess the connection. You may want to prompt students with ideas, but don't give the correct answer at this stage.

3b Divide the class into groups to read about the wedding and answer their questions. Group A should discuss their answers together and Group B should discuss their answers together.
- Walk round the class and check each group has answered their questions correctly.

Group A:
1 press photographers and security guards
2 smart hotel, guests in smart clothes, flowers, beautiful wedding dress
3 they have never met, never seen photos of each other and only talked on the phone for 40 seconds

Group B:
1 they won a competition on a radio station
2 the radio station
3 hopeful about a successful and happy marriage

4 Regroup the students (As and Bs work together now). Encourage them to tell each other their answers, not just to read the other text.
- Ask students for their reaction to the wedding.

Vocabulary focus

5 Focus attention on the table and ask them which definition goes with *got married* (d – *become husband and wife*).
- Students complete the activity and check their answers with a partner.
- Go over the answers. See also **Language notes**.

1 d   2 h   3 a   4 g   5 b   6 e   7 i   8 c   9 f

6 Ask students to divide the expressions into the correct category. If students are aware of the four types of phrasal verbs ask them to categorise these too.

get + adjective	*get* as a fixed expression	*get* as a phrasal verb
get married	get to know	get on with (Type 4)
get engaged	get on someone's nerves	get over (Type 2)
get upset	get back together	
get divorced		

Practice

7 Refer students to the example and point out they may have to change the tense of the verb or use the infinitive.
- Students do the activity and check with a partner.
- Go over the answers

1 to get over   2 gets on my nerves   3 get to know
4 get engaged   5 get divorced   6 got upset
7 get on with   8 got back together

Get talking ...

8 Focus attention on the picture of Carla and Greg and ask a volunteer to remind the class of the facts of their strange wedding.
- Walk round the class while students discuss the questions. Make a note of any common mistakes to correct at the end.
- Ask a few students to report back with reasons for their opinions.

Carla and Greg's marriage did not last. Three months after they got married, Carla and Greg separated. Their honeymoon was very difficult; reporters, security guards and TV cameras followed them everywhere. They had arguments and got on each other's nerves. They moved out of the flat and gave back the sports car. They don't say they regret it, but Carla says she would never do it again. Greg says he's sad the marriage is over.

... and writing

9 Elicit ways of starting an informal letter:
Dear..., *Hello...*, *Hi...*
- If time, start the letter in class. Students could finish it for homework.
- For an example of an informal letter, see **Writing Bank 4** page 149.

Vocabulary	*Waste, use, spend, save* + noun
Grammar	Modal verbs for giving advice
Language to go	Giving advice

Less is more

Language notes

- Modal verbs are difficult because they have many functions. The three verbs in this lesson focus on giving advice.
- Point out that negative and question forms of *ought to* are unusual, e.g. It is more typical to say: *I don't think you ought to do that* than *You ought not to do that* and *What should I do?* than *What ought I to do?*

Way in

- Draw attention to the picture and ask students to name as many things as possible. Use this time to teach any new vocabulary the students will need for Exercise 2.

Vocabulary and speaking

1 Focus attention on the spidergram and check students understand the relationship of the verb *waste* to the surrounding nouns (*waste* collocates with all these nouns).

- Tell students to draw three more spidergrams. Warn them to think carefully about which of the nouns from Exercise 1 can and can't collocate with each of the verbs.

use /juːz/ collocates with all the nouns.
These are *not* typical collocations:
spend: *paper, space, opportunities* save: *opportunities*

- Encourage students to store vocabulary items with typical collocations, as this will help them remember how individual words connect with other words to make useful 'chunks' of language.

2 Read the instruction and example with the students. Recheck the meaning of *wasting electricity* (use too much electricity unnecessarily).

- Students work together to make as many sentences as possible. Set a time limit of about five minutes.
- Go through the answers.

Possible answers
They are wasting energy because all the heat is going out of the window.
The women are wasting time talking.
A woman is spending a lot of money.
They aren't using the space well because the files are on the floor and the shelves are empty.

3 Read the sentences and check students understand what to do.

- Students work in pairs to discuss the statements.
- Encourage them to give reasons for their answers but don't give the correct answers at this stage.

Listening

4 🔲 Elicit ideas about where the text is from. (*A TV guide / TV magazine*).

- Ask students to discuss question 2, but don't give the correct answers at this stage.
- Play the recording (more than once, if necessary) so students can check their answers.

1 less   2 less   3 shorter   4 less

5 Play the recording again.

- Students work with a partner and discuss the advice given in the listening.
- Ask if they agree with any of Laura Evans' suggestions or not.

Grammar focus

6 Check students are clear about the function of giving advice by asking if the speaker is *making a suggestion* or *telling people they have to do something* (answer: *making a suggestion*).

- Students work alone to complete the rules, before checking with a partner.
- Go through the answers. See also **Language notes**. Remind students about the pronunciation of *should* /ʃʊd/, *could* /kʊd/ and *ought to* /ɔːt təː/.

1 *should; could*
2 an infinitive without *to*
3 it uses *ought*, which is followed by an infinitive with *to*.

Practice

7 Read the instruction and example and check students understand the correction (*should* is followed by the infinitive without *to*).

- Students do the activity and check with a partner.
- Go through the answers.

1 You could **open** the window for more fresh air.
2 Perhaps you ought **to** go to bed earlier.
3 You **shouldn't** watch horror movies before going to bed.
4 Perhaps you **should** do more exercise.
5 You **ought to** read a book in bed.
6 You **shouldn't** drink so much coffee.
7 Couldn't you **try** drinking warm milk?

8 🔲 Pause the recording after each sentence to allow students time to repeat.

- Remind students that the modal verb is not usually stressed. (See page 9 for ways to deal with pronunciation.)

Get talking ...

9 Give each student a letter (A, B or C) and ask them to look at the appropriate page to find out their problems.

- Clarify any difficult vocabulary and elicit ways of asking for advice (e.g. *What should I do? I don't know what to do, can you help? Have you got any suggestions?*).
- When students are ready, they work in groups of three (A+B+C) and take it in turns to explain their problems and ask for advice. The others in the group should listen and give appropriate advice.

... and writing

10 Ask students to choose one of the situations they spoke about (or think of a different one) and write a short, informal letter to a friend describing the problem and asking for advice.

- For an example of an informal letter, see **Writing Bank 4** page 149.

Vocabulary   The five senses
Grammar   Defining relative clauses
Language to go   Defining people, things, time and place

Looks good!

Language notes

- The vocabulary highlighted in Exercise 1 is used to describe personal reactions to do with the senses. Some of the verbs are the same as the nouns: *taste / to taste*; *smell / to smell*, while others differ from the nouns: *sight / to look*; *touch / to feel*; *hearing / to sound*.
- There are two types of relative clauses: defining and non-defining. Defining clauses tell us which person or thing the speaker means. (See Lesson 36 for non-defining relative clauses). When the relative clause refers to the *object* of the sentence, a relative pronoun is *not* necessary, e.g. *This is the information (that) you need.*

Way in

- Ask students to close their eyes and imagine they are lying on a beautiful beach. After about twenty seconds ask *What is the strongest sensation; the view, the feel of the sun, the sound of the waves or the smells?*
- Students compare answers in small groups. Ask a few students to report back to discover which sensation was the strongest for the class.

Vocabulary and speaking

1 Focus attention on the pictures and check students know the word for each (shell, flower, chocolates, sunset, bird). Tell students that there can be more than one sense associated with each picture. Encourage them to give reasons.

Suggested answers:
A Shell: *touch, sight, hearing (when put to your ear)*
B Flower: *smell, touch, sight*
C Chocolate: *taste, smell, sight, touch*
D Sunset: *sight, hearing (the waves)*
E Bird: *sight, hearing,*

2a Read the instruction and do an example with the class: ask them which picture goes with the first sentence (Picture C).
- Students work in pairs to complete the activity.
- Go over the answers.

1 Picture C   2 Picture A   3 Picture D
4 Pictures A, C   5 Picture D   6 Pictures B, C
7 Pictures A, E

2b Tell students to look at sentences 2, 3, 5 and 7 to help them answer the question about *looks / looks like* and *sounds / sounds like*.

Looks like and *sounds like* are used with a noun. They are used to compare the look or the sound of something with something else.
Looks and *sounds* are used with an adjective. They are used to describe the look or the sound of something.

Reading

3 Ask students to discuss the question about how different smells can be used to help businesses.
- Students read the text to see if they were right. Encourage them to read quickly and not to worry about unknown words at this stage.

Smells like bread can make people want to buy. Coconut smells can persuade people to buy holidays to sunny destinations. Lemon can increase people's energy and therefore production.

4 Ask students to read the questions before reading the text again.
- Allow a few minutes for the students to discuss the questions in pairs.

1 the part which controls memory and emotions
2 banks and hotels
3 vanilla and lavender
4 lemon increases energy and flower smells improve concentration

Grammar focus

5 Ask students to look back at the text to complete the sentences.

A: which   B: where   C: what
D: no relative pronoun needed / that

- Check that students understand why we use defining relative clauses by asking them if they a) *give you extra information* or b) *tell you which person or thing you're talking about* (✓). See also **Language notes** above.
- Students work to find four other defining relative clauses.

… that used the smell of … (para. 3) …who attended … (para. 3) … who are nervous… (para. 3) … when your business … (para. 5)

6 Ask students to match the pronouns and functions.

1 c *where*   2 e *who*   3 b *when*   4 a; d *that / which*
5 f *whose*

7 See **Language notes** above.

the object

Practice

8 Check that students understand the example: ask them why we use *who* (because we are defining which girl).
- Point out the changes in the combined sentence, i.e. we don't need to repeat the subject pronoun, *she*.
- Students do the activity and check with a partner.
- Go through the answers.

1 You made me happy when you said you loved me.
2 Look at that guy (who is) driving an old Chevrolet.
3 That's the woman whose daughter plays the clarinet.
4 I loved the smell of the flowers (which / that) you sent me.
5 I don't like those nightclubs where they play techno.
6 I love the quiet of the night when it's very calm and peaceful.
7 Did you like the CD (which / that) I lent you?

Get talking

9 Focus attention on the symbols and elicit the five senses. Ask students to think of things they really like the smell, taste, sound, sight and touch of, and one thing for each they hate.
- You may want to give an example *I love the smell of coffee but I can't stand the taste!*
- Students compare ideas in groups.

Vocabulary Lifestyle: word building
Grammar Present perfect simple with *yet, already, just*
Language to go Describing recent changes

Changes

Language notes

- This is the second lesson on the present perfect (see also Lessons 7, 27 and 37). The focus here is on recent actions and the uses of the adverbs *already*, *just* and *yet*.
- Typical learner difficulties may include using *yet* in positive statements, e.g. ~~I've done it yet~~ and *already* in negative statements, e.g. ~~They haven't already done it.~~

Way in

- Focus attention on the picture and ask students what they can see. Also ask: *What is the most interesting part of the picture? Why? Do you think it is a relaxing picture? Why / Why not?*
- Ask students to discuss the picture in pairs. After a few minutes ask for a few suggestions from the class.

Vocabulary and speaking

1 Tell students that all the words are connected to lifestyle in some way. Read out the new vocabulary paying attention to pronunciation.
  - Students briefly discuss which of the items they have in their lives.

2 Read out the questions and ask students to discuss them in pairs.
  - Walk round the room while students are talking and check that they are using the new vocabulary accurately.
  - At the end, ask a few students about the three most important things. Encourage them to give their reasons.

Reading

3 Ask students to read the questions before reading the text about Feng Shui /fʌŋ ʃweɪ/.
  - Remind students to read quickly at this stage just to answer the questions.

1 China.
2 Go to the park, get some fresh air, start your day with a glass of water, tidy your home and workplace.
3 Grey is a sign of confusion.

4 Look at the example with the students: tell them to underline *happy* in the text.
  - Students work to find the other adjectives in the text.

happiness – happy, (good) health – healthy, calm – calm, success – successful, stress – stressful, (good) luck – lucky, noise – noisy, energy – energetic, wealth – wealthy

  - Tell students that this kind of word-building exercise is a useful way of extending their vocabulary.

Listening

5 ☐☐ Tell students that they are going to listen to a man, Graham, being interviewed about Feng Shui on a radio programme. Tell them to tick the advice in the text.
  - Play the recording.

He has tried these:
✓ Take up a sport …
✓ Tidy your home and your workplace every day …
✓ Stop wearing grey clothes. …

6 Allow time for students to read the questions before playing the recording again.
  - Allow a few minutes for students to check their answers with a partner.
  - Go through the answers.

1 T   2 F   3 F   4 T

Grammar focus

7 Ask students to check the recording script on page 120 in order to complete the sentences.

1 I've <u>already</u> tried one or two of the ideas.
2 Have you bought any fish <u>yet</u> ?
3 I've <u>just</u> bought myself a new black suit.

  - Make sure students are clear on the meaning of the present perfect simple. Ask: *When we use the present perfect simple, which is more important, the action or the time it happened?* (The action).
  - Write this sentence on the board *I've changed my job last week.* Ask students if it is correct. (No – I changed my job last week **or** I've changed my job.)

8 Encourage the students to use the examples from Exercise 7 to help them to match the words to the explanations.
  - Students do the activity and check with a partner.

1 *yet*   2 *just*   3 *already*   4 *Just*   5 *Yet*   6 *Yet*
7 *Already*

Practice

9 Check that students understand the example by asking: *Why do we use the present perfect here?* (Because it is a recent action and there is no time reference.)
  - Students do the activity and check with a partner.

1 She's already done her homework.
2 Michael hasn't phoned me yet.
3 My neighbour has just rearranged his living room.
4 I don't know – I haven't decided yet.
5 I've just finished it.
6 No, he's already gone.
7 I've already learnt those English verbs.
8 Have you seen it yet?

Get talking

10 Tell students to make notes individually first, then discuss their opinions in groups.
  - At the end, ask a few students to report back.

Vocabulary   Phrasal verbs: *turn; switch; go*
Function   Informal and polite requests
Language to go   Making and responding to requests

How polite are you?

Language notes

- Refer also to **Language notes** about phrasal verbs in Lessons 13 and 34. All these phrasal verbs are associated with technology but can be used in other contexts too (e.g. *turn on the car engine*). *Go off* is a Type 1 phrasal verb. *Turn on, switch on, turn off, turn up, turn down, turn over* are all Type 3 phrasal verbs. Students should be encouraged to store these items in the format: *turn something on*. This will show that they are separable.
- There are a number of ways of making requests in English. Students need to be aware of formality to avoid sounding either rude or over-polite. Requests with *Would you mind …?* and *Do you mind …?* may cause problems. Draw attention to the fact that the response *No* means *OK, it's no problem* and the response *Yes* means *It's not OK, there is a problem*.

Speaking and vocabulary

1   Ask students to sit quietly for a minute and to listen to the noises in and around the classroom. They should then describe what they heard to a partner.

2   Play the recording and ask students to write down what they think each noise is, and if they like it or not.
   - Students discuss the noises in pairs.

1 mobile phone   2 someone sniffing   3 whistling
4 walkman played too loudly   5 contemporary classical music

3   Students discuss the questions with a partner.
   - At the end, ask a few students to report back.

4   Tell students that these are all common phrasal verbs to do with technology.
   - Students work to complete the sentences.
   - Go over the answers, drawing attention to what Type each phrasal verb is. See **Language notes** above.

1 off   2 on   3 on   4 off   5 over   6 up   7 off
8 down

Reading

5   Elicit the meaning of *polite* and its opposite (*rude* or *impolite*). Make sure students understand they are to answer the quiz as if they were their partner. You may want to demonstrate, e.g. *I think Maria would say b) in question 1*.
   - Students then discuss what they have put for each other and say if they agree with their partner's answers for them or not.
   - Read out the scoring and interpretation for the quiz.

Score: 3 points for every 'a'; 2 points for every 'b' and 1 point for every 'c'.
Interpretation: 9–12   =   You know how to be polite. Well done.
   5–8   =   You are quite polite but could be better.
   1–4   =   You are rude and need to be careful if you don't want to offend people!

Language focus

6   Ask for another way of saying *request* (*to ask someone to do something for you*) and ask students to find the first example in the quiz. (*Would you mind turning your music down, please?*)
   - Students work in pairs to find other requests.

1 <u>Can you stop</u> that …   <u>Stop</u> that …   <u>Could you stop</u> Mitzy …   <u>Would you come</u> … <u>Shut up!</u>
<u>Do you mind</u> moving …   <u>Please tell</u> this man …

   - Tell students to look at the examples in question 2 and discuss the answer in pairs.

2 *OK, it's no problem.*

7   Ask students if all the requests are equally formal (No). It depends on *what* you are requesting and *who* you are talking to.
   - Elicit which of the four requests is the most formal (*Would you mind …*), and the most informal (*Turn the …*). Ask for situations when you might say this, and who to.
   - Remind students of the importance of intonation if they are to sound *polite*.
   - Play each sentence once allowing time for students to listen and repeat.

Practice

8   Focus attention on the first cartoon and ask students what else they could say in this situation, e.g. *Could you turn the music down, please?* Check students understand how formal each situation is. Situations 1, 3 and 4 are more formal than situation 2.
   - Students do the activity and check with a partner.
   - Go over the answers, accept any correct alternatives.

Possible answers:
1 A: Do you mind if I open the window?
   B: No, not at all.
2 A: Could I borrow your dictionary, please?
   B: Yes, here you are.
3 A: Would you mind turning your TV down, please?
   B: Actually, I would.
4 A: Could you be quiet, please? I'm trying to study.
   B: Sorry! Of course.

Get talking

9   Divide students into two groups (Groups A and B). Allow groups sufficient time to read their relevant information and discuss any problems.
   - Regroup students into pairs (A+B) to say the dialogues.
   - Encourage them to repeat the dialogues without looking at their notes.

Vocabulary   Adjectives describing loneliness and fear
Grammar   Second conditional
Language to go   Talking about hypothetical situations

Going alone

Language notes

- Conditional structures are also covered in Lessons 9, 29 and 39. This lesson focuses on the second conditional, which is used to talk about situations that are unlikely or even impossible. It may help students to point out that the past tense is used to distance the speaker from the subject matter, e.g. *If I were there* (but I am not), *I'd ...*
- The verb *to be* can be confusing in the *if* clause. In the language 'chunk', *If I were you ...*, *were* is correct. In other uses, *were* is usually considered 'more correct', e.g. *If she were here...* , but nowadays, *was* is frequently used and often acceptable, e.g. *If she was here ... .*

Way in

- Write the word *claustrophobia* /ˌklɔːstrəˈfəʊbiə/ on the board and ask if anyone can explain what it is a fear of (very small spaces).
- Divide the class into small teams and ask them to make a list of as many words as possible from this word (e.g. *stop, cab, boat*). Set a time limit of about five minutes. The team with the most words is the winner.

Vocabulary and speaking

1   Tell students that all the words in Exercise 1 are to do with fear or loneliness.
- Ask students to work together to try and explain the difference in meaning between the words in italics.
- Draw attention to pronunciation and the prepositions which follow *worried, nervous* and *scared*.

> 1 *alone* /əˈləʊn/ means 'without others' and is neutral in register, while *lonely* /ˈləʊnli/ means 'unhappy because of being alone'.
> 2 *worried* /ˈwʌrid/ (*about*) and *nervous* /ˈnɜːvəs/ (*about*) both mean a little *scared* (*of*). You are *nervous about something* in general, e.g. *I'm nervous about my exams*; but *worried about something* more specific, e.g. *I'm worried about my history exam* (*because I haven't studied enough*).

2   Read the instruction and ask students to describe how they feel in these situations.
- Walk round the class as students discuss the situations. Make sure they use the new vocabulary accurately.

Reading

3   Focus attention on the photo and ask students to describe the situation.
- Students discuss the questions.
- Ask a few students to report their ideas to the rest of the class.

> *Background information*
> - The *Vendée Globe* yacht race starts and finishes in France. It runs every four years and is the ultimate solo test. It lasts for 100 days as the sailors battle through the storms of the southern ocean. Even to finish the race is an enormous achievement. Ellen MacArthur's boat in the race was called *Kingfisher*. At 18.3 metres long, it is one of the new types of yachts, capable of 30 knots (55 km/h) or double the speed of traditional yachts.

4   Students read the text to check their ideas.
- Encourage students to read quickly and not to worry about unknown words at this stage.
- Go through the answers.

> 1 In a yacht in the middle of the ocean.
> 2 She's taking part in a race, sailing single-handed, non-stop around the world.
> 3 Tired, not lonely, determined to finish.

5   Make sure students read the questions before reading the text again.
- Students answer the questions then check with a partner.

> 1 T   2 F   3 T   4 F   5 F

Grammar focus

6   Students complete the rules about the second conditional. Take this opportunity to revise the first conditional and compare differences in form and meaning. See also **Language notes** above.
- Go through the answers.

> 1 *unlikely / hypothetical*
> 2 a) *past simple;* infinitive   b) *would*

Practice

7   Read the instruction and example and check understanding by asking students if a) *there is a real possibility of going swimming* or b) *we are thinking about an unlikely situation* (✔).
- Remind students that the two clauses can be written in either order.
- Students complete the activity and check their answers with a partner.
- Go through the answers.

> 1 I'd miss other people too much if I took part in the race.
> 2 He'd go out more if he knew more people.
> 3 I'd phone him if I knew his number.
> 4 If John were (was) here I'd ask him about the weekend.
> 5 If I wasn't (weren't) scared of small spaces, I'd use the lift.
> 6 People would always understand me if I spoke English very well.

8   📼 Stop the recording after each sentence to give students time to repeat.
- Remind them about the contraction of *would*.

Get talking

9   Check understanding of *desert island* and *luxuries*.
- Tell students to make notes about question 2 individually, before discussing their ideas in groups.
- If time, do the second part of question 2 as a 'pyramid discussion'. Divide the class into pairs and give them a time limit of three minutes. Tell students that they must agree on five luxuries. Then students must agree in groups of four (with a time limit). Finally they must agree in groups of eight (with a time limit).

Vocabulary	Food and cooking
Grammar	Verb constructions with -*ing*/infinitive
Language to go	Talking about food and cooking

What's in the fridge?

Language notes
• Verb constructions with -*ing*/infinitive always cause difficulty. The best advice for learners is to use their memory rather than try to apply grammar rules. Repetition exercises in class can help. Learners should also be encouraged to store these items in sentences, and not as individual words, e.g. *I keep on forgetting what comes next.*

Way in
• Revise food and drink vocabulary by writing the following anagrams on the board: *team, hesece, atsap, marce, ejicu, rebe, odofase, sifh, hisus, tegbavesel*
• Set a time limit (e.g. three minutes) and ask students to work out the anagrams. Check the answers with the whole class, using visuals to clarify meaning if necessary.

meat, cheese, pasta, cream, juice, beer, seafood, fish, sushi, vegetables

Vocabulary and speaking
1 Students work in small groups to discuss the differences.
• Encourage them to use monolingual dictionaries if they have them to hand.

1 a *cook* is a person who cooks; a *chef* is a professional cook in a restaurant; a *cooker* is a machine for cooking (the inside part is called an oven).
2 a *fridge* keeps food cold, but above 0°C; *frozen* means below 0°C; frozen food is kept in a *freezer*.
3 breakfast, lunch and dinner are *meals*; a *course* is part of a meal, e.g. soup, starter, main course, dessert. You eat food off a *plate*.
4 *fast food* comes from places like McDonald's®, usually hamburgers, chips, pizza etc; *raw* means uncooked, e.g. meat, fish or vegetables; *fresh* means in good natural condition because (the food) hasn't been kept too long.
5 You *boil* food in water; you *roast* food in the cooker (oven) in oil; you *fry* food on the top of the cooker in oil.
6

Knife   Fork   Spoon

7 a *vegetable* is a potato or carrot etc.; a *vegetarian* is a person who eats no meat or fish; a *vegan* is a person who eats no animal products (meat, fish, cheese, milk, eggs etc.)

2 Read out the questions and ask students to discuss.
• Walk round the class as students talk in pairs, giving help where needed.
• Ask two or three students to say something about their partner.

Listening
3 Focus attention on the photos and ask them where the person is from, what their job is and what their kitchen is like. (Takanori is from Japan; he's a chef; his kitchen is modern and organised. Gabriela is from Italy; she's also a chef; her kitchen is homely and more traditional.)

• You may want to prompt students to think about Japanese and Italian food in particular when discussing the questions.
• Ask students for their opinions and ideas but don't do feedback at this stage.

Background information
Typical Japanese food and drink includes seafood, raw fish (*sushi*), seaweed, rice, soy sauce, rice wine (*sake*). Typical Italian food and drink includes pasta, pizza, cold meats and cheese (*antipasti*), red and white wines.

4 Play the recording for the students to identify what is in the fridges.

Takanori's fridge:	seafood, raw fish, fresh vegetables, French wine
Gabriela's fridge:	cold meat, cheese, ingredients for pasta, ice cream, juices, drinks, cans of beer

5 Ask students to read the questions and answer any they can at this stage.
• Play the recording (more than once, if necessary).
• Students do the activity and check with a partner.
• Go through the answers.

1 T   2 F   3 T   4 F   5 F   6 F   7 T   8 F

Grammar focus
6 Students read the examples and answer the questions.

1 the infinitive   2 the -*ing* form

7 Read out the verbs in the box. Refer students to the recording script and ask them to find the verbs. See also **Language notes**.
• Go through the answers.

Infinitive	-*ing* form
I'm *planning* to get a larger one.	I won't *waste time* sightseeing.
You can't *afford* to stand still …	I *spend time* relaxing with friends.
That's why I've *decided* to visit …	I've *given up* trying to keep it tidy.
They *offer* to do the cooking for me.	I *keep on* filling it so full.
I don't often *manage* to have an evening off.	I *avoid* cooking complicated meals …

Practice
8 Students do the activity and check with their partner.
• Go through the answers.

1 to eat   2 eating   3 to eat   4 reading   5 to do
6 going   7 shopping; cooking   8 buying   9 to find

Get talking
9 Divide the class into small groups.
• Walk round the class as students discuss the questions, giving help if needed and listening for any mistakes with -*ing* forms and infinitives.
• At the end, find out: the most popular food(s), if most people eat out a lot, how many people like cooking etc.
• Write a few mistakes you heard on the board and ask students to correct them.

LESSON **21**
The past

Vocabulary Travel and airports
Grammar Past perfect simple
Language to go Recounting events in your life

Airport

Language notes

- In Exercise 1, all the items are nouns (*journey*, *trip*, *flight*, *tour*, *cruise*) except *travel*, which is a verb. A common mistake is to use *travel* as a noun, e.g. *I hope you had a good travel.* [trip] A *journey* /dʒɜːni/ refers to the time spent and distance covered when you go somewhere, especially if it is long or travelled regularly. A *trip* /trɪp/ is a journey to a place and back that is not made regularly, and is perhaps short. A *flight* /flaɪt/ refers to a journey by plane. A *tour* /tʊə/ and a *cruise* /kruːz/ are both journeys for pleasure, during which you visit several different places. A *cruise*, however, refers specifically to boats.
- The grammar focused on in this lesson is the past perfect. See also Lesson 31. It is often used when we are already talking about the past and want to refer to an earlier past for a moment. It is useful to emphasise the sequence of events. Be aware that sometimes when teachers focus on the past perfect, students start over-using it. When telling a story, the main verb tense is usually the past simple.

Way in

- Ask a few students about the last time they went to an airport. *Were you going somewhere, or meeting someone? Was the plane on time? Did you have a good journey?*

Vocabulary and speaking

1 Tell students that the words in the box are all to do with travelling.
   - Students complete the sentences and check their answers with a partner.
   - Go through the answers. See **Language notes** for information on usage.

   1 flight   2 trip   3 journey   4 tour   5 travel   6 cruise

2 Focus attention on the picture of the airport and ask students to identify the labelled items using the words in the box.
   - Check that students know how to pronounce the words correctly and highlight the stress.

   1-f de<u>par</u>ture <u>lounge</u>   2-d duty-<u>free</u> <u>shops</u>
   3-b <u>check</u>-in <u>desk</u>   4-g <u>pass</u>port con<u>trol</u>
   5-f <u>hand</u> <u>lug</u>gage   6-h <u>board</u>ing <u>card</u>
   7-e <u>flight</u>-infor<u>ma</u>tion <u>screens</u>   8-a <u>cab</u>in <u>crew</u>

3 Read out the questions and ask students to discuss them in pairs.
   - After a few minutes, ask a few students for their ideas and opinions.

Reading

4 Explain (or get a student to tell you) the meaning of *hub* (the central part of a system or area to which all other parts are connected).
   - Read the instruction and ask students to read the text quickly to answer the question. Remind them not to worry about unknown words at this stage.

   The traveller had a negative experience.

5 Allow time for students to look at the sentences before reading the text again.
   - Students mark the statements true or false and check their answers with a partner.
   - Go over the answers. Ask students to justify their answers by reference to the text.

   1 T   2 T   3 F (he realised before he got on the plane)
   4 F (he found it)   5 T

Grammar focus

6 Tell students to use the example and the timeline to help them answer the questions.

   1 *before*   2 *past participle*

Practice

7 Read the example and ask students which action happened first; *I / arrive* or *flight / leave* ? (*the flight had left* is the first action, so we use the past perfect).
   - Remind students to think about the correct past participles. Refer them to the irregular verb list in the Phrasebook.
   - Students check their answers with a partner.
   - Go through the answers at this stage or, if you prefer, students can listen for the answers in Exercise 8.

   1 wanted; hadn't packed   2 decided; 'd enjoyed
   3 realised; 'd met   4 had finished; went
   5 asked; 'd lost   6 hadn't studied; saw

8 ▭ Tell students to listen to check their answers. Remind them to listen carefully for the contracted forms of *had*.
   - Stop the recording after each sentence to give them time to repeat.

Get talking ...

9 Ask students to draw seven boxes in which to write the key events of their story. Prompt and help students with ideas and words if necessary. You may want to tell your own story, or use this one, as an example.
   1 *asleep*   2 *hear a noise*   3 *get out of bed*   4 *turn on light*   5 *go downstairs*   5 *see a light in kitchen*
   6 *ring police*   7 *see husband making a sandwich*
   Last night I turned on the light in my bedroom. I'd been fast asleep but then I'd heard a noise, which had woken me up. So, after I'd turned the light on, I went downstairs. I saw a light in the kitchen and thought it was a burglar. However, it was only after I'd rung the police that I saw it was my husband. He was making a sandwich.
   - Put students into pairs to tell their stories and remind them to think carefully about the verb tenses.
   - As they tell their stories, make a note of any mistakes with the past perfect. Write these on the board and ask students to correct them at the end.

... and writing

10 Ask students to write their story, again starting at event four.
   - For an example of a story, see **Writing Bank 1** page 146.

LESSON 22
The present

Vocabulary   Fame and success
Grammar   Passive constructions
Language to go   Describing a process

A star is born...or made?

Language notes

- Passive constructions are not just grammatical alternatives to active constructions. We use the passive when we want to highlight certain aspects of something we are talking about. The passive is generally used in the following situations: when we are talking about processes; in more formal contexts; and when the agent is unknown or not important.

Way in

- Ask students to think of someone they admire (e.g. a singer, an actor, a sportsperson etc.) and to tell a partner a little bit about them, and why they like them.

Vocabulary and speaking

1 Ask students if they can identify any of the people in the photos. (Left to right: Spice Girls (British pop group – Exercise 4 has further information); Venus Williams (US tennis player – see **Get talking** activity for more information); Oasis (British pop group – see below); Macaulay Culkin (US actor – see also below).
  - Students discuss the questions in pairs. If the stars are not known to your students, you may want to ask them about celebrities from their own country.

  Background information
  Oasis the British rock band was started by Liam and Noel Gallagher, and three friends. Their first album, *Definitely Maybe* was released in 1994.
  They became huge in the USA as well as the UK after their second album. Also famous for controversy: fighting between the brothers, drugs charges, rude and arrogant to the press and not turning up to concerts.
  Macaulay Culkin: child film star. When he was ten years old, he starred in *Home Alone*, which became the most commercially-successful comedy ever. By 1994, he had been in fourteen films.

2 Students read the statements and discuss them briefly.
  - Ask a few students to report back at the end.
3 Draw two columns on the board headed *Adjectives* and *Nouns*. Refer students to the words in italics in Exercise 2 and ask them to write down the corresponding noun for each adjective.
  - Encourage students to help each other and to use monolingual dictionaries, if available.
  - Go through the answers, drawing attention to word stress and to the 'silent' syllables in *brill(i)ant*, *legend(a)ry* and *fash(io)nable*.

  famous – fame; successful – success;
  talented – talent; brilliant – brilliance; skilful – skill;
  fashionable – fashion; legendary – legend;
  original – origin; popular – popularity

Listening

4 Students read the question and programme guide and discuss the question in the context of the Spice Girls.
  - Ask a few students for their opinions.
5 [cassette] Tell students they are going to hear part of the programme and ask them to listen for the presenter's viewpoint.
  - Play the recording once.

  The Spice Girls were made into stars. The presenter doesn't feel that they are really stars, because they haven't got much talent.

6 Allow time for students to read the questions before playing the recording again.
  - Students complete the activity and check their answers with a partner.
  - Go through the answers.

  1 T   2 F   3 F
  4 F (she left because of disagreements)   5 T

Grammar focus

7 Focus attention on the grammar box and tell students to refer to this when answering the questions about the passive. See also **Language notes** above.

  1 passive   2 active   3 Passive

8 Students underline the correct alternatives to show how the passive is formed.
  - Refer students to the recording script on page 121 to find other examples of the passive.

  be; past participle

Practice

9 Remind students that we don't always need to include the agent in passive sentences (e.g. ... *by the director* is not necessary in the example).
  - Students do the activity and check their answers with a partner.
  - Go through the answers.

  1 The brilliant album *Skill* was released last year.
  2 The new president was interviewed by a journalist from *Time* magazine.
  3 Different celebrities are always invited to present the film awards.
  4 Two children are needed for the TV show, 'Fun House'.
  5 The winning lottery numbers are announced every Saturday.
  6 The singers are taught how to dance by the dance instructor.
  7 10,000 tickets for the concert were sold in an hour.
  (*Sentences 1, 3, 4, 5 and 7 do not need the agent.*)

Get talking

10 Divide the class into As and Bs. Ask them to look at their relevant information and prepare their questions.
  - When they are ready, divide the class into pairs (A+B). Remind them **not** to look at each other's information, but just to ask and answer the questions.

Vocabulary   Toys and games
Grammar   Modal verbs to talk about future probability
Language to go   Making predictions about the future

The future of toys

Language notes

- *Will* is used to show that we think something is very probable (e.g. 90% chance of something happening) in the future. *May*, *might* and *could* are used when something is seen as less probable (e.g. 40–50% chance). Some people feel that *might* is less probable than *may*.
- *Will*, *may*, *might*, *could* are all examples of modal verbs: they are followed by an infinitive without *to*, and they do not change for the third person, e.g. *She may be late.*

Vocabulary and speaking

1 Students match the words to the pictures. You may need to check understanding further by asking concept questions like *What other board games do you know?*

> 1-c jigsaw puzzle   2-d construction kit
> 3-a board game   4-g dolls   5-f skateboard
> 6-e cards   7-b computer game

2 Read out the questions. With questions 1 and 2, you may want to use this opportunity to extend the vocabulary of toys and games further.
- At the end, ask students for their ideas about toys of the future. Write a few suggestions on the board for use in Exercise 3.

Reading

3 Ask students to think about their ideas from Exercise 2 and to read the text quickly to see if the text agrees with them.

> In the future toys and games will use a lot more technology, e.g. allowing communication between people, and communication of information.

4 Allow time for the students to read the sentences before reading the text again.
- Students do the activity and check their answers with a partner.
- Go through the answers. Ask students to justify their answers by reference to the text.

> 1 T   2 F   3 F (only gives us *examples* of languages)
> 4 T   5 F

- Ask students which of the toys they think will be most successful (i.e. sell well).

Grammar focus

5 Ask students to complete the sentences by referring back to the text.

> A *The Navigator Game®* **will** connect to a child's bicycle.
> B It *may* be done in many ways.
> C The Globe *could* be used as a night light.
> D Footballs of the future *might* contain video cameras.

6 Point out that the choice of modal verb to use depends on how sure you are in your opinion / feeling about something. See also **Language notes** above.

> 1 will   2 may, could, might   3 infinitive (without *to*)

- Check that students understand which of the phrases used to express opinions can **only** go with *will* (*I'm sure*, *I don't think*, *I doubt if*).

Practice

7a Students do the activity then check their answers with a partner.
- Go through the answers.

> 1 I expect it will soon be possible to connect computers to *Lego®* models.
> 2 Skateboards could have electric motors soon.
> 3 Personal flying machines might be available by the year 2015.
> 4 Famous people may become characters in computer games.
> 5 I doubt if people will buy teddy bears with computers inside them.
> 6 I think most children will have mobile phones before long.
> 7 I don't think people will read paper books for much longer.
> 8 Children might be very unfit in the future.

7b Do the first sentence as an example with the class by telling them your opinion, or ask one or two students to give their opinions.
- Students then discuss if they agree with the statements or not.

Get talking ...

8 Check understanding of *multi-media equipment* by asking students to give examples of current equipment. (TV, DVDs etc.)
- Give students a few minutes to think about their own ideas before dividing the class into small groups. Prompt and help with ideas if necessary.
- Walk round the class while students are speaking, giving help if necessary, and listening for mistakes with the future forms.
- At the end ask a few students about one or two of the topics, and write a few of the mistakes you heard on the board for students to correct.

... and writing

9 Students choose one item from their discussion (or think of something else) to describe as part of a catalogue advertising products of the future. Use the reading text in the lesson as a model for this writing task.
- Encourage students to edit their own writing and to check their partner's.
- At the end, pin all the descriptions up around the class so students can read about each other's products.

LESSON 24
Vocabulary

Vocabulary 1 Telephoning expressions
Vocabulary 2 Phrasal verbs about telephoning
Language to go Communicating by phone

I'll call you

Language notes

- Some of the expressions may need extra clarification: *mobile phones* are usually known as *cell phones* in the US. In the UK, people often just call them *a mobile*, e.g. *I'll call you on my mobile. To text someone* (*texting*) is to send written (text) messages from one mobile phone to another.
- This lesson also focuses on phrasal verbs (see Lesson 13 for a description of the four types of phrasal verbs). *Hang up* and *hold on* are examples of Type 1 (intransitive – no object). *Call someone back* and *put someone through* are examples of Type 3 (transitive and separable). Remind students that when the direct object is a pronoun, the two parts of the verb must be separated, e.g. *Please tell him I'll call **him** back later.*

Way in

- Focus attention on the photo of the three girls. Get students to describe what is happening and get their reaction to the use of mobile phones. *Do they like them / hate them? Should children have them? Why? / Why not?*
- Alternatively, if you think it won't cause embarrassment, ask students who they last phoned and what they spoke about.

Speaking and vocabulary

1   Ask students to discuss the questions in pairs and help each other with any problematic vocabulary. See also **Language notes**.
    - Ask a few students to report back to the whole class.
    - If time, and of relevance to your students, you may want to point out ways of saying telephone numbers in the UK and in the US.

    ### Background information
    There are certain conventions for saying telephone numbers: '0' is pronounced as 'zero' in the US, and as 'oh' in the UK. Two numbers the same together are pronounced as 'double' e.g. '007' is *double oh seven.* It is usual to pause where there is a space between the numbers, e.g. 011 3272 4489 is pronounced as *oh double one   three two seven two   double four eight nine.*

2a Tell students that there are some fixed expressions we use on the phone and these should be learned as 'chunks'.
    - Do the first one as an example with the class.
    - Students do the activity and check their answers with a partner.

1 leave	2 This is	3 busy	4 afraid	5 I'd like
6 It's	7 press	8 returning		

2b Tell students that these expressions form part of a telephone conversation. Ask them to put them in an appropriate order, but do not give the correct answers at this stage.

Listening

3   [cassette] Tell students to listen carefully to the conversation and to check their answers to Exercise 2.
    - Play the recording (more than once, if necessary).

    Order of expressions: 7, 2, 5, 6, 4, 8, 3, 1

4   [cassette] Allow time for students to read the questions before playing the whole of the conversation.
    - Students do the activity and check with a partner.
    - Go through the answers.

    1 Donna, the receptionist.   2 Jon is not there.
    3 She is put through to one of his colleagues.
    4 Jon's colleague.   5 Jon

Vocabulary focus

5   Tell students that there are also some phrasal verbs specifically used about telephoning. Do the first one together with the whole class.

    A 2   B 4   C 3   D 1

    - Refer students to the recording script and ask them to find the phrasal verbs in the dialogue.

6   Remind students that there are different types of phrasal verbs. If students are familiar with the four types, ask them to categorise these verbs. See **Language notes**.
    - If you prefer not to go into too much theory here, recommend that students focus on learning phrasal verbs in a context.
    - Go through the answers:

1 call me back	2 Hold on	3 hang up
4 put you through		

Practice

7   Remind students that although the sentences are grammatically correct, they are not the accepted language for telephoning, and would therefore sound strange to a native speaker.
    - Students work to complete the activity and check their answers with a partner.
    - Go through the answers, or if you prefer, students can listen to the answers in Exercise 8.

    1 I'd like to speak to Michael, please.
    2 The line's busy.   3 I'm afraid she's not here at the moment.   4 Please hold on.   5 I'll just put you through.   6 Can I take a message? *or* Do you want to leave a message?   7 I'm returning her call.   8 Could you call her back later?   9 It's me!

8   [cassette] Stop the tape after each sentence to give time for students to repeat.
    - Encourage them to listen carefully and repeat the sentences with polite intonation.

Get talking

9   Ask students to look at the prompts on page 85 and say which situation is more formal, (the first).
    - If possible, ask students to sit back to back (i.e. not looking at each other) to simulate a 'real' phone conversation.
    - Encourage students to practise the dialogues several times first **with**, and then **without**, the prompts.

LESSON **25**
Modals

Vocabulary *Make* and *do*
Grammar Modal verbs for necessity and obligation
Language to go Describing rules in the present

Do the right thing

Language notes

- Students may find it helpful to know that we use *make* to talk about building and creating (e.g. *make a good impression*) and we use *do* when we do not say exactly what the activity is (e.g. *do your best*).
- Modal verbs of obligation can be confusing, because the choice may depend on the speaker's opinion or feeling.
- *Must* is a stronger obligation than *should*. *Must* is sometimes described as an 'internal' obligation, e.g. *I must remember to phone you*, whereas *have to* is described as an 'external' obligation, e.g. *We have to pay taxes*. Students tend to over-use *must*.
- The negative constructions (*mustn't* and *don't have to*) are not direct opposites of the positive forms: *mustn't* is an obligation **not** to do something (i.e. there is no choice) whereas *don't have to* means there is **no** obligation to do something (i.e. there is a choice).

Way in

- Write *correct, write, true, right, accurate* on the board. Ask students which word is the odd one out and why (*write* because all the others have a similar meaning). Ask them for the opposites of the other four words (*correct – incorrect; true – false; right – wrong; accurate – inaccurate*).

Vocabulary and speaking

1 Explain (or get a student to tell you) the meaning of *etiquette* – the rules of social and professional behaviour (i.e. doing the right thing in particular situations).
   - Students discuss the questions in pairs or small groups. If students are from different countries take this opportunity for cross-cultural comparisons.
   - At the end, ask a few students to report back on what happens in their country. Encourage the students to give reasons for their answers.
   - Students may be interested to know what happens in the US or the UK.

   ### Background information
   1 In the UK people often take a bottle of wine, flowers or chocolates. However, customs vary considerably from country to country and it is always best to find out what the local customs are, to avoid embarrassment.
   2 In Europe and the USA you can make 'small talk' about the weather, your family and any neutral subject which is not too personal or potentially controversial. It is generally best NOT to talk about politics, religion, health, money or very personal matters at first.
   3 It is not very strict in the USA and Europe. Other cultures often do things very differently.

2 Tell students they're going to look at some expressions with *make* and *do*.
   - Although there are some guidelines for when to use *make* and *do* (see **Language notes**), it is best to learn the expressions. Suggest that students make a list of these expressions.

1 make 2 do; make 3 do 4 make 5 make

Expressions with *do*	Expressions with *make*
do the right thing (unsure) what to do do your best	make a good impression make (it) more formal make a point make sure

Reading

3 Invite suggestions from the class as to the meaning of *Netiquette*. (A combination of the word 'Net', short for the Internet, and etiquette. It means the rules of behaviour for e-mails, the Internet, chat rooms, etc.)
   - Students discuss the questions from Exercise 2. Ask for ideas but do not give answers at this stage.

4 Students now read the text to see if their ideas about *Netiquette* are confirmed by the text.
   - Go through the answers. Explain that *emoticons* comes from the words *emotions* and *icons*.

1 F 2 T 3 F 4 F 5 T

Grammar focus

5 Do the first example together. Then ask students to underline the others in the text.

I <u>must</u> make it plain and simple.
You <u>mustn't</u> overuse punctuation.
You <u>have to</u> use plain English.
You <u>don't have to</u> use abbreviations.
Your messages <u>should</u> be short.
The way you start <u>shouldn't</u> be too formal.

6 Students use the examples from Exercise 5 to complete the explanations.
   - Check students understand the meanings, particularly the differences between: *must / should; must / have to; must / mustn't; have to / don't have to*. See **Language notes** above.

1 must   2 have to   3 shouldn't   4 don't have to 5 mustn't   6 should

Practice

7 In the example, remind students that *have to* is seen as an obligation from 'outside' (in this case the computer).
   - Students do the activity and check in pairs.
   - Go through the answers.

1 don't have to   2 mustn't   3 have to   4 should 5 must / should   6 don't have to   7 shouldn't / mustn't

Get talking …

8 Divide the class into pairs. Students work in pairs then compare their ideas with another couple.

… and writing

9 If possible, students write and send real e-mails.
   - For an example of an e-mail, see **Writing Bank 2** page 147.

Vocabulary Expressions with *time*
Grammar Ways to express contrasting ideas
Language to go Comparing attitudes

Six and a half hours

Language notes
- Students will need to learn the expressions with *time* as fixed expressions. Some of the expressions may be more problematic (*on time* = at exactly the right time; *in time* = at or before the required time). Point out that *spend time* is to use time doing something, while *waste time* is to use time badly.
- Exercise 5 focuses on different ways of showing contrast. Be prepared to spend time on the form, as *despite, in spite of, however*, etc. are followed by different structures.

Way in
- Ask students to think of the advantages and disadvantages of having a regular routine in their job (or studies). Find out if they think it is a good idea to have a lot of routine, or very little routine in their lives.

Vocabulary and speaking
1 Tell the students all the expressions in italics include the word *time*.
- Students match the two halves of the expression.
- Go through the answers, checking meaning further if necessary. See **Language notes** above.

   1 d   2 g   3 f   4 c   5 a   6 e   7 b

- Encourage students to discuss the questions in reference to their own situation.
- Make sure that students use the new phrases accurately.
- At the end, ask a few students to report what their partner said.

2 Focus attention on the photograph and ask students to describe the scene. Explain (or get a student to tell you) the meaning of the word *commuter* (n.) and *commute* (vb.)
- Ask students to predict if the statements are true or false for Tadao Masuda.
- Encourage them to give reasons for their answers, but do not spend too long on this activity.

Reading
3 Students read the article and check their answers from Exercise 2.

   1 T   2 T   3 T   4 F   5 F   6 T   7 F

4 Allow time for students to read the questions before asking them to read the article again.
- Students compare answers in pairs, before going over the answers.

   1 6 hours 30 minutes. (3 hours 15 minutes plus 3 hours 15 minutes)
   2 15 hours 55 minutes (4.55 a.m. to 8.50 p.m.)
   3 He likes to relax, think and be on his own.
   4 He works hard and doesn't complain.
   5 He might like more time, but he might miss the routine of travelling.

Grammar focus
5 Check that students understand the concept of *contrasting ideas* by telling them to look at example A. Ask if each part is positive, or negative (*You arrive at work tired,* is negative, but *it could be a lot worse,* is more positive). Clarify that the word *however* is used to contrast the two statements and show they are different. Draw attention to the position of *however* in the sentences and also to the punctuation.

   1 You arrive at work tired. *However*, it could be a lot worse.
   2 *Although* he knows the journey time to the minute, he leaves nothing to chance.
   3 *Despite* many problems at work during the day, I've always forgotten them by the time I get home.
   4 *Despite not* enjoying the journey, he does not complain about it.
   5 *In spite of* staying with the same company all his life, he still only gets ten days off a year.

- Draw students' attention to the form of these contrasting expressions: *However,* + subject + verb, *Although* + subject + verb, *Despite (not)* + noun / -ing form, *In spite of* + noun / -ing form.

6 ▭▭ Pause the recording after each sentence to give students time to repeat.
- Use a backchaining drill if students have problems with the long sentences. (See page 9 for ways to deal with pronunciation.)

Practice
7 Remind students that they may need to make changes with the word structures depending on which contrasting word they are using.

   1 Although I like work, I don't like commuting. (*work is a noun here **not** a verb*)
   2 I don't really like my job. However, I need the money.
   3 Although she works hard all week, she takes it easy on Sundays.
   4 Despite being very busy, he manages to take some time off.
   5 In spite of leaving on time, I'm always late.
   6 Despite not having an alarm clock, he always wakes up on time.
   7 Vocabulary is not easy to remember. However, it is essential.
   8 In spite of English verbs being easy, I have problems remembering the irregular ones.
   9 Despite wanting to learn English, I don't do any homework.
   10 Although I enjoy my English lessons, I'm often tired.

Get talking ...
8 Give students time to think about their own answers before dividing the class in pairs or small groups.
- Encourage students to give reasons for their attitudes.

... and writing
9 Remind students of ways of apologising and how to write a formal letter for a work situation.
- For an example of a formal letter, see **Writing Bank 5** page 150.

Vocabulary   Achievements and projects
Grammar   Present perfect simple and continuous
Language to go   Discussing personal achievements and projects

Achievement

Language notes

- The vocabulary in Exercise 1 looks at verb + noun combinations (or collocations) to do with achievement. Point out that other variations may be possible, but they are not the most typical, e.g. *win a machine*, *invent an exam* etc.
- Reassure students that the difference in meaning between the present perfect simple and the present perfect continuous can be very slight, especially when talking about an activity or state than can last a long time (*live*, *work*, *study* etc.). If an activity is completed, then we can **only** use the present perfect simple. Compare *I've been writing a letter* (I may or may not have finished it) and *I've written a letter*. (I've finished it).

Way in

- Give an example of a topical or famous achievement in your country. From this context elicit the idea of *achievement* (something successfully finished through skill and hard work). Ask students to tell each other about an achievement they really admire, and why. It could be to do with architecture, sport, inventions etc.

Vocabulary and speaking

1a Focus attention on the picture and ask students to describe any achievements they can see.
- Students match each verb with the most suitable noun. See also **Language notes** above.
- Go through the answers.

1 c   2 d   3 b   4 e   5 f   6 a

1b Students discuss the statements. At the end, ask a few students to report back, giving reasons for their choice.

2a Tell students to look at the nouns in the sentences to make some more verb + noun combinations.

1 working on   2 revise for   3 train to be   4 develop

2b Allow a few minutes for the students to discuss these statements, but do not spend too long on this activity.

Listening

3 Focus attention on the three photographs of radios. Elicit suggestions as to the differences between them, but do not go into detail about the connection to Trevor Baylis at this stage.
- Play the recording for students to choose the correct radio.

Picture B – the wind-up radio

4 Allow time for the students to read the questions and answer any they can at this stage.
- Play the recording again (more than once, if necessary) for students to answer the questions.
- Students check their answers with a partner.
- Go through the answers.

1 He's creative, outspoken, wild-haired. He's always working on new projects.
2 He realised that in many parts of Africa they could not use radios because there was no electricity and batteries were expensive.
3 A wind-up torch and a wind-up computer.
4 A power device which creates electricity as you walk (to power a mobile phone) and a wind-up system for roller-blades.
5 The programme is on at four o'clock.

Grammar focus

5 Read the example sentences and ask students to identify the tenses.
- Students do the activity and check with a partner.
- You may want to check further the difference in meaning between the two tenses (see **Language notes**).

1 Example A   2 Example B   3 The present perfect simple   4 The present perfect continuous
5 *past participle*   6 *been + present participle*

Practice

6 Read the example and elicit why the present perfect simple is used here (we're talking about *results* of past achievements).
- Students work to complete the activity.

7 Students listen and check their answers to Exercise 6.
- Remind students that *have*, *has* and *not* are usually contracted in speech.
- Pause the recording after each answer to allow students time to repeat accurately.

1 I haven't revised for my exam tomorrow, and now it's too late.
2 Mick's received a gold certificate for lifesaving.
3 I've been working on my typing skills, but I still make mistakes.
4 They're exhausted because they've been training for next week's marathon.
5 I've passed all my exams and now I'm going on holiday!
6 At last, I've finished working on that project.
7 He's been trying to get a new job but he hasn't had a single interview so far.

Get talking ...

8 Tell students to make notes individually first. Set a time limit (five minutes) and emphasise that their projects and achievements can be fairly small things.
- Students work in groups to ask and answer about their achievements and projects.
- At the end, ask a few students to report back.

... and writing

9 You may want to help students with ideas for a job (or club) they are going to apply for, and also what projects and achievements are relevant.
- For an example of a formal letter, see **Writing Bank 5** page 150.

Vocabulary   Prison
Function   Prohibition, obligation and permission in the past
Language to go   Discussing freedom

Long walk to freedom

Language notes
- Point out that *had to* is the past of both *must* and *have to*. It signals there was an obligation and therefore no choice. *Didn't have to* signals a lack of obligation and therefore a choice.

Way in
- Write the word *prison* on the board and ask students what other words it brings to mind, e.g. *criminals*. Construct a spidergram around the word. Don't spend too long on this warm-up.

Vocabulary and speaking

1 Focus attention on the photos and elicit some general information about Nelson Mandela (see below). You may want to pre-teach *arrested*; *cells*; *warders*; *freedom*; *prisoners* and *strict* at this stage. Add these words to the spidergram started in the warm-up exercise.
- Ask students to read the questions. Reassure them that it doesn't matter if they don't know about Mandela, as they are only required to make predictions at this stage.
- Ask a few students for their ideas but do not give any answers at this stage.

Background information
Nelson Mandela was an opponent of the old *apartheid* /əˈpɑːtheɪt/ (segregation of blacks and whites) system in South Africa. He fought for equal rights and opposed the government. In 1964 he was given a life sentence and spent the next 27 years as a political prisoner at Robben Island prison, near Cape Town. Meanwhile outside prison, his wife Winnie, and thousands of people worldwide, campaigned for his freedom. After his release from prison, he became President of the newly-independent state of South Africa.

2 Play the recording for students to check their predictions from Exercise 1.

1 He was arrested as a political prisoner for his violent fight against apartheid in South Africa.
2 Robben Island off the coast of South Africa. Conditions were terrible.
3 Very small and cramped – cells were six feet (1.8 m) wide.
4 They forced the prisoners to work in silence. They told them to break stones up with hammers.
5 Half an hour a day supervised by the warders.

Reading

3 Read the question and ask students to predict the rules to do with letters and visits.

4a Divide the class into two groups: Group A reads the extract about *letters* on page 58; Group B reads the extract about *visits* on page 85.
- Ask students to read their text and answer their questions.
- Walk round the class and give answers for each group separately.

Group A: 1 F   2 F   3 F   4 T
Group B: 1 F   2 T   3 F   4 T

4b When students are ready, divide the class into pairs (A+B).
- Tell them to share their information about their texts. Remind them to listen to their partner, not to read the other text.

Language focus

5 Go through Example A with the class. Draw attention to the form and remind students that the past of *must* is *had to*. See also **Language notes**.

A He *didn't have to break* stones.
B They *didn't make him work* in silence.
C They *didn't let him write* a letter every six months.
D He *wasn't allowed to have* visits of 30 minutes.

6a Ask students to complete the sentences using the examples (and negative forms) from Exercise 5.
- Students do the activity and check with a partner.
- Go through the answers.

1 had to; made
2 didn't have to; didn't make
3 was/were allowed to; let
4 wasn't/weren't allowed to; didn't let

6b Refer students back to the examples in order to complete the rule of form.

1 *object* (him/her/them etc.)
2 *infinitive* (without *to*)

Practice

7 Check understanding of the example by asking students if it is past *prohibition*, *obligation* (✓) or *permission*.
- Students do the activity and check with a partner.

8 Stop the recording after each sentence to give students time to check their answers. (Alternative answers are given in italics.)
- Play the recording again and ask students to repeat each sentence with the correct pronunciation.

1 Mandela's prison warders only let him exercise / *allowed him to exercise* for 30 minutes a day.
2 In the past, many prisoners had to wear / *were made to wear* chains.
3 Our family was very relaxed about rules and I was allowed to come home any time I wanted.
4 My grandmother was very strict – she didn't let us talk at the dinner table at her house.
5 My parents gave me no choice. I had to keep / *was made to keep* my room tidy.
6 There was a 'no smoking' rule at my school. The teachers and the students weren't allowed to smoke anywhere.
7 Some warders were kind. They didn't make me work when I was ill.

Get talking

9 Ask students to make notes about different times in their lives, and to give examples of things they were (and weren't) allowed to do.
- At the end, find out when people had the *most* or *least* freedom.

LESSON 29
Conditionals

Vocabulary   Doing business
Grammar   First and second conditionals
Language to go   Talking about likely and unlikely situations

Shaking hands

Language notes

- This lesson contrasts the first and second conditional. See **Language notes** in Lessons 9 (First conditional) and 19 (Second conditional) for further points. Students may be confused by the form not matching the meaning:
  First conditional: *If + present tense, will + infinitive* – to talk about likely events in the future.
  Second conditional: *If + past tense, would + infinitive* – to talk about unlikely or hypothetical (unreal) events in the present or future.

Way in

- As this lesson looks at ways of doing business around the world, take this opportunity to revise different countries and nationalities. Ask students to tell a partner about a country they enjoyed visiting and to name a country they would like to visit in the future, and why.

Speaking and vocabulary

1 Focus attention on the photograph and ask students to think of words to describe the scene.
   - Students work in pairs to discuss the questions. For students with no experience of meetings, ask *What do you imagine are the good and bad things about meetings?*
   - At the end, ask a few students to report back.

2 Tell students that the highlighted vocabulary is about *doing business*.
   - Ask students to read the text quickly before trying to complete the gaps. Remind them of possible tense changes.
   - Go through the answers. Encourage students to record verb + noun collocations like these in contexts. If time, ask students to think of other nouns which collocate with these verbs (e.g. *go on a course, do a good job, offer someone a drink*).

   1 do   2 made   3 made   4 offering
   5 exchanged   6 negotiate

Reading and listening

3 Students work with a partner (if possible, from a different country) to discuss the quiz and decide if they think the statements are true or false.
   - Do not go through the answers at this stage.

4 🎧 Play the recording for students to check their answers from Exercise 3.

   1 T   2 F   3 T   4 F   5 T   6 T   7 T   8 F

5 Focus attention on the statements that are false and ask students to try and correct these before they listen again.
   - Play the recording again for students to check their answers.

   2 It takes a long time to negotiate a deal in the Middle East.
   4 Business lunches in the US will probably only last an hour.
   8 In Thailand, a business person wouldn't open a present straight away.

Grammar focus

6 Read out the example sentences and ask students to identify the form and the meaning. See also **Language notes**.

   1 first conditional – *present tense, will + infinitive*
   2 second conditional – *past tense, would + infinitive*
   3 *likely*
   4 *unlikely*

7 Ask students to look at the recording script on page 122 and find other examples.

   First conditional:
   You probably won't have so many problems if you travel close to home.
   If someone invites you to the pub, they'll expect you to buy some drinks.
   If you have a business lunch, it'll probably only last an hour.

   Second conditional:
   If I visited an office there, they would almost certainly offer me a hot drink.
   If I wanted to negotiate a deal there, I would expect it to take some time.
   If you gave them a present, they'd probably think it was a bribe.
   If you gave a present in Thailand, they wouldn't open it straight away.

Practice

8 Do the example with the class. Check they understand the meaning of *likely* and *unlikely*.
   - Remind students that sometimes there isn't a 'correct' answer as it depends on how you feel about a situation.

9 Focus attention on the examples and tell students to write sentences about what they *will* or *would* do in these situations.
   - Walk round the class giving help and suggestions, but don't discuss the answers with the class, as students will do this in the next exercise.

   Suggested answers (for guidance only):
   1 If a friend asked me to give his nephew a job, I would refuse.
   2 If I decide to get a new job this year, I'll have to write my CV.
   3 If I were an hour late for an important business meeting, I'd lie and say that my train had been cancelled.
   4 If I was still in a meeting two hours after my finishing time, I wouldn't say anything.
   5 If it's sunny tomorrow, I won't go to work.
   6 If a business partner offered me a bribe, I'd pretend I hadn't heard.
   7 If my boss asked me to move to another country, I'd say yes.
   8 If one of my employees makes a lot of private phone calls, I'll tell them to stop.

Get talking

10 Divide the class into small groups and ask them to discuss their answers from Exercise 9.
   - At the end, find out how many of the issues they agreed on.

	Vocabulary	The weather
	Grammar	Reported statements
	Language to go	Reporting what you hear or read

Sunshine and showers

Language notes
- In reported speech, tenses usually 'jump back' in time; for example the present becomes the past, past simple changes to past perfect, *will* becomes *would*, *can* becomes *could*. If the statement remains true when reported, then it is not necessary to change the tense, e.g. *I love you* can be reported as *He said he loved me* or *He said he loves me*.
- Other changes include time expressions (e.g. *last night* becomes *the night before*; *this morning* becomes *that morning*) and pronouns (e.g. *I love you* becomes *He said he loved me*).
- *Say* and *tell* usually cause problems for students at this level. *Tell* is **always** followed by an indirect object but *say* is not. *She said ~~me~~ it was raining.*

Way in
- Make a statement about the weather and how it affects you, e.g. *Rain always makes me feel sad.* Ask students if the weather affects their mood, and if so, how?

Vocabulary and speaking
1. Focus attention on the weather map and ask students to tell you which country it is. (The US.)
   - Students match the words to the weather symbols.
   - Go through the answers. Check some of the vocabulary further, especially *fog* (cloudy air near the ground making visibility difficult), *showers* (rain, heavy or light, lasting a *short* time) and *thunderstorms* (heavy rain, lightning and thunder).

   1-e snow   2-f sunshine   3-b fog   4-h wind
   5-d showers   6-c rain   7-g thunderstorms   8-a cloud

2. Refer students to the first question and ask which adjective in the box goes with *rain*. In the context of question 1 it must be *heavy* (although it is possible to talk about *light rain*). Point out that these adjective-noun combinations are collocations, and are not necessarily logical and students must therefore learn them.
   - Students do the activity and check with a partner.

   1 heavy   2 light   3 severe   4 thick   5 heavy
   6 strong   7 thick   8 bright

3. Do the first question open class, encouraging students to use appropriate collocations.
   - At the end, ask a few students to report back

Listening
4. Ask students to match the statements to the pictures.
   1 B   2 C   3 A
5. Check understanding of the context (from the wedding invitation), especially that the reception will be outside, if the weather is nice.
   - Ask one or two students for their suggestions at this stage.

Play the recording for students to complete the table with the three predictions.

	What weather do they predict?
Danuta's grandmother	rain for most of the day
Steve's friend	warm weather and sunshine
The weather reporter on TV	rain, strong winds, thunderstorms, low temperatures

6. Play the rest of the recording (more than once, if necessary) and ask students to decide whose prediction was the most accurate.

   The weather reporter was the most accurate.

Grammar focus
7. Remind students that the first part of the recording script is *direct speech*.

   A The sky was very red this morning.
   B There will be rain and winds in the next 24 hours.

8a and b
Using the direct and reported speech from Exercise 7, students work to discover the rules. See also **Language notes**.

   a 1 told   2 said   b *don't need*

9. Write one or two examples from the recording script on the board to highlight the changes we make to tenses and time expressions.

   1 move one back   2 change

Practice
10. Remind students to think about *say* and *tell*, verb tenses and time expressions.
    - Students do the activity and check with a partner.

    1 She told us she felt sure about that.
    2 She told them they would just have to have the party inside.
    3 He said dreams could tell us a lot.
    4 He told us he had been dreaming about blue.
    5 He said he had been lying on a tropical beach the night before.
    6 He told them he was never wrong.
    7 She said the weather for the following day was looking very changeable.
    8 She told us thunderstorms would be everywhere by the following morning.
    9 She said they would be back after the late news.

Get talking
11. Check that all the groups understand their information, and that individuals within the groups know what they are going to say.
    - When students are ready to report their information, make new groups (A+B+C).
    - At the end, find out how students got on. Did they decide to have the party?

Vocabulary   Things we read
Grammar   Past perfect simple and continuous
Language to go   Talking about important moments

Turning points

Language notes

- Students sometimes confuse the past perfect continuous with the past continuous for setting the scene in a story. Compare *The sun was shining* (at the time of the main events of the story) with *The sun had been shining* (before the main events of the story).
- The past perfect simple is dealt with in more detail in Lesson 21. Both the simple and the continuous forms are used when we are already talking about the past. The past perfect simple to talk about an earlier past *action*. The past perfect continuous to talk about an earlier past *activity* or *repeated event*.

Way in

- Encourage students to read more in English. Remind them that it is an excellent way of improving vocabulary (as well as their reading and writing skills). If possible, take in examples of books, graded readers, newspaper articles etc. for students to read.

Vocabulary and speaking

1 Tell students that the highlighted vocabulary is to do with things we read. Refer students to the first speech bubble and ask what the speaker is talking about.
- Students do the activity and check with a partner.

1-g poetry   2-f a play   3-e a novel   4-c a newspaper
5-a a best-seller   6-d a textbook   7-h websites
8-b magazines

2 Divide the class into pairs and ask them to discuss the questions. Set a time limit of about five minutes.
- At the end, ask two or three students to report back about their partner.

Reading

3 Focus attention on the photograph and ask if the students recognise the person. (The author of the *Harry Potter* novels, J.K. Rowling.)
- Draw two columns on the board as shown and ask students to add things to either column.

Things I know about J.K. Rowling	Things I'm not sure about / would like to know about her
Wrote Harry Potter books	British?

4 Students read the text to discover what the title means, and to see if any of their ideas from Exercise 3 were correct.
- Remind students to read quickly and not to worry about any unknown words at this stage.

The title refers to the fact that J.K. Rowling brought the original Harry Potter stories back to Britain when she returned from Portugal.

Background information
The *Harry Potter* books have been hugely successful with more than 90 million copies sold all over the world. The books follow the adventures of Harry Potter; the orphaned son of two powerful wizards who possesses unique magical powers of his own. Harry enrols at *Hogwarts School of Witchcraft and Wizardry* where he meets a close circle of friends. Together they have magical and dangerous adventures.
J.K. Rowling plans to write more *Harry Potter* books. The film of the first book (*Harry Potter and the Philosopher's Stone*) stars Daniel Radcliffe as Harry.

5 Make sure students understand they are to put the events in chronological order, not the order they appear in the text.
- Students discuss their answers in pairs.
- Go through the answers.

1 f   2 d   3 b   4 a   5 i   6 e   7 c   8 h   9 g

Grammar focus

6 Use the timeline and check that students understand the past perfect is used when we are already talking about the past. Both tenses refer to things that happened *before* a particular time but the continuous form is used to talk about an earlier past activity or repeated event. See also **Language notes**.
- Focus attention on Example B: *Before 1996, she had been living in Portugal.* Ask: *Is 1996 in the past?* (Yes.) *Was living in Portugal before then?* (Yes.) *So, what tense do we use to show that?* (Past perfect.)
- Highlight pronunciation of both forms: *had* is often contracted and *been* is pronounced as a weak form /bɪn/.

1 action   2 activity

Practice

7 Check that students understand the tenses in the example (*had been working* – past perfect continuous for an activity *before* the main event – *became the director*).
- Students work to complete the activity then check their answers with a partner.

1 scored / had been playing
2 passed / had been studying
3 had been going out / decided
4 won / had been buying
5 had been hoping / had
6 had been planning / was
7 understood / had been studying

Get talking

8 If students are short of ideas, help them by telling them something from your own life, or suggesting further categories (sport, exams, chance meetings etc.). Remind them to think carefully about the tenses.
- Walk round the class listening to the groups as they share stories and make a note of any mistakes with the language of the lesson. Write these on the board and ask students to correct them at the end.

Vocabulary Housework and cleanliness
Grammar *Have something done* and reflexive pronouns
Language to go Things you do, and have done for you

Clean and tidy

Language notes

- Reflexive pronouns are often used for emphasis, e.g. *I cut my hair* **myself** (*I usually go to the hairdresser*). However, they are not usually used with these verbs: *wash, shave, dress, feel, hurry, relax, concentrate, meet. I felt ~~myself~~ very sad.*
- Students at this level often under-use causative constructions with *have*. A common mistake is: *I ~~cut my hair~~ at the hairdresser* [I had my hair cut at the hairdresser.] Word order can also be a problem, so be prepared to spend time on pattern drills.

Way in

- Ask students what their least favourite job or task around the house is (e.g. *doing the ironing*), and how they avoid doing it.
- Students mingle (i.e. walk round the room) and ask each other these questions, in order to find someone who agrees with them.
- Ask one or two students to report back to the whole class.

Vocabulary and speaking

1   Students do the activity and check their answers with a partner.
- Encourage students to help each other with the words they are not sure about.
- Point out that *homework* and *housework* are both uncountable nouns. If you've already done Lesson 25, encourage students to add to the expressions with *do* to their notebooks (*do the ironing, do the dishes, do the gardening*).

> 1 housework; tidy   2 wash; do   3 messy
> 4 do   5 do; wash

2   Where possible, ask male and female students to work together for this exercise. At the end, ask a few students to report back, encouraging students to give reasons for their opinions.

Reading

3   Write *Maid4U* on the board and invite students to suggest what it means, e.g. *Made for you / (a) maid for you.*
- Ask students to read the introduction as far as *Then read on …* and then close their books.
- Check students understand what the leaflet is (an advertisement for a domestic services agency) and elicit ideas about what services *Maid4U* might offer, e.g. *They clean the house for you. They do your washing.*
- Students now read the advertisement to see if their ideas were correct.

> washing and ironing; house cleaning; shopping; writing your shopping list and preparing menus (deciding what to buy); cutting hair; doing nails (manicure); picking children up from school; reading children bedtime stories.

4   Read out the titles and check they understand the meaning of *treat* (to buy or give something special to someone, or to yourself, as a friendly act).

- Students read the text again and match the headings to the paragraphs.

> 1 Home Services   2 Shopping special
> 3 Treat yourself   4 School's out

Grammar focus

5a   Focus attention on example A and ask what kind of word *yourself* is. (A reflexive pronoun.) You may want to ask students to compare the following sentences:
He's such a clever boy, he did it all.
He's such a clever boy, he did it all **himself**.
- Ask how the word *himself* makes it stronger. (He got no help.)
- Students work to complete the questions.

> 1 the same   2 stronger

5b   Ask students to complete the list of reflexive pronouns.

> me – *myself*   it – *itself*
> you – *yourself*   we – *ourselves*
> him – *himself*   you – *yourselves*
> her – *herself*   they – *themselves*

6a   Refer students to example B in the box and the highlighted structure: *have + something* (washing and ironing) *done*.
- Ask *who* does the action; *you*, or *someone else* (✓), and if you usually pay for the service or not. (Yes, you usually pay.)

> 1 No   2 Yes

6b   Draw attention to the construction:

> subject + *have* + object + past participle.

Remind students to use this structure in other tenses, the verb *have* changes while the other parts stay the same.
- Ask students to find examples in the text.

> … **have** all the boring things **done** … **I had** it (the house) **cleaned** … **Have** all your weekly shopping **done** … **Have** you ever **had** your hair **cut** … I've been **having** my hair and nails **done**

Practice

7   Ask students about the example: which part means you pay someone else to do it for you (*… have your feet massaged*).
- Students work to complete the activity and check their answers with a partner.
- Go through the answers.

> 1 did you have it cut; cut it myself
> 2 clean it myself; have it cleaned
> 3 organising it all themselves; having things organised
> 4 repair it myself; had mine repaired

Get talking

8   In pairs students think of other services. Ask them to share their ideas with the class, and write these on the board.
- Put students into small groups to discuss the questions.
- If time, you could do a class survey, e.g. *How many people do which services themselves? How many people have which services done for them?*

Vocabulary Describing changes
Grammar Future with *will* and *will have done*
Language to go Predicting future events

Tomorrow's world

Language notes

- As the expressions in Exercise 1 are similar, point out the following: *climb / drop*: implies a large increase / decrease; *improve / deteriorate*: implies an increase / decrease in quality; *go up / go down* and *get better / get worse* are more informal than the other expressions.
- We use *will have done* (the future perfect) to say that something will already be completed by a certain point in the future. We are talking now, but viewing things from a point in the future. We often use expressions beginning with *by*, meaning at or before that time, but not after that time, e.g. *I'll have finished it by Friday.*

Way in

- Write on the board: *Are you a technophobe or a technophile?* Check that students understand the meanings (*technophobe = someone who hates technology*; *technophile = someone who loves technology*).
- Prepare a handout (or write on the board) and let students test each other with these questions to find the technophobes and technophiles:

  1 Do you read about new developments in technology?
  2 Do you know how to use all the functions on your video, microwave oven, TV, hi-fi, mobile phone etc.?
  3 Do you use the Internet every day?

Vocabulary and speaking

1 Tell students that the expressions are all related to *change*. You may want to check meaning further.

good / bad changes	up / down changes
improve / deteriorate	go up / go down
get better / get worse	decrease / increase
	fall / rise
	climb / drop

2 Read out the topics for discussion and check understanding of *pollution, birthrate* and *life expectancy*.
- Walk round the class while students are talking and make sure they use the new language accurately.
- At the end, ask a few students to report back, giving reasons for their opinions.

Listening

3 Focus attention on the pictures and elicit ideas from the students as to what the inventions are. Accept any suggestions at this stage.

4 ▭ Play the recording for students to match the invention to the speaker.

A: Speaker 4   B: Speaker 3   C: Speaker 2
D: Speaker 1

5 Check understanding of *edible* (something you can eat).
- Play the recording again.
- Students listen for the year the speakers predict that these inventions will become available.

Prediction	Year
'Brainlink' computer	2035
More robots than people	2020
Edible computers	2020
Communication by brainwaves	2050

- Play the recording for a final time. Ask students which (if any) of the inventions they think will happen.

Grammar focus

6 Ask students to look at the examples of different ways of talking about the future and to find other examples in the recording script.

> Future with *will have done*
> By 2020, scientists *will have produced* computers…
> By 2050, scientists *will have developed* a technique …
>
> Future with *will*
> A tiny computer *will be implanted* … (passive) *It will tell* your brain … The number of schools *will fall* … They *will record* everything …
> These systems *will be* invaluable to doctors …
> The boundaries between people and machines *will disappear* … These *will allow* us to communicate …

7 Draw the following timeline on the board if necessary, to help students answer the questions. See also **Language notes**.

I'll have finished it by Friday

		✓?	✓? ✗
	today		Friday

> 1 before or at (not after)   2 at

- Point out that *will* is usually contracted and *have* is a weak form:
  I'll have /ailəv/ *finished it by Friday.*
- Drill as necessary.

Practice

8 Check that students understand the mistake in the example (the past participle is wrong).
- Students do the activity and check with a partner.
- Go through the answers.

> 1 won't <u>have</u> finished   2 will have <u>become</u>
> 3 <u>by</u> 3.30   4 they will have <u>built</u>   5 they <u>will</u> have developed   6 he'll <u>have</u> gone out   7 They will <u>have</u> <u>designed</u>

Get talking

9 Ask students to complete the table about themselves and their partner. Help students with ideas if necessary, e.g. exams, jobs, travel.
- Ask students to discuss their ideas.
- At the end, ask students to report back on any strange or amusing predictions their partner had made for them.

Vocabulary 1   Medical problems and symptoms
Vocabulary 2   Phrasal verbs about illness
Language to go   Describing symptoms of an illness

Honeymoon horrors

Language notes

- In Exercise 1 point out that the verb and noun are often the same word: *to ache / an ache, to bite / a bite, to itch / an itch, to sting / a sting, to cut / a cut.*
- You may need to check the specific meaning further, e.g. *What kind of creatures sting?* (bees, wasps, jellyfish) *What can bite?* (anything with teeth, also mosquitoes, spiders, snakes) *What makes you itch?* (wool, certain foods, fleas)
- The phrasal verbs in this lesson are as follows. See also Lesson 13.
  Type 1 Intransitive: *swell up, pass out, throw up* (inf.)
  Type 2 Transitive and inseparable: *turn into something, get over something.*
  Type 4 Transitive and inseparable with two particles: *come down with something, come out in something.*

Way in

- Ask students to name their *favourite*, and *least favourite* animals. Tell students that in this case 'animals' can include all animals, insects, birds and fish.
- Students discuss, giving reasons for their answers. Help with new vocabulary as necessary.

Vocabulary and speaking

1a Do the first sentence as an example with the class (sting). Use concept questions to check meaning further (see **Language notes**).

1 sting	2 swell up	3 bite	4 ache	5 itch	6 cut

1b Encourage students to help each other and, if possible, provide monolingual dictionaries for students to use.

to ache	an ache	achy
to bite	a bite	bitten
to cut	a cut	cut
to itch	an itch	itchy
to sting	a sting	stung
to swell up	a swelling	swollen

2 Ask students to look at the questions. Check the meaning of *precautions* (things you do, or have, to avoid possible danger, e.g. get medical insurance, have vaccinations against diseases like cholera, take antiseptic cream etc.).

Listening

3 Read the instruction and focus attention on the pictures. Check the meaning of *honeymoon* (a holiday for a newly married couple).
- Ask students for suggestions, but don't give the answers yet.

4 🔲 Make sure students understand they are just to listen for the correct picture at this stage.
- Play the recording once.
- Go through the answers (see column two of table).
- Check the meaning of *symptoms* (a noticeable sign of a disease, e.g. spots, pain).
- Play the recording (more than once, if necessary).
- Students complete the table and check their answers with a partner.

Speaker	Picture	Country	What happened?	Symptoms
1	C	Tanzania	bitten by a snake	leg swelled up; felt faint
2	B	Australia	stung by a jellyfish	leg came out in red spots
3	D	Ecuador	bitten by a mosquito	itchy; body ached
4	A	the USA	bitten by a spider	sickness, high fever; pain

Vocabulary focus

5a Write the phrasal verbs from the box on the board. Refer students to the recording script to find examples.
- Ask students to tell you the example (or get them to write it on the board).

a) I thought I was going to *pass out*.
b) It started to *swell up* straightaway.
c) My whole leg had *come out* in huge red spots.
d) It might have *turned into* something worse.
e) I didn't know what I had *come down* with.
f) I had a very high fever and *threw up* several times.
g) It took me almost a year to *get over* it.

5b Remind students to look at the examples in context and try to discover the meaning themselves.

1 d	2 e	3 a	4 b	5 g	6 c	7 f

6 Remind students of the different types of phrasal verbs.
- Ask them to divide the verbs into two groups. If students are familiar with the four types (see **Language notes**), you could ask them to categorise them in this way. Point out *throw up* is very informal.

Transitive	Intransitive
turn into; come down with; get over; come out in	swell up; pass out; throw up

7 🔲 Tell students that they are now going to listen to the examples that they found in the recording script. They should underline the stressed word as they listen.
- If time, play the recording again pausing after each item to allow students time to repeat.

See answers for Exercise 5a which show stress marked. The stress is on the second part, i.e. the (only) particle in two-part verbs and the first particle in three-part verbs.

Practice

8 Students complete the exercise, paying attention to any tense changes.
- Go through the answers.

1 Last year, I *came down with* a ...   2 it *swelled up* and I couldn't ...   3 ... – he *threw up* all night.
4 ... an infection can suddenly *turn into* something very bad.   5 ... – I *come out in* red spots if I eat it.
6 She'll be back at work when she *'s got over* the flu.

Get talking

9 Tell students to look at both parts of their rolecard. Monitor and help with their preparation, if necessary.
- Students then do the roleplay, changing roles when they are ready. Encourage them to set up the chairs for a 'doctor's surgery'.

LESSON **35**
Modals

Vocabulary   People and groups
Grammar   Past modal verbs of deduction
Language to go   Drawing conclusions about the past

Ice maiden

Language Notes

- Students at this level may have some trouble using past modals of deduction. Be prepared to spend some time on this and to give extra practice, if necessary.
  could have … and *might have …* mean something is possibly true (in my opinion).
  must have … means it is certainly true (in my opinion).
  can't have … means it is certainly <u>not</u> true (in my opinion). NB *Can't have …* is generally considered correct, but in some places *mustn't have …* is also used.

Vocabulary

1   Ask students to match the definitions with the words in the box and check their answers with a partner.

> 1 family   2 team   3 culture   4 generation
> 5 society   6 status

- If time, provide dictionaries and ask students to find collocations with these words (e.g. *pop culture*; *nuclear families*; *generation gap*; *high society*; *status symbol*; *team effort*; etc.).
- Write some of these on the board and suggest the students also put them in their vocabulary books.

Speaking and reading

2   Ask students to look at the photographs to help them make predictions.
- Ask students for suggestions, but don't give the answers at this stage.
- You may want to pre-teach *archaeologist* (a person who works and studies buried remains of ancient times) at this stage.

3   Students read the introduction to the article quickly in order to find the answers. (NB the meaning of *people* here is similar to *nation*. *Maiden*, meaning a young woman, is not a word of modern usage.)

> 1 A team of archaeologists. Excavating a burial ground in Siberia.
> 2 The body of a woman 2,500 years old.

4   Tell students that before they read the rest of the text, you'd like them to try and come up with explanations for various facts about the Ice Maiden. Check the meaning of *headdress* (a covering that decorates the head) and *tattoo* (a pattern or picture on the skin made with ink and needles).
- Read out number one and invite students to give reasons (*maybe she was very healthy, maybe she was from a different country* etc.).
- Students discuss the other facts, but don't give the answers at this stage.

5   Ask them to read the rest of the article to find the answers.

> 1 Possibly because she had extra food because of her high status.
> 2 Possibly because she was a soldier.
> 3 Possibly because she was important and she was almost certainly rich and powerful.
> 4 Probably because she was preserved in a special way when she died, because she was important.
> 5 Probably because she was a storyteller and used the tattoos to illustrate her stories.

Grammar focus

6a   Ask students where the first example comes in the text. Then let them work individually to find and underline the others. Write the answers on the board.
- Remind students that *might* and *could* have a very similar meaning. Draw attention to the pronunciation of *have* – usually pronounced as a weak form, e.g. *He must have* /mʌstəv/ *gone*.

> A She might have had extra food because of her status.
> B She could have worked as a soldier.
> C She can't have been an ordinary member of society.
> D She must have been a storyteller.

- Ask if the examples are talking about the present, or the past (✓).

6b   Students use the examples to match them with the meanings.

Sentence	Meaning of modal phrases
C	It's certainly not true
A or B	It's possibly true
D	It's certainly true
B or A	It's possibly true

Practice

7   Explain (or get a student to tell you) the meaning of *draw conclusions* (make educated guesses based on facts).
- Refer students to the example and ask: *How sure are we that she was rich? What reasons do we have for this?* (We are *sure*, because we have the information that she had a *gold* headdress).
- Students do the activity and check with a partner.

> 1 She might/could have had special medical care.
> 2 She must have had a good memory.
> 3 He might/could have run out of petrol.
> 4 He can't have heard his alarm clock.
> 5 He must have gone out.
> 6 They might/could have got lost.
> 7 Someone might/could have borrowed it.
> 8 She can't have studied much.

Get talking …

8   Focus attention on the cartoon and elicit a few ideas about life 2,500 years ago. Remind them to also think about the text while they're making notes.
- Reassure them that it doesn't matter if they don't know the 'answer', as the idea is to make an educated guess.
- Divide the class into groups to discuss their ideas. Encourage students to give reasons.

… and writing

9
- Remind students to use the language from the lesson.
- Encourage students to edit their own writing and to check their partner's.

LESSON 36
Connecting

Vocabulary Business processes: word building
Grammar Non-defining relative clauses
Language to go Giving extra information

A winning formula

Language notes

- Non-defining relative clauses give extra (non-essential) information. (Defining relative clauses are covered in Lesson 16). Using the same sentence with commas (non-defining) or without commas (defining) can produce a very different meaning. Compare: *His wife, who is from Hong Kong, cooks wonderful Chinese food* with *His wife who is from Hong Kong cooks wonderful Chinese food*. In the first sentence, he has only one wife and incidentally she is from Hong Kong. Hong Kong is non-essential information. We are not **defining** which wife. In the second sentence, he has more than one wife. *This* wife is from Hong Kong. The others are not. So it is important to **define** which wife.
- Non-defining relative clauses are more common in writing where they are separated by commas before, and after, the clause. In speaking, the same affect can be achieved using pauses and intonation.

Way in

- Show students pictures or real pieces of clothing with famous brand names on them, e.g. a pair of Levi® jeans, some Nike® trainers etc. Tell students that Levi's, Nike etc. are *brand names*. Ask students to suggest why some people prefer to buy famous brand-named products.

Vocabulary and speaking

1   Refer students to the highlighted vocabulary. Point out the word stress, particularly any shifting word stress:
    a <u>pro</u>duct / pro<u>duc</u>tion / to pro<u>duce</u>
    a <u>mar</u>ket / <u>mar</u>keting / to <u>mar</u>ket
    a <u>bus</u>iness / <u>bus</u>iness / to do <u>bus</u>iness
    an ad<u>ver</u>tisement / <u>ad</u>vertising / to ad<u>ver</u>tise
    - Students complete the sentences choosing words from the box.
    - Go over the answers.

    1 products   2 Business   3 marketing; advertising
    4 planning   5 business plan   6 market   7 advert

2   Ask students to read the statements and discuss them with a partner.
    - At the end, ask a few students to report back.

Reading

3   Focus attention on the article and check comprehension of *a winning formula* (a successful idea).
    - Students read the introduction to answer the question.

    creating short, memorable messages on T-shirts

4   Ask students to read the whole of the text quickly to find out the significance of the numbers.
    - Students check their answers with a partner.

    5 – the number of words on a T-shirt
    20 (years) – how long he has known his friends
    36 – how old Toby Mott was when he had the idea
    40 – the number of T-shirts he sold in (the first) week
    60,000 – the number of T-shirts sold in the last 12 months

5   Allow time for students to read the questions before reading the text again.

    1 Because the first T-shirts sold so quickly.
    2 From things he thinks about and what his friends say.
    3 They still treat him the same and they are surprised by his success.

    - At the end, ask: *Would you wear a T-shirt like this? What message would you write on yours?*

Grammar focus

6   Read out the example sentence. Students work together to answer the questions.
    - Take this opportunity to revise defining relative clauses and to point out the importance of punctuation. See **Language notes** above.

    1 it adds extra information
    2 *who*
    3 it will still make sense, but the meaning changes
    4 commas before and after the clause (or a full stop at the end of a sentence)

7   Students look back at the text to find other examples of non-defining relative clauses.

    His customers, <u>*who include the rich and the famous*</u>, enjoy his imaginative phrases.
    … <u>*which he sold to the top international model*</u>, Kate Moss.
    … on the same small desk, <u>*where I produce all the designs*</u>.

    Relative pronouns used: *who, which, where*

    - Remind students about other relative pronouns (*when, whose*) and point out that the relative pronoun *that*, cannot be used with non-defining relative clauses.

Practice

8   Check students understand the changes necessary in the example. Ask: *What word is **new**, and what word is **missing**?* (*which* is new and *it* is missing).

    1 Her home town, which has a population of 50,000, is in the north of the island.
    2 Budapest, where I went on business last year, has a large river.
    3 His wife, who is from Hong Kong, cooks wonderful Chinese food.
    4 My football team, who I have supported for years, keeps on losing.
    5 That woman, who is only 25, has opened her own shop.
    6 My friend, whose parents live in Cape Town, has decided to move to South Africa
    7 That programme 'Entrepreneurs', which is on at 8.00 p.m., is really good.

Get talking …

9   Monitor and help students with ideas for a product if necessary.
    - Ask students to explain their business plan to other students.

… and writing

10 Remind students about the layout and language of a formal business letter.
    - For an example of a formal letter, see **Writing Bank 5** page 150.

> PHOTOCOPIABLE ACTIVITY PAGE 126

Vocabulary Verb expressions about friendship
Grammar Present perfect with *for* and *since*
Language to go Describing friendship

Old friends

Language notes
- Other lessons on the present perfect are 7, 17 and 27. This lesson looks at both the simple and the continuous forms with reference to *for* and *since*. Remind students that *for* refers to a **period** of time and *since* refers back to a **point** in time.
- Students at this level often have difficulty in choosing between the simple and continuous forms. There is a general tendency for the continuous form to be preferred when we refer to something *temporary*, *recent* or *unfinished*. Reassure students, however, there are many situations when you can use either form.
- Point out that as with other tenses, we don't usually use state verbs in the continuous form, e.g. *believe*, *know*, *understand*. *I've ~~been knowing~~ Martin for three years.* [known]

Way in
- Ask students to tell their partner about the last time they sent (or received) a greetings card, e.g. a birthday card. What was the occasion, and who did they send a card to / receive a card from?

Vocabulary and speaking
1 Tell students that the highlighted vocabulary is to do with friendships.
   - Ask students to read all the sentences before trying to fill the gaps.
   - Encourage them to help each other, or to use monolingual dictionaries if they have them to hand.

   1 send   2 lost contact with   3 keep in touch with (*continue to be in contact with someone*)   4 rely on
   5 keep up with (*continue to know what is happening in someone's life*)   6 remain   7 am in touch with (*be in contact with someone*)

2 Divide the class into pairs and ask them to say if the sentences are true for them or not. If not, what is?
   E.g. *I'd like to send cards to all my friends but I often forget because I've got a bad memory.*
   - At the end, ask a few students to report back to the whole class.

3 Encourage students to describe the appearances and possible characters of the men in the photograph. Ask for ideas but don't give any answers at this stage.

Listening
4 📼 Tell students they will hear the men talking separately about their friendship. Check they understand they are to listen to see if the men agree with each other or not.
   - Play the recording (more than once, if necessary) for students to listen and make notes.

James says...	Richard says...
1 60 years	1 55 years
2 at school	2 they were neighbours
3 yes, but not in the 70s (too much work)	3 they lost touch when he moved to Scotland in the 70s
4 about once a month	4 about once a week
5 go to the park; have drinks in the evenings	5 go to the park; meet for lunch

5 Play the recording once through for a final time and ask students to find any other differences.
   - Students check their answers with a partner.

   They disagree about:
   Schools – James says: *He started at my school.* Richard says: *He went to a different school.*
   Weddings – James says: *Richard was my best man when I got married.* Richard says: *I didn't go to James' wedding, but he came to mine.*
   Living in Brighton – James says: *We've both been living in Brighton since we retired in 1995.* Richard says: *I've been living in Brighton since '99.*

Grammar focus
6 Focus attention on the timelines. Ask students to work together to discover the rules. See also **Language notes**.

   1 *actions or states which started in the past and continued until now*
   2 *present perfect continuous*
   3 *since*
   4 *for*

Practice
7 Check students understand the example by asking why *for* is correct (*two hours* is a *period* of time).
   - Students do the activity and check with a partner.
   - Go through the answers or, if you prefer, students can listen for the answers in Exercise 8.

   1 We've <u>known</u> them for more than twenty years.
   2 She's <u>won</u> the competition for the last five years.
   3 <u>Have</u> you visited your grandmother since her accident?
   4 They haven't <u>phoned</u> me for ages.
   5 I've <u>been</u> doing my homework for two hours.
   6 I've <u>liked</u> her for a long time.
   7 How long <u>have you</u> been living here?

8 📼 Ask students to listen to check their answers.
   - Remind them that *have / has* and *been* are not stressed.
   - Stop the recording after each sentence to give students time to repeat.

Get talking
9 Draw a circle on the board and write '*me*' in the middle.

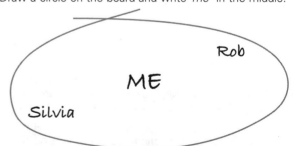

   - Write the names of two of your friends in the circle (the closer the friend the nearer they go to the middle). Tell the class a little bit about them and invite them to ask you questions, e.g. *How long have you known Rob?*
   - Ask students to do the same. Remind them to look at the questions in the table in Exercise 4.

Don't worry, be happy

Language notes
- Word order in indirect questions can be confusing for students at this level. For *Wh-* questions, the subject and verb are reversed, e.g. *What time is it?* → *Could you tell me what time it is?* For *Yes / No* questions, the subject and verb are reversed and we use *if*.
Are you married? → *Can I ask if you are married?*
- Remind students that the construction *Would you mind ...* is followed by the *-ing* form and that the response *No* means it **isn't** *a problem*, and *Yes* means it **is** *a problem*.

Way in
- Write the words *Happiness is ...?* and *I feel really happy when ...* on the board. Students complete the sentences in their own words, then discuss with a partner. Ask a few students to report back to the rest of the class.

   ### Background information
   Bobby McFerrin was born in New York in 1950. Throughout his career he performed all over the world. He was very successful commercially with his one-man vocal act; he sings all the words and plays or creates all the sounds. In 1988, he released his most famous album, *Simple Pleasures*, which included the hit *Don't worry, be happy.*

Speaking and vocabulary
1   Focus attention on the photograph and ask students if they know anything about the singer pictured. (Bobby McFerrin.)
   - Ask students to discuss the questions with a partner. Reassure students they do not have to talk about any uncomfortable issues.
   - At the end, ask a few students to report back.
2   Ask students to read the sentences and to put the words in italics into the correct columns.
   - Go through the answers, drawing attention to the number of syllables, and any 'silent' syllables: *pleas(e)d* (O); *thrill(e)d* (O); *depress(e)d* (oO); *mis(e)rable* (Ooo); *delighted* (oOo); *satisfied* (Ooo).

very unhappy	happy	very happy
depressed	satisfied	delighted
miserable	in a good mood	thrilled
in a bad mood	pleased	
	glad	

3   Ask students to discuss the graph with their partners and when they are ready to look at the answers on page 87.
   - Ask students if they were surprised by any of the results.

Listening
4   📖 Play the recording once through. Students make a note of any of the topics from the graph which are mentioned.

   health, money, marriage, job

5   Allow time for students to read through the sentences.
   - Play the recording again (more than once, if necessary).
   - Students check their answers with a partner.

   1 F   2 T   3 F   4 T

Language focus
6   Ask students why we use indirect questions (to be *polite*, e.g. when we are asking something *personal*, or if we don't know the person very well).
   - Refer students to the recording script to complete the questions, then to think of the equivalent *direct* question.

   A Would you mind **telling me** if you've ever seen ... ? (Have you ever seen ... ?)
   B Could you **tell me** which you worry about more? (Which do you worry about more?)
   C Can I **ask you** how you feel about ... ? (How do you feel about ... ?)
   D I'd like **to know** how you feel about your job. (How do you feel about your job?)

   - Point out that indirect questions starting with *I'd like to ...* do not need a question mark at the end.

7a   Tell students to use the examples to help work out the rules. See **Language notes**.
   - If necessary, check form further by asking if auxiliary verbs (*do, have* etc.) are used with direct (✔) or indirect questions.

   1 *Wh-*questions: **question word** + subject + (modal verb) + **main verb**.
   2 *Yes / No* questions: **If** + subject + (modal verb) + **main verb**.

7b   Remind students that these are *polite* ways of saying you don't want to answer a question.

   I'd **prefer** not to answer that one. I'd **rather** not say.

Practice
8   Students work to complete the activity and check their answers with a partner.
   - Go through the answers or, if you prefer, students can listen for the answers in Exercise 8.

   1 I'd like to know if you're generally an optimistic person.
   2 Can I ask you if you are happy with your job?
   3 Could you tell me if you woke up in a good mood this morning?
   4 I'd like to know how you'd react if someone damaged your car.
   5 Would you mind telling me how you'd feel about winning the lottery?
   6 Could you tell me if you worry about getting old?
   7 Can I ask you if you like answering personal questions?

9   📖 Play the recording for students to check their answers to Exercise 8.
   - Allow time for students to listen and repeat.

Get talking ...
10   Remind students that if they don't want to give an answer, they need to refuse *politely*.
11   📖 Get students to look at the words (or sing along) as they listen.

> PHOTOCOPIABLE ACTIVITY PAGE 130

Vocabulary   Shopping
Grammar   Third conditional and *I wish / If only*
Language to go   Talking about past regrets

If only …

Language notes

- Some of the expressions in Exercise 1 may need further clarification: *shop around* – compare goods before buying; *go window shopping* – look at goods without intending to buy; *get a bargain* – buy something for less than its real value; *haggle* – negotiate a cheaper price (usually in street markets, not in shops in the UK or US); *the sales* – a period when shops sell the goods more cheaply (usually at the end of a season).
- *If only*, *I wish* and the third conditional are used to express regret about the past (you are talking *now* about something you did / didn't do in the past). The third conditional is also used to speculate about how past events might have been different. Be prepared to spend time on the conditional clause of the third conditional and give extra practice if necessary.

Way in

- Ask students about the most expensive thing they've ever bought. What was it? Why did they buy it? Are they glad now?

Vocabulary and speaking

1   Ask students to read all the sentences before trying to fill the gaps.
- Encourage them to help each other and to try and discover the meanings from context.
- Go over the answers. See also **Language notes** above.

> 1 go window shopping   2 buy things on impulse
> 3 the sales; get a bargain   4 shop around
> 5 take things back; refund   6 haggling
> 7 try clothes on

2   Set a time limit (about five minutes) for students to discuss the questions. Walk round the class as students talk, giving help as necessary. Make sure they use the new vocabulary accurately.

Reading

3   Ask students to read the questions. Check understanding of *souvenirs* (objects kept to remind you of a place you've visited).
- At the end, ask a few students to report back.

4   Focus attention on the pictures and ask students to describe the situation. (They are tourists in India, the photograph is of the Red Fort in Delhi.)
- Ask them to read the text quickly and name the people in the picture. (Liz, Dave, the hatseller, other tourists.)
- Point out that *You buy hat?* and '*you give price*' is not standard English but is used here to show that the hatseller is not a native speaker.
- Allow time for students to read the sentences, before reading the text again.

> 1 F   2 T   3 T   4 T   5 F

Grammar focus

5   Focus attention on the grammar box and ask students to answer the questions.

> 1 Yes, he bought the hat.
> 2 He regrets / is sad and angry that he bought the hat.

6a   Refer students to the examples to help them answer the questions.
- You may want to point out that *wish + past perfect* can be used with other subject pronouns, e.g. *He wishes he hadn't bought the hat. They wish they hadn't gone to France.*

> 1 *past perfect simple*
> 2 *may have been different in the past*

6b   Draw attention to the fact that *had* and *would* are usually contracted and *been* is usually pronounced as a weak form.

> *If + had + past participle, would + have + past participle*

Practice

7   Check that students understand the example sentences by asking: *Did I buy that skirt on impulse?* (Yes); *Did I waste my money?* (Yes); *How do I feel now?* (I regret buying it).
- Students do the activity and check with a partner.

> 1 I wish / If only I hadn't gone to bed late.
>   If I hadn't gone to bed late, I wouldn't have felt tired in the morning.
> 2 I wish / If only I'd started my homework early enough.
>   If I'd started my homework early enough, I'd have finished it.
> 3 I wish / If only I hadn't forgotten my mother's birthday.
>   If I hadn't forgotten my mother's birthday, she wouldn't have got upset.
> 4 I wish / If only I'd paid more attention at school.
>   If I'd paid more attention at school, I wouldn't have failed my exam.
> 5 I wish / If only I hadn't arrived late for the interview.
>   If I hadn't arrived late for the interview, I would have got the job.
> 6 I wish / If only I hadn't told my friend she looked fat.
>   If I hadn't told my friend she looked fat, she would have spoken to me again.

Get talking

8   Tell students that 'you only regret what you don't do' is a saying that some people believe is true. Give an example, *I had the chance to go to the US. But I didn't go. Now I wish I had gone.*
- Ask students to make notes individually first before dividing the class into small groups.
- At the end, find out how many people in the class believe the saying is true.

Vocabulary   Job applications and interviews
Grammar   Reported questions
Language to go   Reporting a conversation or interview

How did it go?

Language notes

• For notes on reported statements see Lesson 30. Many of the issues discussed there are also true for reported questions, e.g. the verb jumps back one tense, pronouns change and time expressions change. Draw students' attention to the different ways of starting reported statements. This lesson focuses on: *She asked me ...*; *He wanted to know ...*; *She wanted me to tell her ... .*

Way in

• Tell students you are thinking of a profession (e.g. a doctor) and they have to guess what it is, asking as few *Yes / No* questions as possible. For example: *Do you wear a special uniform? Do you work long hours? Do you earn a big salary? Did you have a lot of training?*
• Once they have guessed correctly, divide the class into pairs and tell them to play the game with their partner.

Speaking and vocabulary

1   Focus attention on the photo of the girl on the left. Elicit what she is doing (preparing for an interview) and ask how she might be feeling (nervous, confident etc.)
   • Ask students to discuss the questions in pairs, but do not spend too long on this activity.

2a Explain (or get a student to tell you) the meaning of *tips* (advice) and ask where this extract comes from (a book about how to get a job).
   • Tell students to read the extract quickly to get an idea of its content before trying to fill the gaps.
   • Go over the answers.

   1 strengths   2 weaknesses   3 experience
   4 qualifications   5 references   6 promotion prospects
   7 long-term goals

2b Give students a few minutes to try and decide on the top three tips, with reasons.
   • Ask a few students to report what they agreed on.

Listening

3   🎧 Tell students to look at the second photo and discuss the questions briefly before listening.
   • Play the recording for students to check their ideas.

   1 She doesn't think she has done well and so won't be offered the job.
   2 Yes. She forgot things and she said things she didn't really want to say.

4   Allow time for students to read the questions before playing the recording again.
   • Students listen and tick the questions that Madeline was asked.

   Questions 1, 3 and 5

Grammar Focus

5   Tell students that they are going to look at reporting questions. If they've studied Lesson 30 recently, point out that many of the rules are the same. See also **Language notes** above.

   1 She asked me + *question word* + *subject* + (modal verb) + *main verb*.
   2 She wanted to know + *if* + *subject* + (modal verb) + *main verb*.

6   Refer students to the examples if necessary.

   one tense back from

7   Ask students to look at the recording script to find different ways of starting reported questions.

   She asked me ...
   She wanted to know ...
   She wanted me to tell her ...

Practice

8   Remind students about the different ways of starting reported questions (as in the example), and also to think carefully about verb tenses, pronouns and time expressions.

   Suggested answers
   1 He asked me what qualifications he needed for the job.
   2 I wanted her to tell me if they offered a training programme.
   3 He wanted to know where he'd work.
   4 She asked me if there was a uniform.
   5 She wanted me to tell her who she would work with.
   6 He asked me what type of work would be involved.
   7 She wanted to know what the salary scale was.
   8 He wanted me to tell him when the job started.
   9 I asked him if there were any promotion prospects.

Get Talking

9   You may need to help students think of an appropriate situation to report. (If students have done Lesson 7 they could use the interview in the *Get Talking* section.)
   • Tell students to make notes individually first.
   • When students are ready, divide the class into pairs and ask them to report their situation.
   • Walk round the class listening and giving help, if necessary. Make a note of any mistakes with the language of the lesson and write these on the board. Ask students to correct these at the end.

Photocopiable material

Vocabulary Adjectives and intensifiers
Grammar Past simple and continuous
Language to go Telling stories and exaggerating events

Hold the front page!

Aim

To give students practice at using the past simple, past continuous and intensifiers when telling stories

Materials

One story (A or B) per student

Time

30 minutes

Preparation

Copy and cut up one worksheet per two students

Procedure

1 Introduce the topic by eliciting the kind of stories you find in tabloid newspapers. Ask students to tell the class about a strange or funny story they have read about in the newspaper.

2 Tell students that they will receive a story in picture form with some vocabulary to help them. The story is about something that happened to them which they want to sell to a tabloid newspaper by making the story as interesting as possible.

3 As an example, write on the board: *... quite a cold night ... a little snow on the ground.* Ask the students to make the story sound more interesting. For example: *It was a freezing night / extremely cold night and there were three metres of snow on the ground.* If students have done the lesson in the Students' Book, remind them of the language they studied.

4 Put students into pairs. Give half of the pairs Story A and the other half Story B.

5 Give them seven to ten minutes to prepare their story. They should **not** write whole sentences but they can write notes. Help students if / when necessary. If some pairs finish early, ask them to practise telling the story quietly to their partner.

6 Ask each student who has worked on Story A to find a new partner who has worked on Story B.

7 In turns, they phone a local English-speaking newspaper and try to sell their story. Their partner is the newspaper editor. Put students back to back if possible, to simulate telephoning. Tell the students that they should only look at their story if they need help.

8 Once both students have told their stories, ask them to work in pairs to think of possible dramatic headlines that would be suitable.

9 Write their suggestions on the board.

Extension

Writing: Students write their story in the form of a tabloid newspaper article.

Story A

1 home from the pub / with my girlfriend / last night / twenty-minute walk / across the fields

2 no stars / dark / couldn't see well / only small torch

3 while walking / suddenly / a roar / large animal

4 couldn't see well / but two eyes / looked like a big black cat

5 afraid / started running / up the hill / not stop until / home / tired

6 back to the field / this morning / big pawprint

Story B

1 husband and I / back to Britain from France / ferry / after a good holiday

2 hungry / fish and chips / restaurant / crowded

3 while eating / sea / rough / husband seasick / side of the boat / as fast as possible

4 unfortunately / false teeth / fell out / into the sea / awful

5 next day / home / radio / interview with a fisherman / found false teeth / fish

6 surprised / phoned him / husband's teeth

 © Pearson Education 2002

Vocabulary Sleep
Grammar Subject and object questions
Language to go Asking about and describing routines

Any answers?

Aim

To give students practice at asking about and describing routines using subject and object questions

Materials

One set of cards per group of three or four students

Time

30 minutes

Preparation

Copy and cut up one worksheet per group

Procedure

1 Tell students that they are going to play a question and answer game in groups of three or four. Every student will receive four or five cards, each one with a sentence written on it connected with things that people do in the home or in their daily lives.

2 As an example, write the following on the board:
Something that people do when they go out in the evening
1)
2)
3)
What _____ *?*

3 Ask students to write down what they think would be the three most popular answers. For example: *Go to a bar, go for a meal, go to a disco.* Write up their suggestions on the board. Establish the three most popular answers.

4 Elicit the question for the example sentence above: *What do people do when they go out in the evening?*

5 Explain that each card will have a similar sentence beginning either with *something* or with *someone*. Make it clear to students that *someone* means a type of person or the title of a job, not a person's name.

6 Give each group their pile of sixteen cards face down. Each student should take four or five cards, think about the most popular answers for each sentence, write his / her three answers underneath the sentence, then write the question. Allow seven to ten minutes.

7 When students have finished writing their questions, they should check them with you.

8 Students now play the game. In turn, they ask the questions on their cards. The first student asks the student on his / her left. If this student gives one of the three answers on the card, he / she gets a point. Then the next student has a chance to answer, and so on until the three answers on the card have been found (or until each student has had three guesses). Every answer that matches an answer on the question card receives a point. The student with the most points at the end wins.

Something that people do when they get home from work/school
1)
2)
3)
What _____ ?

Someone who works sometimes at night and sometimes during the day
1)
2)
3)
Who _____ ?

Someone who people write to
1)
2)
3)
Who _____ ?

Something that people do when they are watching TV
1)
2)
3)
What _____ ?

Someone who uses the phone a lot in his/her work
1)
2)
3)
Who _____ ?

Someone people complain to
1)
2)
3)
Who _____ ?

Something that people do when they're ill
1)
2)
3)
What _____ ?

Something that makes people laugh
1)
2)
3)
What _____ ?

Something that wakes people up in the morning
1)
2)
3)
What _____ ?

Something that people do to relax
1)
2)
3)
What _____ ?

Something people do when they can't sleep
1)
2)
3)
What _____ ?

Someone who travels a lot in his/her job
1)
2)
3)
Who _____ ?

Something you see people doing in a bus or a train
1)
2)
3)
What _____ ?

Someone you go to when you have a problem
1)
2)
3)
Who _____ ?

Someone you watch in a theatre, a stadium or a concert hall
1)
2)
3)
Who _____ ?

Someone you buy presents for
1)
2)
3)
Who _____ ?

LESSON **3**

The future

Vocabulary Associations
Grammar Future with *will* and *going to*
Language to go Making decisions and giving reasons for decisions

Name it

Aim

To give students practice at using *will* and *going to* for making decisions about the future, and at giving reasons for their decisions

Materials

One set of cards per group of three or four students

Time

25–30 minutes

Preparation

Copy and cut up one worksheet per group

Procedure

1 Introduce the activity by asking students to suggest different things that they have to make decisions about in their lives.

2 Tell them that they are going to play a decision-making game which tests how quickly they can make decisions. They will play the game in groups and each group will have sixteen question cards.
The answer to each card will require the name of a person, place, type of food, etc.

3 Explain the rules of the game. The sixteen cards are shuffled and placed face down in the middle of the table. Students take it in turns to pick up a card and read it to the group. The first student to respond correctly with *will* and give a reason gets five points. (If no one responds within ten seconds, the card is put to the bottom of the pile.) The other students then have a chance to respond, also with *will* and giving a reason, for two points. Finally, the student who read out the card has to summarise his/her group's responses, using *going to*. This student gets one point per correct sentence.

4 As an example, tell students you are going to read them a card. If they want to respond, they have to call out their name; the first person to say his/her name will get the first chance to respond. Say: *You have a new dog/cat. Decide what to call it.* Follow the procedure above, awarding five points to the first correct response and two points for other correct responses. Then ask students to summarise the responses, for example: *Laura is going to call it 'Snowy' because it's white. David is going to …*

5 Put students into groups of three or four. Check the rules. If there is any disagreement about an answer, the group should call you.

6 Students play the game for twelve to fifteen minutes. Establish the winner in each group (the student with the most points).

7 Then put the following questions on the board and ask students to discuss them in their groups:
Which questions were the most difficult for you to answer and why?
Do you like making decisions quickly or do you prefer to think about something first? Why?
When should you think about something before making a decision?

You're in your favourite restaurant. Decide what to have.

You're in a disco or wine bar. Decide what drink to have.

You've received £100 for your birthday. Decide what to buy.

You're on a TV game show. You need some help with a question about history. Decide who to phone.

You're on holiday. You buy some postcards. Decide who to send them to.

You've won a holiday for two. Decide who to take.

A friend from another country is coming to visit you. Decide what to show him / her.

A friend asks you to recommend a book to read. Decide what to recommend.

It's your best friend's birthday next week. Decide what to buy him / her.

You want to relax by listening to some music. Decide what to listen to.

You're in the video shop. Decide what to take out.

You have a personal problem and you want to discuss it with someone. Decide who to talk to.

It's a really hot day. You see an ice cream shop. Decide what kind of ice cream to buy.

You want to take up a new sport. Decide what to try.

You're in a newsagent's. Decide what newspaper / magazine to buy.

You want to cook a special meal for your partner. Decide what to cook.

Vocabulary Education
Grammar Comparatives and superlatives
Language to go Comparing careers

Contrasting careers

Aim

To give students practice at using comparatives and superlatives when discussing different jobs

Materials

One worksheet per student

Time

30 minutes

Preparation

Copy the worksheet

Procedure

1 Ask students to write down two jobs, one they would really like to have and one they would hate. Now write the following sentences on the board and ask students to write one or two similar sentences about their two jobs:
   A film star is better paid than a nurse.
   A nurse has a more important / stressful job than a film star because …
   A film star has a more enjoyable life than a nurse because …
   A nurse needs better qualifications than a film star because …
2 Ask individual students to tell you the jobs they have written down and one of the sentences comparing the two.
3 Briefly review how to form comparatives.
4 Tell students that they will be given a worksheet with five pairs of jobs illustrated. For each pair, they should talk about the similarities (if any) and the differences, using the expressions in the table on the worksheet and any others that they want to use.
5 Put students into pairs and give them each a copy of the worksheet. Ask them to check the meaning and pronunciation of the vocabulary first. They then have about ten minutes to discuss the five pairs of jobs.
6 Ask for brief feedback. **NB** For stronger students, see extension below.
7 Form groups of three or four students to discuss the questions in Part B of the worksheet.

Extension

Speaking:

1 With stronger students, you could write the following on the board before you move on to Part B:
   the most exhausting   the most important   the most skilful
   the most difficult   the most dangerous   the riskiest
   Explain that these are different ways of deciding how much people should be paid for their jobs. For example:
   People with the most exhausting / the riskiest jobs should be paid the most.
2 Ask students to find a new partner. In pairs, they should discuss which is the best way of deciding what people should be paid and give their reasons. They do not have to agree. They have about three minutes. Ask for feedback.

Contrasting careers

Part A

a racing driver / a military officer

a doctor / a computer programmer

a police officer / a pilot

a bank manager / a hairdresser

a lawyer / a musician

have a / an	easy / difficult / exciting / enjoyable / boring / safe / dangerous / stressful / important	life / job
have a	long / short	career
be	well-paid / well-dressed	
need	good qualifications / smart clothes	

Part B

Which jobs should be better paid?

Which jobs are the most useful?

Which jobs are the most stressful?

Which jobs are the most popular?

 © Pearson Education 2002

LESSON **5**
Modals

Vocabulary Levels of difficulty
Grammar Modal verbs for ability
Language to go Describing abilities and difficulties

I can do it!

Aim

To give students practice at using *can*, *could*, *be able to* and *manage to* when talking about past and present abilities and difficulties

Materials

One rolecard per student (A, B, C or D); several pairs of scissors

Time

30 minutes

Preparation

Copy and cut up one worksheet per four students

Procedure

1 Write *I can … I can't …* on the board. Ask students to tell you some things they can/can't do. Ask why, to elicit the word *confidence*.

2 Tell students you are going to read them an advertisement about a company. Write these questions on the board:
What does the company do?
How does it do this?
How long does it take?

3 Read the advert aloud twice. Students listen and answer the questions. Check the answers.

THE CONFIDENCE COMPANY
Improve your life in seven days!
• Do you find it difficult to talk to people at parties?
• Do you get nervous when you have to give a presentation?
Our experts will help you to be more confident by teaching you to relax, to visualise success and to find the 'real' you.

---

4 Tell students that they are going to play the role of someone who has done the course. Copy Rolecard A onto the board. Explain that the 'before' information is about Anna, before she did the course; the 'after' information is about two different people, after they did the course. The students will each be given a similar rolecard. They have to collect two pieces of information about themselves after the course and give away the information about the two other people, by going around and meeting different partners. With each partner, they read aloud the information on their 'before' card. If they have information about their partner, they give him/her the piece of paper with the 'after' information on it.

5 Hand out a rolecard to each student and let them check that they understand the information on it.

6 Distribute scissors. Ask students to cut up their cards so that they have one 'before' card and two 'after' cards.

7 Check the instructions. Students then start finding partners and exchanging information.

8 When they have all collected the correct 'after' information, form groups of four students – one Anna, one Marian, one Paul and one Brad.

9 Write the following questions on the board:
What couldn't you do before the course?
Have you managed to overcome your problem?
How do you feel now?

10 In their groups, students take it in turns to interview each other. They should try to answer without looking at their cards.

ANSWER KEY
Anna Martin: 4, 5   Marian Severa: 1, 7   Paul Bodin: 2, 8
Brad de Marco: 3, 6

Rolecard A

Anna Martin

BEFORE

- I can't go out without make-up on. I feel undressed.

- I can't do simple things like cook for friends or family. I get too worried.

Rolecard B

Marian Severa

BEFORE

- I can talk to people one-to-one, but in my job I have to give presentations which make me nervous.

- I also find it difficult to answer questions that people ask me about the presentation.

Rolecard C

Paul Bodin

BEFORE

- I can't get my message across very easily. For example, it took me three years to ask my wife out.

- I can't get my bosses to listen to and understand my ideas.

Rolecard D

Brad de Marco

BEFORE

- I can't chat up women. I just don't know what to say to them.

- I can't make decisions very quickly. For example, last week I failed my driving test because I couldn't decide when to turn into the main road.

1

AFTER

I really enjoy my job now. Two weeks ago I managed to talk to an audience of fifty people.

2

AFTER

The day after the course I was able to have my first real conversation with my wife, after five years of marriage.

3

AFTER

I went on my first date last week. After three years, I was able to ask a woman in my office out on a date.

4

AFTER

I don't worry how I look now. Last week I managed to go to the cinema without wearing any lipstick.

5

AFTER

Last Saturday I invited my parents over for dinner and I was able to cook a three-course meal without worrying.

6

AFTER

I also managed to decide where to go. We went to a new French restaurant.

7

AFTER

I was also able to deal with their questions without a problem.

8

AFTER

I got promoted last month and I was at a meeting in Paris where I managed to communicate my ideas clearly.

Vocabulary   Crime
Grammar   Adverbs of purpose
Language to go   Describing reasons for actions

Be safe not sorry

Aim

To give students practice at using adverbs of purpose in the context of writing up a report from a sales meeting

Materials

One worksheet per student

Time

30 minutes

Preparation

Copy the worksheet

Procedure

1 Introduce the lesson by asking students to suggest what happens in meetings. This should elicit *take notes*.
2 Write *FAQs* on the board. Ask students to tell you what this stands for. (*Frequently Asked Questions.*)
3 Tell students that they will receive the notes of a sales meeting at a company that sells security and safety products. The meeting discussed how to answer questions often asked by customers. They have to use the notes to write full answers to the questions.
4 Give each student a copy of the worksheet. Tell them to look at the illustrations of security and safety equipment at the top of the page. Check that they understand what each object is. (A *satellite tracking device* is a device used for pinpointing someone's exact position anywhere in the world.)
5 Ask students to look at the section entitled *FAQs* in the memo to sales staff, and at the meeting notes below. Explain that the meeting notes give the answers to the FAQs, but are not in the correct order. Ask students to find the answer to the first question and expand it into a full sentence: *We recommend you install smoke alarms and buy fire extinguishers in case you have a fire.*
6 Put students into pairs. They have to expand the other answers in note form and write them next to the correct questions. Allow them seven to ten minutes. Then check the answers.
7 In pairs, students roleplay being customers and sales staff. They take turns to ask and answer the questions. Encourage the sales staff to answer the questions from memory rather than reading from their worksheets.

ANSWER KEY

1 We recommend you install smoke alarms and buy fire extinguishers in case you have a fire.
2 We advise this so that you can keep all your important documents in a secure, fireproof place.
3 We suggest this in case someone steals your car.
4 You can use them for spying on a babysitter or workman.
5 We suggest this so that you can record and listen to the conversations of your employees.
6 You can use the camera to catch someone stealing expensive plants.
7 We recommend you do this so that your passengers feel safer.

BSNS – SECURITY AND SAFETY PRODUCTS

smoke alarms   fire extinguishers   safes   external secret video cameras   satellite tracking devices   miniature video cameras   micro telephone recorders

TO: ALL SALES STAFF
FROM: TRAINING MANAGER
SUBJECT: ANSWERING CUSTOMER FAQs

FAQs   **Suggested answers**

1 What things can we do to make our home safer?

2 Do I really need to have a safe at home?

3 Why do I need a satellite tracking device in my car?

4 How can I use miniature cameras in my home?

5 Why should we buy a micro telephone recorder for the office?

6 Why do we need a secret camera in the garden?

7 Why should we install miniature video cameras in trains and buses?

Notes from sales meeting, 18th June

- You can use them for / spy on / babysitter or workman

- We recommend you install smoke alarms and buy fire extinguishers in case / have / fire

- You can use / camera / catch someone stealing expensive plants

- We recommend you do this so that / passengers / feel safer

- We advise this so that / keep all / important documents / secure, fireproof place

- We suggest this in case / steal / your car

- We suggest this so that / record / listen / conversations / your employees

LESSON 7

The perfect

Vocabulary   Work
Grammar   Present perfect simple
Language to go   Talking about your experience

Who's the best candidate?

Aim

To give students practice at using the present perfect simple for experience in the context of choosing the best candidate for the job

Materials

One copy of Sheets A, B and C per two students

Time

25–30 minutes

Preparation

Copy and cut up Sheets A, B and C per two students

Procedure

1 Tell students that you are going to give them a job advert to read. Write the first line of the advert on the board: *EDITOR FOR NEW WEEKLY NEWS MAGAZINE WANTED*. In pairs, students write down any other information that they think they will find in the advert. Allow two or three minutes and then write up their ideas on the board.

2 Give each pair a copy of Sheet A. Ask them to check the vocabulary and then see if the advert includes all the information they were expecting. Ask a few students to report back.

3 Tell students that, in pairs, they will roleplay two colleagues who work for the agency that placed the advert in the newspaper. They had so many good applicants that they had to interview half the applicants each. They will each receive the interview notes of the best candidate they interviewed. They first have to tell their partner about their candidate and then together choose the best candidate for the job by discussing the strengths and weaknesses of each candidate. They should use the advert to help them. Finally, they have to present their recommendation to their client, giving the reasons for their choice.

4 Give a copy of Sheet B to one student in each pair, and Sheet C to the other. (Emphasise to students that they should tell their partner about their candidate, not just show him/her their notes.) Give them seven to ten minutes to choose their candidate and prepare their recommendation.

5 After seven minutes, make sure that all pairs are preparing their recommendation. They should both be involved in presenting their recommendation.

6 Put pairs together into groups of four. Each pair presents their recommendation to the other pair, who play the role of the client.

7 Class feedback.

Sheet A

EDITOR FOR NEW WEEKLY NEWS MAGAZINE WANTED

❏ Previous experience essential
❏ Must be good at managing teams
❏ Must have good interpersonal skills
❏ Must be good at working under pressure

Company car, company pension, salary negotiable.
Apply to Executive Jobs, PO Box 150, New York.

Sheet B

NAME:
Patrick O'Dolan

MARITAL STATUS:
Married / 2 children

AGE:
38

PRESENT JOB:
Editor of national sports magazine, in charge of 9 full-time journalists

WORK EXPERIENCE
has worked for a local newspaper (news reporter)

has worked as a journalist for several magazines (Pop Stars, Sport Crazy)

has written sports and music articles for several national newspapers

FURTHER TRAINING
has done courses on team building and time management

OTHER RELEVANT EXPERIENCE
has been the manager of a youth basketball team

has worked as a volunteer DJ on a local radio station

REASONS FOR WANTING JOB
has always been interested in news reporting

PERSONALITY
easy going and self-confident

Sheet C

NAME:
Anna Schiavella

MARITAL STATUS:
Single

AGE:
33

PRESENT JOB:
Editor of regional newspaper, in charge of 6 full-time journalists

WORK EXPERIENCE
has worked for other local newspapers

has been a political journalist, sports journalist, arts journalist

FURTHER TRAINING
has taken workshops on people management

OTHER RELEVANT EXPERIENCE
has directed some plays for an amateur theatre group

has worked as a volunteer helping people with their reading and writing

REASONS FOR WANTING JOB
would like the opportunity to report on national and international news

PERSONALITY
seems very ambitious and enthusiastic

© *Pearson Education 2002*

LESSON 8
Functions

Vocabulary Topics of conversation
Function Managing a conversation
Language to go What to say in social situations

Lovely day, isn't it?

Aim

To give students practice at using the functional language involved in managing a conversation

Materials

One situation card per student, plus some spares (more for a very strong class)

Time

30 minutes

Preparation

Copy and cut up one worksheet per three to six students (see Procedure 4)

Procedure

1 As an introduction, ask students to get into groups of three or four and tell each other about a social event/situation that they enjoyed or that they hated. They have three to five minutes.

2 Ask each group to report back and write the situations on the board.

3 Tell students that in pairs they will receive some cards. Each card shows a social situation, for example, in a restaurant. Underneath the picture there are three lines of dialogue. First they have to decide where the situation takes place and the relationship of the people. Then they read the lines of dialogue and decide how they might be used in a conversation (for example, to end the conversation).

4 Put students into pairs and give each pair two cards (or four if you have a very strong class; one if you have a very weak class). Give them two to three minutes to look at the cards.

5 Tell them that they have to prepare a conversation for each situation which includes the lines of dialogue on the card. They shouldn't write out the whole conversation, but can make brief notes about how the conversation will develop. For example: *1) Start conversation, 2) ask about the weather*, etc. They should practise the conversations so that they can act them out to other pairs. Allow about seven minutes for this. If some pairs finish more quickly, give them another card to work on.

6 If you have a small class, you can ask each pair to present one or both of their conversations to the rest of the class. If you have a big class, form groups of four (two pairs), each with different situations if possible, and ask each pair to act out one or both of their conversations. If time, make new groups so students can act out their conversations to other pairs.

Situation A

1 Lovely day, isn't it?
2 Are you over here on business?
3 Have a nice stay.

Situation B

1 You haven't phoned me for ages.
2 I've been busy.
3 Can't we try again?

Situation C

1 I love the new hairstyle.
2 You're looking really happy today.
3 I'm sorry. I have to go. Are you free for lunch?

Situation D

1 How is everything?
2 I've got some news.
3 Congratulations!

Situation E

1 Pleased to meet you.
2 So what's it like in New York?
3 I'd love to.

Situation F

1 How's business?
2 Great!
3 This fish isn't hot!

Situation G

1 Hi, John. What's up?
2 That's brilliant!
3 I can't. How about going tomorrow?

Situation H

1 Can I buy you a drink?
2 You're the most beautiful woman in the world.
3 You haven't met my boyfriend, have you?

Explore Canada

Aim

To give students practice at using the first conditional in the context of providing travel information, and to give them guided practice at writing a travel guide

Materials

One worksheet per student

Time

25–30 minutes

Preparation

Copy the worksheet

Procedure

1 Ask students to tell you what kind of information is useful when going to another country. Write their suggestions on the board.
2 Tell students that they are going to enter a travelguide writing competition. Ask what the layout of a page of a guide book might look like. This should elicit the idea of having headings.
3 Write the following headings on the board:

   a) GETTING THERE   d) TRAVEL FACTS
   b) TRAVELLING AROUND   e) WHEN TO GO
   c) ACTIVITIES   f) MONEY AND COSTS

   Elicit from students what kind of information they would expect to find under each heading.
4 Tell students that they will be given a worksheet with information about Canada. They have to read each piece of information and decide which heading it is connected to (see suggested answer key).
5 Put the students into groups of three or four. Give each student a copy of the worksheet. Allow about five minutes.
6 Class feedback.
7 Now tell students that they are now going to use the information to write part of the introduction section of a guide book on Canada. They should first decide the order of their headings and write them in the spaces provided on the worksheet. They should then decide who in their group is going to write each section. Remind them that the information is in note form so they have to expand it. As an example, write the following on the board:

   • Like seafood? Go to Old Town. Fish restaurants.
   • Stay youth hostel = $20/ day
   Ask students to expand the information. This should produce:
   • If you like seafood, go to the Old Town. There are a lot of fish restaurants there. / You'll find fish restaurants there.
   • If you stay in a youth hostel, it'll cost you $20 a day.
   They should write their first draft on rough paper, not on the worksheet. They have about ten minutes.
8 Students check their rough drafts with you. They then complete the sections of the guide book introduction to Canada on the worksheet, using the corrected drafts that they and their partners have written.

Extension

Reading and speaking: Students read the guide book introductions that the other groups have produced. In their groups, they discuss which one should win the competition. Have a class vote to establish a winner.

SUGGESTED ANSWER KEY

a) *Getting there:* 1, 9   b) *Travelling around:* 2, 3, 11, 12
c) *Activities:* 4, 13, 14, 15   d) *Travel facts:* 7, 8
e) *When to go:* 5, 6   f) *Money and costs:* 10

TRAVEL WRITING COMPETITION

Win the chance to become a travel writer for Lonely Globe Travel Guides

1 Not from USA or Europe? Probably need a visa.

2 Six time zones.

3 Spring, summer, autumn - good for touring.

4 Want to ski? Come in winter/spring.

5 Want to visit far north? Come July/August.

6 Spring/autumn cheaper. Some attractions closed.

7 Capital city: Ottawa.

8 Population: 31,281,000.

9 Want to fly direct? Get flights to main cities – Vancouver, Toronto, Montreal.

10 Cheap accommodation + eat in cafés = US$40/day. Motels + sometimes eat in restaurants = US$75/day.

11 Not in a rush? Travel around by land – more interesting. Best way = hire car.

12 Only a short time? Fly.

13 Like adventure sports? Go to National Parks.

14 Looking for great skiing? Go to Ontario, Quebec, Alberta and around Whistler in British Columbia.

15 Like beach activities? Go to Nova Scotia.

Explore
Canada

Situated north of the USA between the Atlantic and the Pacific Oceans, Canada is the world's second largest country. It extends 7,700km east to west and 4,600km north to south. Canada has rivers, lakes, mountains, plains and even a small desert. It has a mixture of French and British traditions as well as traditions brought from Asia, Latin America and Europe.

Vocabulary   Expressions with *take*
Grammar   Verb constructions for likes and dislikes
Language to go   Discussing sport

Love it or hate it?

Aim

To give students practice at using verb constructions for likes and dislikes by talking for thirty seconds about different leisure activities

Materials

One set of cards per group of four students

Time

25–30 minutes

Preparation

Copy and cut up one worksheet per group

Procedure

1 Ask students to suggest leisure activities they think are popular in Britain. Write their suggestions on the board. Then ask them to guess what the most popular is (watching television).
2 Tell students that they are going to play a game in teams where they have to speak about a sport or leisure activity for thirty seconds.
3 Put students into groups of four students. Give each group a set of the cards, and ask them to identify the different sports and leisure activities.
4 Write the word *camping* on the board. Ask students to suggest why they and other people like or dislike camping. Encourage students to use a variety of verb constructions for expressing likes and dislikes. Write up their ideas in two columns, *like* and *dislike*, on the board, numbering each idea.
5 Elicit ways of expressing different points of an argument, for example: *firstly, secondly, another reason is …, finally*, etc.
6 Explain how to play the game:
   • Groups divide into two teams of two students.
   • They shuffle the picture cards and place them face down in a pile.
   • A student from one team picks up a card and shows it to everyone. He / She has to speak about the leisure activity depicted on the card for thirty seconds starting with one of the ways of expressing likes and dislikes on the board, for example: *I like camping because you are in the open air and you are close to nature. Some people might not enjoy camping because you can get cold and wet if the weather is bad, and you don't have luxuries like a bed and bathroom!*
   A member of each team should act as timekeeper. If the student manages to speak for thirty seconds, then the team keeps the card. If the speaker hesitates for more than three seconds before the thirty seconds is up, they have to put the card to the bottom of the pile. Once a member of one team has spoken, then a member of the other team picks up a card and speaks about the next leisure activity.
   • Team members should take it in turns to speak for their team.
7 The aim of the game is to collect as many cards as possible. Students play for a maximum of ten minutes.

Extension

Writing and speaking: As a follow-up, students choose three of the ways of expressing likes and dislikes and write a sentence about three of the leisure activities depicted on the cards. They then walk around the room and try to find someone who agrees with them.

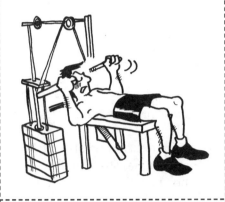

© *Pearson Education 2002*

Vocabulary   Determination
Grammar   *Used to* and *would*
Language to go   Comparing past and present habits

The burglar, the gambler and the rubbish collector

Aim

To give students practice at talking about past habits (with *would* and *used to*) in the context of a talk show

Materials

One rolecard per student (A, B, C or D)

Time

30 minutes

Preparation

Copy and cut up one worksheet per four students

Procedure

1 Ask students if they watch any talk shows, for example *The Jerry Springer Show* (or another show that is popular in your country). Elicit why these shows are so popular.

2 Ask what kinds of subject they discuss. Write some answers on the board.

3 Elicit the format of a typical talk show, for example: First the talk show host introduces the programme. Then he / she introduces the first guest and interviews him / her. Then he / she introduces and interviews the second guest, etc.

4 Tell students that they are going to take part in a talk show about addictions. They will each be given a rolecard. In groups of four, they will play three addicts or former addicts and the talk show host. They should read the information on their rolecard and prepare what to say. The information is in note form so they will have to expand the prompts.

5 Remind students of the format of the talk show. It is the role of the talk show host to introduce the programme and the guest, and to interview each guest.

6 Put the students into groups of four and distribute the rolecards. Give Rolecard D to a stronger student as he / she will have to manage the talk show.

7 Allow students a few minutes to read their rolecards and to expand the prompts. Give them help as required.

8 They then have seven to ten minutes to prepare the talk show in their groups. If a group finishes quickly, ask them to practise the show without looking at their rolecards.

9 They can now act out the talk show. For classes of up to twelve students, each group acts it out in front of the class. The other groups are the audience. For classes of more than twelve students, one group acts it out to another group, not the whole class.

10 At the end of each group's performance, students who have been watching vote for their favourite participant. Choose one of the following criteria:
- the most entertaining person
- the person they respect the most
- the person who has done the most to change

Rolecard A

THE BURGLAR

What is your name? (Choose a name for yourself.)

_____

Read this information and think of answers to the questions.

- burglar / now work as / security adviser
- gave up after / sent to prison
- break into 2 or 3 houses / day
- only steal small things / sell in markets

What kind of things did you use to steal?

_____

Why did you use to enjoy burglary?

_____

What's your life like now?

_____

Rolecard C

THE RUBBISH COLLECTOR

What is your name? (Choose a name for yourself.)

_____

Read this information and think of answers to the questions.

- collect rubbish as / hobby / now collect rubbish as / job
- steal letters and bank statements / from famous people's rubbish bins / sell / information / newspapers

How much do you earn?

_____

- married / wife left / go out every night / 3 or 4 o'clock in the morning
- also smell

Why do you enjoy looking in people's rubbish bins?

_____

Rolecard B

THE GAMBLER

What is your name? (Choose a name for yourself.)

_____

Read this information and think of answers to the questions.

- gambler / now job helping gamblers / give up gambling
- family / nice house / shop / lost everything
- at first / poker only once a month / addicted / then 2 or 3 times a week
- one week / lost so much / sell shop / home

How much did you lose?

_____

- wife left / with daughter
- not gamble now / want wife / daughter / back

Do you think your wife will come back to you?

_____

Rolecard D

THE TALK SHOW HOST

You are going to interview a former gambler, a former burglar and a rubbish collector. Before the talk show, prepare some questions to ask each guest. Use these notes.

The gambler
What / do now?
How often / use to gamble?
How much / lose?
Why / give up?
Wife / come back to you?
The burglar
What / do now?
Why / give up burglary?
How often / use to break into houses?
What / use to steal?
Enjoy it? Enjoy life now?
The rubbish collector
Why / use to collect rubbish?
How much / earn?
Why / collect rubbish now?
Married now? Why not?
Why / enjoy looking in people's rubbish bins?

Find out the names of your guests and then decide how to introduce them. For example: _This is ... . He ..._

You and money

Aim

To give the students practice at using verbs with two objects in the context of a questionnaire about attitudes to money

Materials

One worksheet per student

Time

30 minutes

Preparation

Copy the worksheet

Procedure

1 Write the word *questionnaire* on the board. Check the meaning and then ask students to suggest the kind of questionnaires you find in magazines for men / women.

2 Tell students that they are going to do a questionnaire about their attitude to money. There are ten questions and each question has three possible answers: a), b) or c).

3 They should first read each question and if necessary check the meaning of any word(s) they don't know. Then they should choose the answer that is nearest to how they feel. They should only choose one answer.

4 Form groups of three and give each student a copy of the questionnaire. To complete it, they take turns to ask their partners the questions, then compare answers and give reasons for their answers. Allow seven to ten minutes for this.

5 It's now time to analyse their answers. Each student should calculate his / her score: one point for an a) answer, two for a b) answer, and three for a c) answer. Ask them to add up their total scores.

6 Students read the text at the bottom of the questionnaire, which describes their attitude to money. Ask them to underline anything they agree with or disagree with.

7 They tell their partners what they agree / disagree with.

Read each question and the three possible answers. Then choose the answer that is closest to what you think. Put a tick (✓) in the box next to your answer.

1 You see a beggar in the street. Would you
a) ☐ give him / her everything in your wallet?
b) ☐ give him / her some change?
c) ☐ say you have no change?

2 Your friends ask you if you want to come on holiday with them, but you don't have enough money. Would you
a) ☐ try to borrow money from friends or your bank?
b) ☐ try to earn some extra money?
c) ☐ tell your friends you can't afford it?

3 You receive a cheque for £1,000 as a present. Would you
a) ☐ spend it all immediately?
b) ☐ spend some and invest the rest?
c) ☐ invest it all in a high-interest account?

4 You've just bought a new bicycle so you don't need your old one. Would you
a) ☐ offer it to someone you know who needs one?
b) ☐ try to sell it for a reasonable price?
c) ☐ try to sell it for more than you paid for it?

5 There's an appeal on TV for money to help people in a disaster. Would you
a) ☐ donate some money immediately?
b) ☐ check how much you have in your bank account?
c) ☐ donate nothing?

6 Your friend looks after your house / flat when you're on holiday. Would you
a) ☐ buy him / her a present to say 'thank you'?
b) ☐ send him / her a 'thank you' card?
c) ☐ just say 'thank you'?

7 One of your best employees asks you for a pay rise. Would you
a) ☐ offer him / her what he / she wants?
b) ☐ offer him / her a pay rise in six months?
c) ☐ say the company can't afford it?

8 You're in the red and your son / daughter asks you to buy him / her a new computer. Would you
a) ☐ buy it with your credit card?
b) ☐ tell him / her the truth and promise to buy one when you have the money?
c) ☐ tell him / her to get a job and pay for it himself / herself?

9 You see some lovely clothes in a shop but you don't really need them. Would you
a) ☐ buy them for yourself anyway?
b) ☐ buy them if you can afford them?
c) ☐ walk out of the shop?

10 Your teenage son is living at home with you. You ask him to clean up his room and wash your car. Would you
a) ☐ pay him for both jobs?
b) ☐ pay him for the car but not for his room?
c) ☐ expect him to do the jobs for nothing?

1–14

You're a very generous person and spend money very easily. In fact, you find it difficult not to spend money. You should try to reduce your spending, especially if you haven't got any money in the bank. Perhaps you should consider opening a savings account.

15–25

You're usually careful with your money and don't spend money unnecessarily. However, you don't let money control your life. You can enjoy the benefits of money but find it difficult to buy something spontaneously. It's OK to splash out on yourself from time to time!

Over 25

You really love money and one of your ambitions is to have as much money as possible. If you're not careful, you'll let money control everything you do in your life. What is more important: money or having friends?

Vocabulary   Phrasal verbs about tourism
Grammar   Present simple and continuous for future
Language to go   Describing plans for a trip

I love Edinburgh

Aim

To give students practice at using the present simple and the present continuous for the future

Materials

One information sheet per student (A, B or C); a map of the UK

Time

25 minutes

Preparation

Copy and cut up one worksheet per three students

Procedure

1 Ask students to tell you anything they know about Scotland. Write their ideas on the board.
2 If possible, give the students a photocopy of a map of the UK and point out Edinburgh, Glasgow, Loch Ness and the Highlands.
3 Tell students that they are on holiday in Edinburgh, the capital of Scotland, and are staying in a five-star hotel. It's Tuesday morning and they meet two other friendly tourists in the hotel lobby. They should tell the other tourists what they have arranged to do during the week and describe the tour they are going on. Then they should arrange to go out together one night.
4 Write the following on the board:

ARRANGEMENTS	TRAVEL ITINERARIES
We're going on a trip tomorrow.	The coach leaves at 8 a.m.
I'm staying in the hotel for a week.	We spend two hours at the castle.

Elicit from students which form, present simple or present continuous, we use to talk about arrangements and which form we use for itineraries.
5 Put students into groups of three. Tell them that they will each receive an information sheet. On the sheet is a diary with everything they have arranged to do and a description of a tour they are going on.
6 Give each student in the group a different sheet. Allow them a few minutes to read the information and to check anything they don't understand. Make sure students realise that they will have to expand the prompts in the diary and the tour itineraries. Tell them that where they see '...' in the tour itineraries, they will have to insert a verb.
7 Then write the following on the board to remind students what to do:
   • *Introduce yourself to your partners.*
   • *Talk about your arrangements and ask your partners about their arrangements.*
   • *Describe the tour you are going on.*
   • *Arrange to go out together one evening.*
8 The students give and exchange information.
9 When most groups have finished, ask each group what arrangements they have made.

Extension

Writing: Ask students to write a postcard from Edinburgh describing their experiences, and their arrangements for the rest of the week.

Sheet A

DAY	MORNING	AFTERNOON	EVENING
Tue	NOW	Edinburgh Castle	Dinner with Scottish friends
Wed	COACH TOUR: LOCH NESS AND THE HIGHLANDS		
Thur		Edinburgh zoo	
Fri	Shopping		
Sat	Airport 2 p.m.		

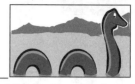

COACH TOUR:
LOCH NESS AND THE HIGHLANDS

8.10 a.m.	Depart – drive north past Stirling Castle
12 p.m.	… lunch near Ben Nevis, Britain's highest mountain
2 p.m.	… a cruise of Loch Ness
3.30 p.m.	Drive to Urquhart Castle – look for the monster!
4.30 p.m.	… north-east to Inverness – capital of the Highlands – 1 hour shopping
5.45 p.m.	… to Edinburgh
8.45 p.m.	… back

Sheet B

DAY	MORNING	AFTERNOON	EVENING
Tue	NOW	Botanical Gardens	
Wed		COACH TOUR: A WHISKY DISTILLERY AND A SCOTTISH PARTY	
Thur	National Gallery of Scotland		Cinema – 'Braveheart'
Fri	Shopping		
Sat	Airport 12 pm.		

COACH TOUR:
A WHISKY DISTILLERY AND A SCOTTISH PARTY

1 p.m.	Leave – drive north to St Andrews
3 p.m.	… the famous university and golf course
4.30 p.m.	… a whisky distillery – … different whiskies
5.30 p.m.	… to Edinburgh
7.30 p.m.	… a coach tour of the city at night
8.30 p.m.	… Scottish party – … Scottish dancing, eat haggis
11.30 p.m.	… to hotel

Sheet C

DAY	MORNING	AFTERNOON	EVENING
Tue	NOW	Shopping	Theatre – 'Macbeth'
Wed		Museum of Scotland	
Thur	COACH TOUR: STIRLING CASTLE, LOCH LOMOND AND BRAVEHEART COUNTRY		
Fri	Edinburgh Castle		
Sat	Airport 1 p.m.		

COACH TOUR:
STIRLING CASTLE, LOCH LOMOND AND BRAVEHEART COUNTRY

10.45 a.m.	Depart – drive north to Stirling – … views of the place where the Scottish beat the English in 1314
11.45 a.m.	… the story of William Wallace, 'Braveheart'
12.30 p.m.	… to Loch Lomond – … lunch
2 p.m.	After lunch – … a boat trip on Britain's largest area of water
3.30 p.m.	… home – on the way, pass through Glasgow city centre
7.30 p.m.	… in Edinburgh

 © Pearson Education 2002

LESSON 14
Vocabulary

Vocabulary 1 Weddings
Vocabulary 2 Uses of *get*
Language to go Talking about relationships

Love on the net

Aim

To give students practice in the different uses of *get* in the context of writing a letter about a friend's new relationship

Materials

One worksheet per student

Time

30 minutes

Preparation

Copy the worksheet

Procedure

1 Ask students to tell you different ways that people meet boyfriends / girlfriends / husbands / wives. Write their ideas on the board.

2 Tell students that they are going to write a letter to a friend about another friend, Elaine, and her new relationship. First they will build up Elaine's story orally with a partner, using cartoon pictures and key vocabulary, and then they will use the information to write the letter.

3 Put students into pairs and give them each a copy of the worksheet. They should only look at the cartoon story, not the bottom section. Tell them to look at the speech bubbles in the first picture and tell you what Elaine is saying. This should elicit:
   1 *Hi Sheila, it's Elaine.*
   2 *I'm in Australia and I've split up with Bob!*
   3 *Why? Well, it's a long story.*
   Make sure students understand that the events in each picture are all in the past.

4 Allow students seven to ten minutes to build up the rest of the cartoon story orally. They shouldn't write anything.

5 When they have finished, ask them to look at the bottom section. They will see a list of sentences labelled a)–e) and the body of a letter, with the numbers 1–5 in different parts of the letter.

6 They have to decide where the sentences go in the letter. Give them three to five minutes to do this.

7 Class feedback.

8 Tell each pair to take a piece of paper and write the letter using the information in the cartoon story and sentences a)–e). As an example, ask students how they would complete the sentence beginning *She's* in the second paragraph. This should elicit: *She's in Australia* (or *She's gone to Australia*) *and she's split up with Bob.*

9 Form groups of four. Each pair reads the other pair's letter.

> **ANSWER KEY**
> 1 c   2 e   3 a   4 d   5 b

a) ☐ Let me tell you the story. Well, …

b) ☐ Take care,
    Sheila

c) ☐ Dear Jane,
    I hope you're well.
    Sorry I haven't written
    sooner, but I've been so
    busy with everything.

d) ☐ Incredible, isn't it?
    Anyway, what about you?
    What's happening in your
    life? I'd love to hear from
    you.

e) ☐ So what's new? Well,
    you'll never guess what's
    happened to Elaine.
    She's …

14 Feb

1 _____

_____

2 _____

_____

3 _____

_____

4 _____

_____

5

Vocabulary   *Waste, use, spend, save* + noun
Grammar   Modal verbs for giving advice
Language to go   Giving advice

Less stress, please

Aim

To give students practice at using *should*, *ought to* and *could* to give advice

Materials

One copy of Sheets A, B, C and D per group of three students

Time

25–30 minutes

Preparation

Copy and cut up one worksheet per group

Procedure

1 Write the following definition on the board:
   Continuous feelings of worry about your work or personal life that prevent you from relaxing.
   Tell students this is a dictionary definition of a word. They write down what they think the word might be. Then ask for suggestions. This should elicit *stress*. If necessary, give students the answer.

2 Draw three columns on the board and write the following three words at the top of the columns: *Symptoms, Causes, Solutions*. Put students into groups of three and ask them to write down any examples of 1) the symptoms of stress, 2) the causes of stress, 3) solutions to stress. Give them about three minutes and then write ideas in the columns on the board.

3 Tell students that each member of their group will receive different information about a real person's daily routine. They should read the information and be ready to tell their partners about the person, so it is important that they check any vocabulary that isn't clear. They should also read the question at the bottom of the sheet.

4 Give each group a copy of Sheets A, B and C. The students take one sheet each. Give them two or three minutes to read their information and check the vocabulary.

5 Tell students that they are stress consultants. The information on the sheets came from three people who have asked for advice about how to reduce stress in their lives. The first student tells his / her partners about the person on the sheet, then they all decide what advice to give the person to reduce stress in his / her life. They should do this for all three people. One student should act as secretary and write down the advice for each person. Tell students they have about ten minutes.

6 Hand out Sheet D, which says what a real stress consultant suggested. Students compare their advice with the advice given by the stress consultant.

Sheet A

NAME *Anne Demontoux, 30 – single mother – works in a museum – lives with 10-year-old son, Bruno, in a flat in Paris*

- **6.30 a.m.** Get up, prepare two packed lunches, put on the washing. Get Bruno ready for school.
- **7.30 a.m.** Take Bruno to school by bus. No car!
- **8.15 a.m.** Take Metro to work.
- **9.00 a.m.** Have sandwich for breakfast.
- **5.00 p.m.** Pick up Bruno from my mother's.
- **6.30 p.m.** Cook dinner. Help Bruno with his homework.
- **9.00 p.m.** Read to Bruno. Have a cup of coffee. Clean flat. No time to phone friends.
- **11.00 p.m.** Go to bed exhausted. Sometimes I can't sleep. Think about problems: money, health …

Can you give me some advice on how to reduce the stress in my life?

Sheet B

NAME *Marcia Bicudo, 18 – studying for university entrance exam – lives at home with her parents in Rio*

- **7.00 a.m.** Wake up.
- **7.30 a.m.** Shower and quick breakfast.
- **8.00 a.m.** Leave home. Traffic jam!
- **9.00 a.m.** Start work.
- **12.00–1.00 p.m.** Have lunch. Check my homework.
- **6.00 p.m.** Leave work.
- **7.30 p.m.** Lessons start (preparation course for university entrance exam).
- **11.00 p.m.** Leave school.
- **12.00 a.m.** Get home.
- **12.30/1.00 a.m.** Go to bed, or study until two or three.

I spend my whole life studying or working. Can you give me some advice on how to reduce the stress in my life?

Sheet C

NAME *Alberto Rossi, 43 – manager for computer company – married with three daughters 13, 14, 16 – lives about one and a half hours from Rome*

- **6 a.m.** Get up, get ready for work. No time for breakfast.
- **7.00 a.m.** Drive to office in Rome.
- **8.30 a.m.** Arrive in Rome. Have a coffee before going to the office.
- **9.00 a.m.** Start work. Have to talk to different customers. Usually no time for lunch. Eat sandwich in my office. Drink six cups of coffee.
- **5.30/6.00 p.m.** Leave work.
- **6.30 p.m.** Drive home.
- **8.00 p.m.** Arrive home. Sometimes later – it depends on the traffic.
- **8.30/9.00 p.m.** Have dinner. Watch TV.
- **11.00 p.m.** Go to bed.

Can you give me some advice on how to reduce the stress in my life?

Sheet D

ADVICE FROM STRESS COUNSELLOR

Anne Demontoux:
You really ought to have something to eat before 9.00 a.m. This would also give you more time to talk to your son. Perhaps you could find another parent with a car who could give Bruno a lift to school, instead of taking him to school by bus. Or could your mother do this for you? You should also try to find some time to talk to your friends about your problems. Good luck!

Marcia Bicudo:
You really have a busy day! First of all, you should try to reduce the amount of hours you work. If you are tired, you can't take in very much information. Is it not possible to work part-time, for example only until lunch? You also ought to go to bed as soon as you get home from school. If you don't get enough sleep, you will feel more stressed. And reward yourself for all your hard work. Once a week you should do something that you really enjoy. Good luck!

Alberto Rossi:
You should try to eat something before you leave for work. It isn't healthy to start your day with nothing to eat. You should also drink less coffee and if possible do more exercise. Your biggest problem is the time you spend travelling. You really ought to think about moving nearer to Rome or finding a job closer to home. You could also try asking your boss about working from home one or two days a week. Good luck!

Vocabulary   The five senses
Grammar   Defining relative clauses
Language to go   Defining people, things, time and place

Define it!

Aim

To give students practice at using defining relative clauses by defining people, places, things and times related to the five senses

Materials

One copy of Sheet A or Sheet B per student; English–English dictionaries (optional)

Time

30 minutes

Preparation

Copy and cut up one worksheet per two students

Procedure

1 Introduce the lesson by asking students to tell you the five senses (taste, touch, hearing, sight, smell).
2 Put students into pairs. Tell them that you are going to read out two dictionary definitions. They listen and write down two or three examples for each definition.
   • *Animals that people touch with their hands*
   • *Things that taste delicious*
3 Put two columns on the board, with the headings *Definitions* and *Examples*. Before asking for answers, elicit the definitions that you read aloud and write them under *Definitions*. Then write three answers next to each definition, in the *Examples* column.
4 Tell students that they are going to play a game in teams. Each team has to think of definitions connected to the five senses from a list of example answers. To demonstrate, remove both definitions from the board and then read out the examples. The students give you the definitions.
5 Put students into pairs. Give half of the pairs Sheet A and the other half Sheet B.
6 Explain that for numbers 1–5, the students look at the examples and write definitions; for 6–10, they read the definitions and write examples. Remind them of the relative pronouns used with places, times, things and people. They have ten minutes. They can use a dictionary or ask you for help.
7 After ten minutes, form groups of four, made up of Team A (a pair that has worked on Sheet A) and Team B (a pair that has worked on Sheet B).
8 They now play the game. Team A should start. For each item (1–10), they say the sense, the example answers and the first word of the definition. Team B have to try and produce definitions for each one. Set a time limit of five minutes. Team A then add up Team B's score. (Two points for each correct definition.) The teams then reverse roles. The team with the most points is the winner.

SUGGESTED ANSWER KEY

Sheet A
1 Things you find in a museum
2 Places where you can listen to music
3 Things that make you feel hungry
4 Things that you eat with
5 People that eat/drink in their job

Sheet B
1 Places where you can see animals
2 People that use their voices in their jobs
3 Things that smell bad
4 Things that you hold in your hand
5 Things you eat as a starter

16

Define it!

Sheet A

👁 **sight**

1 Things _____
Examples: *sculptures, paintings, dinosaurs*

👂 **hearing**

2 Places _____
Examples: *a record shop, a disco, a concert hall*

👃 **smell**

3 Things _____
Examples: *the smell of your favourite food, the
smell of fresh bread, walking past a restaurant*

✋ **touch**

4 Things _____
Examples: *a fork, a knife, a spoon*

👄 **taste**

5 People _____
Examples: *a chef, a wine taster, a restaurant critic*

👁 **sight**

6 Places where you go to watch something or
someone
Examples: *a theatre,* _____

👂 **hearing**

7 Things that you can hear on the radio
Examples: *an interview,* _____

👃 **smell**

8 Things that smell nice
Examples: *a flower,* _____

✋ **touch**

9 People who work with their hands
Examples: *a potter,* _____

👄 **taste**

10 Times when people usually have something to eat
Examples: *breakfast,* _____

Sheet B

👁 **sight**

1 Places _____
Examples: *the zoo, the jungle, a circus*

👂 **hearing**

2 People _____
Examples: *a singer, a teacher, a radio presenter*

👃 **smell**

3 Things _____
Examples: *dirty socks, bad food, cigarettes*

✋ **touch**

4 Things _____
Examples: *a pencil, a telephone receiver, scissors*

👄 **taste**

5 Things _____
Examples: *soup, a salad, a prawn cocktail*

👁 **sight**

6 People that you often see on TV or in films
Examples: *an actor,* _____

👂 **hearing**

7 Times when you listen to music
Examples: *in the car,* _____

👃 **smell**

8 Things that people wear to smell nice
Examples: *aftershave,* _____

✋ **touch**

9 Things that you do with your hand
Examples: *write,* _____

👄 **taste**

10 Places where you can buy something to eat
Examples: *a supermarket,* _____

© *Pearson Education 2002*

Vocabulary   Lifestyle: word building
Grammar   Present perfect simple with *yet*, *already*, *just*
Language to go   Describing recent changes

Fame

Aim

To give students practice at using the present perfect with *just*, *already* and *yet* in the context of describing how success and fame has changed their lives

Materials

One rolecard (A, B, C or D) per student

Time

25–30 minutes

Preparation

Copy and cut up one worksheet per four students

Procedure

1 Ask students for names of famous and successful people. Then put them into groups of three or four and ask them to write down the advantages and disadvantages of being famous and successful. Allow three to five minutes.

2 Write their ideas in two columns on the board and ask them to vote on which they think is the greatest advantage/disadvantage of being famous.

3 Tell students that they are going to play the role of someone who has recently become famous. They are going to take part in a radio interview. The four roles are a writer, a pop star, a footballer and a TV celebrity.

4 Tell students that at the top of their rolecard they will have information about what they do. First they should read the information and choose a name for themselves. Then, using the vocabulary at the bottom of the rolecard, they should write some notes about:
   • what they've just done
   • what they've already done
   • what they haven't done yet
   They should think of reasons for what they've done. They can also add their own ideas.

5 Give each student a rolecard. Allow them three to five minutes to write notes.

6 Elicit typical questions that a famous person might get asked in a radio interview, including: *Has fame/success changed your life? How has fame/success changed your life?* The radio interviewer should try to ask follow-up questions after the famous person says something. As an example, write the following statement on the board: *I've just moved out of New York.* Elicit possible follow-up questions, for example: *Where have you moved to? Why?*

7 You can choose from two alternative procedures for roleplaying the interviews.
   Either: Put students into groups of four (A, B, C and D). They take turns to be the radio interviewer: Student A interviews Student B, then Student B interviews Student C, etc.
   Or: Put students into pairs. They take turns to interview each other. Then they change partners and repeat the process. They change partners a second time and repeat the process again.

8 At the end, ask students to tell you which of the four people they think has the best lifestyle, taking into account the advantages and disadvantages of being famous.

17

Fame

Rolecard A

You're a best-selling writer. A year ago you were a teacher and a part-time writer. Then recently one of your books was made into a film.

What's your name?_____

JUST

ALREADY

NOT YET

- move house
- make a lot of money
- give up job
- sign a new contract with publisher
- start new book
- have job offers in Hollywood

Rolecard B

You're a professional footballer. A year ago you were only an amateur. Now you're the youngest player ever to play for your country. You're seventeen years old.

What's your name?_____

JUST

ALREADY

NOT YET

- buy new house for parents
- get engaged to girlfriend
- sign a new contract with club
- buy a Ferrari
- spend a lot of money
- do some sports adverts for TV

Rolecard C

You won a competition to be a member of a pop group. Two months ago you were working in a restaurant. Now you're a pop star. You're eighteen years old.

What's your name?_____

JUST

ALREADY

NOT YET

- move out of parents' house
- have a holiday
- record a new single
- lose contact with old friends
- meet other famous pop stars
- receive marriage offers from fans

Rolecard D

Three months ago you were a shop assistant. Then you took part in a TV documentary that was very popular. Now you're a TV celebrity.

What's your name?_____

JUST

ALREADY

NOT YET

- be on several TV talk shows
- give up old job
- decide what to do
- do some fashion modelling
- have a lot of job offers
- do a TV presenter's course

Vocabulary   Phrasal verbs: *turn, switch, go*
Function   Informal and polite requests
Language to go   Making and responding to requests

Not at all

Aim

To give students practice at making and responding to informal and polite requests

Materials

One set of cards per student (A, B, C or D)

Time

25–30 minutes

Preparation

Copy and cut up one worksheet per four students

Procedure

1 Ask students to write down examples of situations in which it is really important to be polite when asking for something. The situations could involve friends, family or strangers. Allow two to three minutes for this.
2 Divide students into groups of four and ask them to compare their ideas. If they can remember any real examples of how being polite helped them to get something, they should describe them.
3 After about five minutes, ask a few students to report back.
4 Tell students (in their groups of four) that they are going to play a game which tests their ability to use informal and polite request forms in a variety of situations. Each group of four students is going to receive sixteen picture cards. Each picture card is one half of a situation; there are therefore eight situations in all. Each picture card shows a person or people with some key language in a speech bubble.
5 Give each student in the group a different set of cards. Students shouldn't show their cards to each other. Student A chooses one of his/her cards and describes the situation (but not what the person is saying) to the rest of the group. The student who thinks he/she has the other half of the picture describes his/her card. Both students put their cards down to check. Then, if the cards match, they act out the situation using the language in the speech bubbles to help them. They should try to make the conversation last about thirty seconds if possible – the pictures are just a starting point. After the conversation, Student B then chooses one of his/her cards and describes the situation to the rest of the group. The game proceeds as above until all the cards have been used up.
6 Ask each group to choose their best conversation and act it out for the whole class. Check that they use appropriate request forms.

Vocabulary   Adjectives describing loneliness and fear
Grammar   Second conditional
Language to go   Talking about hypothetical situations

Explorer

Aim

To give students practice at using the second conditional for hypothetical situations

Materials

One worksheet per student

Time

30 minutes

Preparation

Copy the worksheet

Procedure

1 Write *Explorer* on the board. Tell students that it is the name of a TV show. Explain that a group of people are sent to a remote place. They have to do different tasks. Every three days a member of the group is voted off the show by the others. The winner is the last person left.
2 Ask students to list the advantages and disadvantages of being on a TV show of this type.
3 Tell students they are going to be given part of the application form for the TV show, which will be filmed in the wilds of the USA, in places like Alaska and the Arizona Desert. To apply, they have to complete ten sentences connected to surviving alone in different situations.
4 Hand out the worksheet. Tell students to read the ten incomplete sentences and to underline any vocabulary they don't know. Allow two to three minutes.
5 Check any words that students don't know.
6 Then give them five to seven minutes to complete the sentences.
7 Now put students into pairs to talk about situations 1–3. They take turns to ask each other what they would do and why. They have three to five minutes.
8 They find new partners and talk about situations 4–6. Then they change partners again and talk about situations 7–10.
9 Class feedback. Elicit from students some of the best completed sentences for each situation.

Extension

Reading and speaking:
1 Tell students that it is now time to choose the best candidates. Write the following on the board:
We're looking for people who:
 • *are not afraid of wild animals or insects.*
 • *like adventure.*
 • *are independent but can work in a team.*
 • *would be able to kill an animal for food if they had to.*
 • *wouldn't panic in difficult situations.*
 • *can live without luxury items.*
2 Form groups of three or four students. Tell them they will be given the application forms of another group. Using the selection criteria on the board, students should look at each form and select the best candidate.
3 Collect each group's forms and give them to another group. They have five to seven minutes to select their candidate.
4 Ask each group to announce their winner, giving their reasons.

APPLICATION FORM FOR THE NEXT
EXPLORER SHOW
Send your application to: Crazy TV, PO Box 20, Hollywood

1 If I broke down in a snow storm in the middle of nowhere, I _____ _____

2 If I was alone in a big city in another country with no money and nowhere to stay, I _____ _____

3 If I was going to backpack around the world, I _____ _____

4 If I had to spend two months in a remote place, I wouldn't miss _____ _____

5 If I did something dangerous like climb a mountain, my personality _____ _____

6 If I got lost in a forest, I _____ _____

7 If I was trapped alone in a lift, I _____ _____

8 If my plane crashed in a remote place, I _____ _____

9 If I had to kill an animal for food, I _____ _____

10 If I had to survive alone in the jungle for a week, I'd be most afraid of _____ _____

Vocabulary Food and cooking
Grammar Verb constructions with *-ing* / infinitives
Language to go Talking about food and cooking

You are what you eat

Aim

To give students practice at using verb constructions with *-ing* forms and infinitives in the context of discussing controversial statements about food

Materials

One set of cards per group of three or four students

Time

25–30 minutes

Preparation

Copy and cut up one worksheet per group

Procedure

1 Put students into pairs to list any food-related stories they have read about in the newspapers or heard on the TV or radio, e.g. about genetically modified food, mad cow disease. Give them three to five minutes.

2 Ask a few students to report back to the rest of the class. Write the different food-related topics on the board.

3 Put students into groups of three or four. Tell them they will be given ten cards. Each card has a statement about a food-related topic. They will use these statements as a basis for short discussions.

4 Elicit some language for asking for and giving opinions. Write it on the board. For example:
What do you think about …?
I think / don't think that …
In my opinion, …
I agree / disagree.

5 Give each group a set of the ten cards. Tell them to read all the statements and underline any vocabulary they do not know.
NB GM stands for genetically modified.

6 Check the meaning of any new words with the class.

7 Each group chooses four or five statements to discuss. Students take turns to introduce a statement and to lead a discussion about it. They should discuss each statement for about three minutes. If any groups finish much earlier than the rest, ask them to discuss some of the other topics.

8 At the end, ask each group which statements they discussed and whether they agreed / disagreed with them.

Extension

Writing: Ask students to choose two statements from the cards, one that they agree with and one that they disagree with. They should write their opinions on each statement and give their reasons.

'Schools don't spend enough time teaching children to cook.'

'A vegetarian diet is for rabbits. We are humans, so it's stupid to give up eating meat.'

'Nowadays people spend too much time working and watching TV and not enough time eating together.'

'We spend years testing drugs before giving them to patients. So why didn't we test GM foods before giving them to people to eat?'

'We have managed to produce a generation of overweight children because they eat junk food and do no exercise.'

'If you avoid eating everything that's bad for you, you'll starve to death.'

'I've decided to buy only organic meat. There's no other way to be sure that it's free of dangerous diseases.'

'Don't waste time going on a diet. You'll put on weight again as soon as you stop.'

'It's expensive to eat healthily. Poor people can't afford to buy healthy food.'

If the world's population keeps on growing at the same rate, we soon won't be able to produce enough food for everyone to eat.'

Vocabulary Travel and airports
Grammar Past perfect simple
Language to go Recounting events in your life

Lost luggage

Aim

To give students practice at using the past perfect simple in the context of a bad travel experience

Materials

One set of picture cards per group of four or five students.

Time

30 minutes

Preparation

Copy and cut up the worksheet as above.

Procedure

1 Put students into groups of four or five. Give each group a set of cut-up picture cards in jumbled order and ask each student to take two or three pictures.

2 Explain that the pictures make up a story. Tell students to describe their pictures in as much detail as possible to the other people in their group; they should not show them to each other.
The task is to listen to all the descriptions and try to work out what happened in the story, and the order of the pictures. Give students about eight minutes for this.

3 Check the order with the class. Answer: f, g, a, j, b, h, i, c, d, e

4 Explain that the students have to tell the story in the past, but the story begins when the man is in the taxi. Ask them what tense the verbs that describe what happened before will be in. (Answer: the past perfect.)

5 Ask students some questions to help them get the idea of how the past perfect will be used. For example: *What had his boss told him?* (She'd told him he had to go to Moscow.) *What preparations had he made for his trip?* (He'd looked on the Internet to find out the weather in Moscow and he'd packed warm clothes.)

6 Students tell the story (orally) in their pairs. They should start like this:
Max was sitting in a taxi on his way to his Moscow hotel.
He was freezing cold and very unhappy ... . Then they should say what had happened before (using the past perfect) and what happened later (using the past simple). Allow five to seven minutes.

7 Finally, ask students to write the story.

> ### SAMPLE STORY
> Max was sitting in a taxi on his way to his Moscow hotel.
> He was freezing cold and very unhappy. The week before,
> the weather had been hot and sunny in Florida where he lived.
> He'd arrived at work and his boss had told him he had to go to
> Moscow. He had packed plenty of warm clothes because he had
> looked on the Internet and discovered that it was very cold in
> Moscow. The flight had been fine. When he had arrived it had
> been snowing and he had wanted to put on his warm clothes.
> He had waited a long time for his luggage but it hadn't appeared.
> He had explained the situation at the lost luggage desk but the
> attendant hadn't been very helpful. So now he was sitting in a
> taxi going to the hotel. It was so cold that as soon as he arrived
> at the hotel he bought some warm clothes. They were very
> expensive and Max wasn't very happy, but he had no choice.
> His own luggage didn't arrive until two days later.

a
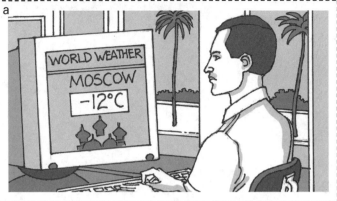

b

c

d

e *Two days later ...*

f

g

h

i

j

Vocabulary Fame and success
Grammar Passive constructions
Language to go Describing a process

Pop stars

Aim

To give students practice at using the present simple passive and past simple passive to talk about the careers of pop stars

Materials

One worksheet per student

Time

30 minutes

Preparation

Copy and cut up the worksheet

Procedure

1 Write on the board:
   a) *When your first single was released?*
   b) *When was your first single released?*
   c) *When was released your first single?*
   Ask students to identify the correct question. (Answer: b) They need to know this to do the following activity correctly.

2 Put students into pairs. Give one student Sheet A, and the other student Sheet B. They have to ask each other questions to complete the missing information. Go through the first one or two questions with the whole class to check they understand the task, then give them five minutes to complete the information.

3 Ask them if they have seen a TV programme like this, or if there is a similar programme in their own country.

4 Divide students into groups of four or five and tell them that they have to imagine they are a pop group. Hand out a copy of Sheet C to each student. Together they invent the information for their group and write it down in the right-hand column. Allow seven to ten minutes.

5 Students now have to find a partner from a different group and take turns to interview each other about their pop groups. They will need to make complete questions from the prompts. Do the first two questions together as examples and write them on the board:
   What is your group called?
   When and where was it formed?
   Allow about five minutes for the interviews.

6 Ask students to write a short article about their partner's pop group for a teenage magazine.

Extension

Speaking: Students tell a partner about a pop group from their country who they like and know something about. You can start by telling them about a group you like, as an example.

Sheet A

The Bardot story

In 1999 auditions were held all over Australia to find twenty-five girls to appear in a TV programme.

The TV programme was called _____ . (*What ...?*)

The programme was designed to find girls to make an all-girl pop group.

Finally _____ girls were chosen to form Bardot. (*How many ...?*)

The girls were called Belinda, Sophie, Sally, Katie and Chantelle.

Their first single was released in _____ . (*When ...?*) It was called *Poison*.

Their first album was called _____ . (*What ...?*) It was released one month later.

In October they were nominated for _____ . (*What ...?*)

In the same month they were welcomed by 500 fans at Singapore Airport at the start of an Asian tour.

In December they were asked to play for _____ . (*Who ... for?*)

Sheet B

The Bardot story

In _____ auditions were held all over Australia to find twenty-five girls to appear in a TV programme. (*When ...?*)

The TV programme was called 'PopStars'.

The programme was designed to _____ . (*What ...?*)

Finally five girls were chosen to form Bardot.

The girls were called _____ , _____ , _____ , _____ and _____ . (*What ...?*)

Their first single was released in April 2000. It was called _____ . (*What ...?*)

Their first album was called *Bardot*. It was released _____ . (*When ...?*)

In October they were nominated for four Australian Recording Industry Awards.

In the same month they were welcomed by _____ fans at Singapore Airport at the start of an Asian tour. (*How many ...?*)

In December they were asked to play for Australian peacekeeping soldiers in East Timor.

Sheet C

What / group called?	
When and where / formed?	
How / discovered by your record company?	
When / first single released?	
What / called?	
When / first album released?	
What / called?	
Where / biggest concert held?	
How many people / attended by?	

Vocabulary Toys and games
Grammar Modal verbs to talk about future probability
Language to go Making predictions about the future

Are you an optimist?

Aim

To give students practice at talking about probability in the future in the context of a questionnaire to discover who in the class is the most optimistic about the future

Materials

One worksheet per student

Time

20 minutes +

Preparation

Copy the worksheet

Procedure

1 Ask students to vote on who they think is the most optimistic person in the class.

2 Hand out the worksheet. For each of the sentences, students circle the degree of probability that most corresponds to their opinion (for example, in sentence 4, if they are pessimistic about their English they might circle *improbable*). Give them about five minutes to do this.

3 Put students into pairs. They should compare their answers using the language they learnt in the lesson in the Students' Book to talk about probability (*may, might, could, I'm sure that ..., I expect that ..., I think that ..., I doubt if ...* and *I don't think that ...*). They should give a reason for each of their answers, for example: *I don't think I'll ever make a lot of money, because I'd have to win the lottery and that's not very probable.* Allow ten to twelve minutes.

4 Students exchange their completed questionnaires with their partner and, using the scoring system at the bottom of the worksheet, add up their partner's score.

5 At the end, see if students guessed correctly the most optimistic person in the class. The maximum score is 50, and the higher the score, the more optimistic the person.

How optimistic are you?

Do this questionnaire to find out.

For each sentence, circle the word(s) which best reflect your opinion.

1   I will live a long and healthy life.

| certain | almost sure | probable | improbable | almost impossible |

2   I will make a lot of money one day and be able to retire early.

| certain | almost sure | probable | improbable | almost impossible |

3   This year will be the best year of my life so far.

| certain | almost sure | probable | improbable | almost impossible |

4   I will be able to speak very good English soon.

| certain | almost sure | probable | improbable | almost impossible |

5   If we make contact with aliens, they will be friendly and help us.

| certain | almost sure | probable | improbable | almost impossible |

6   The number of deaths from heart disease and cancer will decrease dramatically in the next twenty years.

| certain | almost sure | probable | improbable | almost impossible |

7   Technology will permit us to work much less and be happier.

| certain | almost sure | probable | improbable | almost impossible |

8   The situation of impoverished nations in the third world will improve in the next ten years.

| certain | almost sure | probable | improbable | almost impossible |

9   We will find a solution to global warming.

| certain | almost sure | probable | improbable | almost impossible |

10   My national football team will win the World Cup in the next twenty years.

| certain | almost sure | probable | improbable | almost impossible |

SCORE

5 points for *certain*   4 points for *almost sure*   3 points for *probable*

2 points for *improbable*   1 point for *almost impossible*

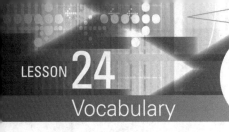
LESSON 24
Vocabulary

Vocabulary 1 Telephoning expressions
Vocabulary 2 Phrasal verbs about telephoning
Language to go Communicating by phone

Can I take a message?

Aim

To give students practice in the language used for telephoning

Materials

One rolecard (A or B) per student

Time

25 minutes

Preparation

Copy and cut up one worksheet per two students

Procedure

1 Explain that students are going to make and receive phone calls and leave and take messages for an absent colleague. Elicit some language that the person leaving or receiving the message might need to use, for example:
I'm afraid she's not here. Can I take a message?
Could you tell me your telephone number?
Could you ask him/her to call me back, please?

2 Put students into pairs. Give out the rolecards (one A and one B for each pair) and ask students to read the instructions.

3 Check that they understand what they have to do, then give them about ten minutes to leave their messages. **NB** If your classroom layout allows it, you may wish to seat the students in each pair back to back to simulate a phone call.

4 Give feedback on good and/or incorrect language use.

5 Put students into new pairs, again pairing a Student A with a Student B.

6 Student A takes the role of Mr Wilkins, who has just returned to the office. He should ask his colleague (Student B) if there were any messages for him. Student B gives him the messages that he/she wrote down, for example: *Your friend Kazuko Hiraki phoned. He would like to play tennis with you next Monday. He wants you to call him back to confirm. His phone number is 0175 200 9874.*
Student A should check the accuracy of the messages against the original instructions on his/her rolecard. Allow about five minutes.

7 Student B then takes the role of Ms Jenkins and Student A gives her the messages that he/she wrote down.

Extension

If you have time, and feel the students can handle the language that will be involved, you could roleplay the follow-up phone calls, for example: Mr Wilkins phones Kazuko Hiraki back to arrange a time to play tennis.

Rolecard A

Take the role of the following people and phone Mr Wilkins at work. You will need to leave a message.

Call 1: Your name is Kazuko Hiraki. You are a friend of Mr Wilkins. You would like to play tennis with him next Monday. You would like him to call you back to confirm. Your phone number is 0175 200 9874.

Call 2: Your name is Anna López from Comesa in Valencia, Spain. You are customers of Mr Wilkins's company. You have a question about a bill you have received. You will call back this afternoon.

Call 3: Your name is June Wilkins. You are Mr Wilkins's wife. You are phoning to tell him you will be late home this evening. You would like him to call you back.

Call 4: You are Jean-Paul Dugommier, a friend of Mr Wilkins from Lyon. You are coming to the UK on business next week and would like to meet him for dinner.

Now take the role of Ms Jenkins's colleague. She's not in the office this morning. She will receive a series of phone calls. Explain that she's not available and offer to take a message. Note down information about the call.

Rolecard B

Take the role of Mr Wilkins's colleague. He's not in the office this morning. He will receive a series of phone calls. Explain that he's not available and offer to take a message. Note down information about the call.

Now take the role of the following people and phone Ms Jenkins at work. You will need to leave a message.

Call 1: Your name is George from George's Motor Repair. You are phoning to tell Ms Jenkins that her car is ready and she can collect it this afternoon.

Call 2: Your name is Martin Schultz from Frankfurt, Germany. Ms Jenkins is coming to Frankfurt for a conference next week. You would like to talk to her about her hotel accommodation. You would like her to call you back. Your number is 00 49 6324 78 11.

Call 3: Your name is Adriana Novokova. You are Ms Jenkins's friend. You are making a personal phone call. You will call her back.

Call 4: Your name is Jan Borowski. You are phoning in answer to a job advertisement in the local newspaper. You would like Ms Jenkins to call you back. Your number is 027 7274 3108.

Vocabulary *Make* and *do*
Grammar Modal verbs for necessity and obligation
Language to go Describing rules in the present

What if ...?

Aim

To give students practice at expressing obligation in the present by talking about the right thing to do in a variety of situations, and by writing an advisory text

Materials

One worksheet per student

Time

30 minutes

Preparation

Copy the worksheet

Procedure

1 Write on the board:
   You receive an e-mail attachment which you think may contain a virus. What's the right thing to do?
   Elicit ideas and write some sentences using obligation expressions on the board, for example: *You mustn't open it.*
2 Hand out the worksheet and ask the students, in pairs or small groups, to talk about the right thing to do in each situation, using the language given. (If preferred, the boxes could be cut up into cards which students turn over and talk about.) They should describe any real-life experiences they have had of the situations, and what they did. Allow about ten minutes. **NB** It is not necessary for them to use all the expressions for all the situations.
3 As class feedback, ask the groups about what they discussed.
4 Ask students to read the text about what to do if you receive an e-mail that you are suspicious of, and to compare the advice with the sentences on the board.
5 Now tell students to choose one of the other situations and write a similar text about what to do. Give them seven to ten minutes for this.
6 Students can read and comment on each other's texts.
7 Give feedback on good and/or incorrect language use.

What if ...?

You receive an e-mail attachment which you think may contain a virus.

What is the right thing to do?

You mustn't ...   You should ...   You shouldn't ...
You have to ...   You don't have to ...

You have a minor traffic accident in which nobody is injured.

What is the right thing to do?

You mustn't ...   You should ...   You shouldn't ...
You have to ...   You don't have to ...

You smell gas in your house.

What is the right thing to do?

You mustn't ...   You should ...   You shouldn't ...
You have to ...   You don't have to ...

A pan of oil catches fire while you are cooking.

What is the right thing to do?

You mustn't ...   You should ...   You shouldn't ...
You have to ...   You don't have to ...

Your credit card has been stolen.

What is the right thing to do?

You mustn't ...   You should ...   You shouldn't ...
You have to ...   You don't have to ...

You have an interview for a job at a bank.

What is the right thing to do?

You mustn't ...   You should ...   You shouldn't ...
You have to ...   You don't have to ...

You are going on a journey up the Amazon.

What is the right thing to do?

You mustn't ...   You should ...   You shouldn't ...
You have to ...   You don't have to ...

You are going on a fourteen-hour plane journey.

What is the right thing to do?

You mustn't ...   You should ...   You shouldn't ...
You have to ...   You don't have to ...

You want to give up smoking.

What is the right thing to do?

You mustn't ...   You should ...   You shouldn't ...
You have to ...   You don't have to ...

You want to lose weight.

What is the right thing to do?

You mustn't ...   You should ...   You shouldn't ...
You have to ...   You don't have to ...

What to do if you think you've received a virus

Computer viruses can be easily transmitted by e-mail. Viruses can attach themselves to mail without the sender knowing. Viruses are evolving all the time so you must have the latest anti-virus software installed on your computer. If you receive an attachment that makes you suspicious:

- You should send a message to the sender to check if he/she has really sent you the message.
- You should run a virus scan on your computer.
- If you have any doubts, you must delete the message and any attached files.
- You mustn't open any attachments until you are sure they are safe.
- If you receive the message at work, you should inform your systems manager.

Vocabulary Expressions with *time*
Grammar Ways to express contrasting ideas
Language to go Comparing attitudes

A nightmare journey

Aim

To give students practice at expressing contrasting ideas using *although*, *despite* and *however* in a guided letter-writing activity

Materials

One worksheet per student

Time

25 minutes

Preparation

Copy the worksheet

Procedure

1 Ask students: *What problems can you have when travelling by plane?* Write their ideas on the board, for example: *delays, flight cancellations, overbooking, lost luggage* etc.

2 Hand out the worksheet and ask students to read about John and his plans for a holiday in Cuba. Ask a few questions to check students have assimilated the information, for example: *How is he going to the airport? When does he arrive in Cuba?*

3 Explain that, in fact, John had a terrible journey to Cuba and that something went wrong at every stage of his journey. In pairs or small groups, the students have five to seven minutes to talk about what they imagine might have gone wrong. Give them an example on the board to get them started: *The taxi didn't arrive, so he had to take a bus to the station.*

4 Explain that when John got home he wrote a letter to his friend Esther telling her about his terrible journey. Ask students to look at the start of the letter on the worksheet and continue it, using *although*, *despite* or *however* to link what John had hoped would happen with what happened in reality. They should work in pairs or small groups, and have about ten minutes to complete their letter.

> **SAMPLE LETTER**
> Dear Esther,
> I had a great time in Cuba but the journey there was a nightmare. Despite having reserved a taxi to take me to the station, I finally had to take a bus because the taxi never arrived. And although the train was scheduled to leave at 11.30, it was cancelled and I had to wait an hour for the next one. So despite having to check in two hours before departure, I only arrived fifteen minutes before. I had a ticket. However, the plane was overbooked and I had to wait for the next one, and although the weather forecast was good, it began snowing and all flights were cancelled until the next morning. I thought the airline would accommodate me in a hotel. However, they were completely unhelpful and I had to sleep in the airport. Finally I arrived in Cuba on Wednesday, although I was supposed to arrive the day before, and despite having a reservation, I discovered that my luxury hotel was full. So I had to look for somewhere else to stay, which was difficult because I couldn't understand anything anybody said to me, although I thought my Spanish was quite good.

John is planning a holiday to Cuba. He's very worried about the journey and he's thinking of the preparations he has made to ensure he gets from his house to Cuba without any problems.

- I've reserved a taxi to take me to the station.
- The train to the airport leaves at 11.30.
- I have to check in two hours before departure.
- I have a ticket, so I'll have a seat on the plane.
- The weather forecast is good for the day of the flight.
- If the flight is delayed or cancelled, the airline will put me on another flight or accommodate me in an airport hotel.
- I arrive in Cuba on Tuesday.
- I have a reservation in a luxury hotel.
- My Spanish is quite good.

Dear Esther,
I had a great time in Cuba but the journey there was a nightmare. Despite having reserved a taxi to take me to the station, I finally had to take a bus because the taxi never arrived.
And although the train . . .

 © *Pearson Education 2002*

Vocabulary   Achievements and projects
Grammar   Present perfect simple and continuous
Language to go   Discussing personal achievements and projects

The clever conference

Aim

To give students practice at using the present perfect simple and present perfect continuous to talk about past achievements and projects in progress

Materials

One rolecard per student

Time

20 minutes

Preparation

Copy and cut up one worksheet per eight students

Procedure

1 Ask students if they have ever been to a conference. What happens at them?

2 Put the class into even groups of up to eight (i.e. if you have ten students, you should have two groups of five; if you have thirteen, one group of six and another of seven etc.). If you have eight or fewer students, this is a whole class activity.

3 Tell students they are going to be guests at the welcoming party of a conference for very clever people. Hand out a rolecard to each student and explain that they will play the person on the card.
Give them a minute or so to read the information on the card (ideally they should memorise it) and to check any items of vocabulary.

4 Explain that they don't know anybody else at the party. They have to move around introducing themselves and finding out the name, profession, achievements etc. of the other guests.

5 If you think it necessary, you could write the following questions on the board:
Hello. What's your name?
What do you do?
What have you achieved in your career?
What have you been working on recently?
What ambition do you have for the future?

6 After about ten minutes, or when they have spoken to everybody else in the group, ask them to sit down and get into pairs.

7 In pairs, they have about five minutes to compare what they can remember about the other people at the party. They should describe anyone they spoke to whom their partner didn't meet.

8 Ask the students who at the party they would most like to be in real life, and to give their reasons.

Rolecard A

Name: Professor Anna Stasiak

Profession: Inventor

Achievements: Invented an indestructible computer – you can hit it when you are frustrated

Current projects: Developing a new system to search for information on the Internet – the last year

Ambition: To be the greatest inventor in history

Rolecard B

Name: GianLuca Tassotti

Profession: Football player

Achievements: Won the league last season

Current projects: Recovering from an injury – the last month

Ambition: To win the World Cup

Rolecard C

Name: Claudine Lefèvre

Profession: Film director

Achievements: Made ten films; nominated for Golden Globe for best foreign film last year

Current projects: Working on latest film – the last year

Ambition: To win an Oscar

Rolecard D

Name: Harriet Harris

Profession: Politician

Achievements: In parliament for ten years; two ministerial positions

Current projects: Working on a new law to increase government spending on international development – the last six months

Ambition: To be Prime Minister

Rolecard E

Name: Chen Fi Ling

Profession: Novelist

Achievements: Wrote six best-selling novels

Current projects: Writing latest novel – the last six months

Ambition: To win the Nobel Prize for Literature

Rolecard F

Name: Andrew Cox

Profession: Architect

Achievements: Designed hundreds of public buildings including hospitals, art galleries, office buildings and libraries

Current projects: Working on the development of a new national sports stadium – the last two years

Ambition: To be happy

Rolecard G

Name: Aki Ichikawa

Profession: Law student

Achievements: President of the university law society – the last six months

Current projects: Revising for final exams – the last month

Ambition: To pass final exams

Rolecard H

Name: Dr María José Martínez Díaz

Profession: Pharmaceutical research scientist

Achievements: Worked on the development of drugs to treat asthma

Current projects: Working on a treatment for cystic fibrosis – the last five years

Ambition: To win a Nobel prize

Vocabulary Prison
Function Prohibition, obligation and permission in the past
Language to go Discussing freedom

The best days of your life?

Aim

To give students practice at talking about obligation and permission in the past

Materials

One copy per student

Time

30 minutes

Preparation

Copy the worksheet

Procedure

1 Write *The Best Days of Your Life* on the board. Ask students which they think the best days of your life are (for example: when you are a child, a teenager, a young adult, a parent, retired) and why.
Tell them that people sometimes say that your schooldays are the best days of your life, and ask them if they enjoyed being at school.

2 Put students into pairs and ask them to work together to match the beginnings and the ends of the questions in Part A to make complete questions. This should take about five minutes.

3 Check their answers.

4 Tell students to find the appropriate reply in Part B to each of the questions in Part A. Give them about seven minutes for this.

5 Check their answers.

6 In pairs, students take turns to ask and answer the questions in Part A. They should note down or remember their partner's answers. Allow about ten minutes.

7 Ask each pair to tell the class whose school they think was better and why. (Students can decide what criteria they will use to judge this!)

ANSWER KEY

Part A

1 How many hours a day did you have to go to school?
2 Did the teachers make you do a lot of homework?
3 Were you allowed to wear your own clothes?
4 What foreign language(s) did you have to learn?
5 Were you allowed to choose which sports you played?
6 At what age were you allowed to choose the subjects you studied?
7 Were you allowed to call the teachers by their first names?
8 Did they let you smoke?
9 Did they let you leave the school at lunchtime?
10 If you did something wrong, how were you punished?
11 What kind of exams did you have to take?
12 Were you allowed to talk to other pupils during lessons?
13 Was there anything else they made you do that you didn't like?
14 At what age were you allowed to leave school?

Part B
1 d 2 c 3 j 4 a 5 e 6 n 7 b 8 g 9 l 10 f 11 i
12 m 13 h 14 k

The best days of your life?

Part A

Match the beginnings and the ends to make questions about your schooldays.

1 How many hours a day did you	do a lot of homework?
2 Did the teachers make you	the teachers by their first names?
3 Were you allowed to wear	have to go to school?
4 What foreign language(s) did you	your own clothes?
5 Were you allowed to choose	you smoke?
6 At what age were you allowed	have to learn?
7 Were you allowed to call	which sports you played?
8 Did they let	to choose the subjects you studied?
9 Did they let you leave	how were you punished?
10 If you did something wrong,	the school at lunchtime?
11 What kind of exams did	to other pupils during lessons?
12 Were you allowed to talk	you have to take?
13 Was there anything else they made	leave school?
14 At what age were you allowed to	you do that you didn't like?

Part B

Here are some answers to the questions in Part A. Decide which answer goes with each question.

a) We had to learn Latin and French.

b) No, definitely not. We were only allowed to call them by their surnames.

c) They made us do quite a lot of homework, especially at the weekends or if we were preparing for exams.

d) We had to go to school from 9 in the morning to 4.15 in the afternoon.

e) They let us choose but there weren't many options. In winter it was either rugby or cross-country running.

f) They made us stay behind for an hour after school in the afternoon.

g) No, smoking wasn't allowed at all.

h) Yes, we had to study religious education. I didn't like it at all.

i) We had to take an internal exam at the end of every term. And when we were sixteen, we had to take exams called GCSEs.

j) No, we weren't. We had to wear a blue and grey uniform.

k) We were allowed to leave school at sixteen. But I stayed on until eighteen because I wanted to go to university.

l) We were only allowed to leave the school if we went home for lunch. They didn't let us hang around in the street.

m) They only let us talk if we had to work together, but if the teacher was talking to the class we had to be quiet.

n) We were allowed to choose some of the subjects we studied when we were thirteen or fourteen.

Now, in pairs, ask and answer the questions in Part A about your secondary education.
Whose school was better, yours or your partner's? Why?

 © Pearson Education 2002

Vocabulary Doing business
Grammar First and second conditionals
Language to go Talking about likely and unlikely situations

Under what circumstances?

Aim

To give students practice at using the first and second conditionals to express likely and unlikely conditions

Materials

One worksheet per group of three or four students; one dice per group; one counter per student

Time

20–25 minutes

Preparation

Copy one worksheet per group

Procedure

1 Put students into groups of three or four. Each group needs one copy of the worksheet (the gameboard), a dice, and a counter per student (they could use coins). One person in each group has to keep score.

2 Explain the rules to students. Put your counter on the start square. Throw the dice and move the number of squares on the dice. Explain that there are four kinds of square:

  • If you land on a 'Complete' square, you have to complete the sentence in a way that is true for you. You get one point for a correct sentence. (Indicated by the star *.)

  • If you land on a 'Verb forms' square, you have to put the verbs in brackets in the correct form to make a sentence. You get one point for a correct sentence. (Indicated by the star *.)

  • If you land on an 'Under what circumstances' square, you have to say under what circumstances you would do what is written in the square. You get two points for a correct sentence. (Indicated by the two stars * *.)

  • If you land on an 'Ask a question' square, you have to ask another player a question in the first or second conditional. You get one point for a correct question and the person you ask gets one point for a correct answer. (Indicated by the star plus star * + *.)

  The winner is the player with the most points when everybody has finished, not the player who reaches the end first.

3 Students play the game, taking turns to throw the dice and move around the board until everyone has reached the end (you don't need to throw the exact number to finish). When they have doubts about whether sentences are correct or not, they should check with the teacher.

4 Find out who got the highest score in the class.

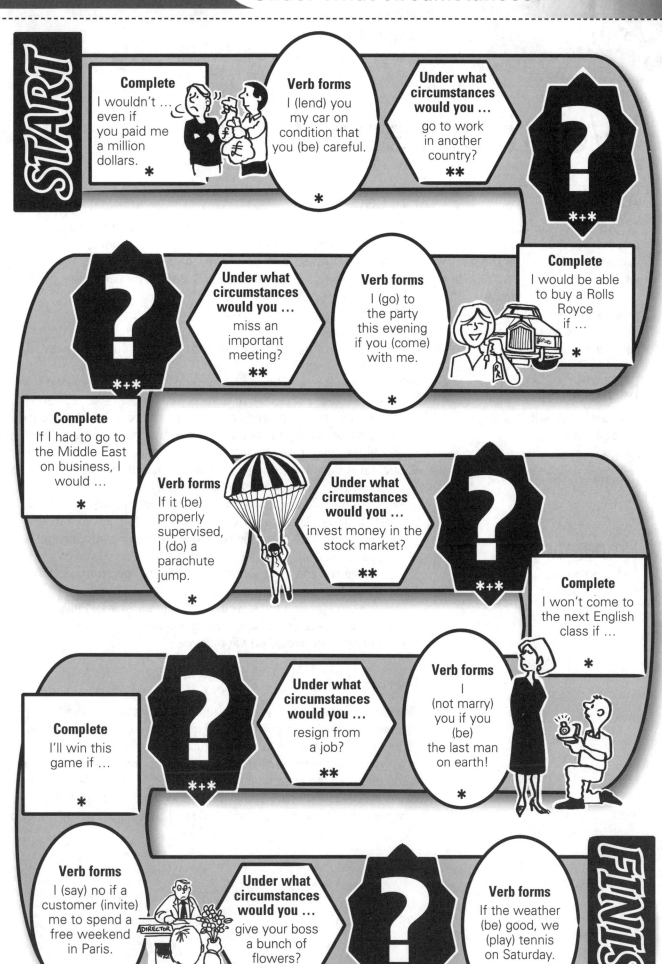

START

Complete
I wouldn't …
even if
you paid me
a million
dollars.
*

Verb forms
I (lend) you
my car on
condition that
you (be) careful.
*

**Under what
circumstances
would you …**
go to work
in another
country?
**

?
+

Complete
I would be able
to buy a Rolls
Royce
if …
*

?
+

**Under what
circumstances
would you …**
miss an
important
meeting?
**

Verb forms
I (go) to
the party
this evening
if you (come)
with me.
*

Complete
If I had to go to
the Middle East
on business, I
would …
*

Verb forms
If it (be)
properly
supervised,
I (do) a
parachute
jump.
*

**Under what
circumstances
would you …**
invest money in the
stock market?
**

?
+

Complete
I won't come to
the next English
class if …
*

Complete
I'll win this
game if …
*

?
+

**Under what
circumstances
would you …**
resign from
a job?
**

Verb forms
I
(not marry)
you if you
(be)
the last man
on earth!
*

Verb forms
I (say) no if a
customer (invite)
me to spend a
free weekend
in Paris.
*

**Under what
circumstances
would you …**
give your boss
a bunch of
flowers?
**

?
+

Verb forms
If the weather
(be) good, we
(play) tennis
on Saturday.
*

FINISH

Vocabulary The weather
Grammar Reported statements
Language to go Reporting what you hear or read

Weather report

Aim

To give students practice at weather vocabulary by exchanging information about weather forecasts in two different continents; also to practise reported speech structures by feeding back on the information gathered

Materials

One copy of Sheet A or Sheet B per student

Time

20 minutes

Preparation

Copy and cut up one worksheet per two students

Procedure

1 To introduce the activity, ask students what they think the weather is like at the moment in different cities around the world, for example: Sydney, Bangkok, New York, Cairo, Stockholm.
2 Write on the board the question and answer format that students will need to complete the worksheet:
What will the weather be like in ... this weekend?
There will be ...
3 Put students into pairs (A and B) and give each student a copy of Sheet A or Sheet B.
4 Tell Student B to ask Student A about the weather forecasted for the places marked on the map of Europe. Tell Student A to look at his/her map of Europe and answer Student B's questions. Student B should draw the appropriate symbols on the map of Europe. This should take five to seven minutes.
5 Student A then asks Student B questions about the weather in Asia and draws the appropriate symbols on his/her map.
6 Put students into new pairs, with two As together and two Bs together. They have five minutes to compare the answers they received and check that they were given the same information. For example:
 – *Ludmilla told me there would be severe thunderstorms in the Ukraine this weekend.*
 – *Yes, and Olga said there would be bright sunshine in Italy.*
 – *Yes, Ludmilla said the same. What about France?*
 – *She said there would be thick cloud.*

Extension

Reading and speaking: If you have an Internet classroom available, students could make predictions about the day's weather in various countries around the world and then use a weather site (e.g. www.weather.com) to check their predictions. Then ask individual students to tell the class what they found out, for example: *I said it would be cold with heavy snow in Moscow, and I was right. But I thought there would be sunshine in Cape Town, and in fact it's raining.*

Sheet A

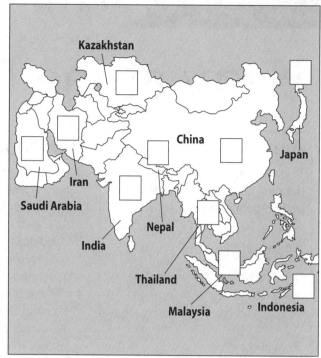

KEY TO WEATHER SYMBOLS	light showers	heavy rain	severe thunderstorms	heavy snow
	thick cloud	thick fog	strong wind	bright sunshine

Sheet B

KEY TO WEATHER SYMBOLS	light showers	heavy rain	severe thunderstorms	heavy snow
	thick cloud	thick fog	strong wind	bright sunshine

Vocabulary   Things we read
Grammar   Past perfect simple and continuous
Language to go   Talking about important moments

Harry at the Dursleys'

Aim

To give students practice at using the past perfect simple and past perfect continuous

Materials

One worksheet per student

Time

30 minutes

Preparation

Copy the worksheet

BACKGROUND INFORMATION

Harry is living with his aunt and uncle because his parents, who were wizards, were killed by the evil wizard Voldemort. Voldemort also tried to kill Harry but he miraculously survived. This is how Harry really got his scar. Harry is unaware of this and his aunt and uncle, who are ordinary people, do not want him to know and lie to him about the death of his parents. The Dursleys treat Harry very badly and make him sleep in the cupboard under the stairs. Harry finally gets away from the Dursleys when he is eleven and, despite the Dursleys' protests, is taken to Hogwarts, the school for wizards, by Hagrid, the school's giant caretaker. At Hogwarts, Harry has many exciting and dangerous adventures.

Procedure

1 Ask students if they know anything about Harry Potter, a character from a children's book. (See background information.)
2 Half the students are As and half are Bs. Put them into small groups, As together and Bs together.
3 Hand out the worksheet and ask students to fold it so that Student As have Extract A and the questions visible, and Student Bs have the questions and Extract B visible.
4 Ask students to read their text. Student As should answer questions 1–5 and Student Bs questions 6–10 (the answers to the other questions are in the other text). They should try to use the past perfect to answer the questions.
5 In their groups, students compare their answers.
6 Put students into pairs (A+B). In each pair, Student A summarises his/her text for Student B, without looking at it. B should look at questions 1–5 and see which ones can be answered from A's summary. Student B then summarises his/her text for Student A, who tries to answer questions 6–10.
7 They can then unfold the worksheet and read the other text. Ask them if they think their partner's summary was good. They should also answer any of the questions that they couldn't answer from their partner's summary.
8 Finally, discuss some or all of the following questions:
How do you think the Dursleys feel about Harry?
What does Harry feel about Dudley?
Do you think Harry is a happy boy?
Would you like to read the rest of the book?
Do you think adults can enjoy books for children?

SUGGESTED ANSWER KEY

1 Harry had arrived at the Dursleys' house. / The Dursleys had woken up to find their nephew on the front step.
2 It had hardly changed at all.
3 He had grown from a baby to a large boy.
4 He had been sleeping and dreaming. / He had been having a dream.
5 It had been a good dream. / There had been a flying motorbike in it.
6 Probably because he had been living in a dark cupboard.
7 Because he had been punched on the nose by Dudley many times. / Because Dudley had punched him on the nose many times.
8 He had had it as long as he could remember.
9 How he had got his scar.
10 According to his aunt, they had died in a car crash.

Extract A (questions 1–5)

Nearly ten years had passed since the Dursleys had woken up to find their nephew on the front step, but Privet Drive had hardly changed at all. The sun rose on the same tidy front garden, and lit up the brass number four on the Dursleys' front door; it crept into their living room, which was almost exactly the same as it had been on the night when Mr Dursley had seen that fateful news report about the owls. Only the photographs on the mantelpiece really showed how much time had passed. Ten years ago, there had been lots of pictures of what looked like a large pink beach ball wearing different-coloured bobble hats – but Dudley Dursley was no longer a baby, and now the photographs showed a large, blond boy riding his first bicycle, on a roundabout at the fair, playing a computer game with his father, being hugged and kissed by his mother. The room held no sign at all that another boy lived in the house, too.

Yet Harry Potter was still there, asleep at the moment, but not for long. His Aunt Petunia was awake, and it was her shrill voice which made the first noise of the day.

'Up! Get up! Now!'

Harry woke with a start. His aunt rapped on the door again.

'Up!' she screeched. Harry heard her walking towards the kitchen and then the sound of the frying pan being put on the cooker. He rolled on to his back and tried to remember the dream he had been having. It had been a good one. There had been a flying motorbike in it. He had a funny feeling he'd had the same dream before.

From Harry Potter and the Philosopher's Stone

1 What had happened ten years earlier?
2 How had Privet Drive changed since then?
3 How had Dudley Dursley changed?
4 What had Harry been doing when his aunt woke him up?
5 What kind of dream had he had?
6 Why was Harry small and skinny?
7 Why were his glasses held together with Sellotape?
8 How long had he had his scar?
9 What was the first question he had asked Aunt Petunia?
10 How had his parents died, according to his aunt?

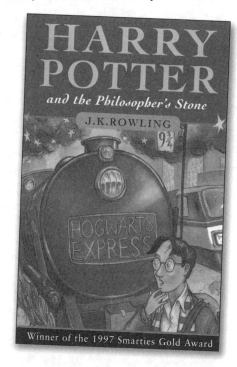

Extract B (questions 6–10)

Perhaps it had something to do with living in a dark cupboard, but Harry had always been small and skinny for his age. He looked even smaller and skinnier than he really was because all he had to wear were old clothes of Dudley's and Dudley was about four times bigger than he was. Harry had a thin face, knobbly knees, black hair and bright-green eyes. He wore round glasses held together with a lot of Sellotape because of all the times Dudley had punched him on the nose. The only thing Harry liked about his own appearance was a very thin scar on his forehead which was shaped like a bolt of lightning. He had had it as long as he could remember and the first question he could ever remember asking his Aunt Petunia was how he had got it.

'In the car crash when your parents died,' she had said. 'And don't ask questions.'

From Harry Potter and the Philosopher's Stone

Vocabulary Housework and cleanliness
Grammar *Have something done* and reflexive pronouns
Language to go Things you do, and have done for you

Do it yourself – or have it done?

Aim

To give students practice at using *have + something + past participle* and reflexive pronouns

Materials

One copy of Sheet A, B, C or D per student

Time

25 minutes

Preparation

Copy and cut up one worksheet per four students

Procedure

1 If necessary, you may wish to pre-teach some of this vocabulary: *dye, pierce, have your blood pressure taken, photo booth, car wash*.

2 Distribute the cut-up copies of the worksheet so each student has one 'Find someone who …' box.

3 Tell students that they will have to find people in the class for whom the sentences in their box are true. (They only need to find one name per sentence, and the names can be different for the different sentences.) They do this by moving around the room and asking other students yes/no questions, for example: *Have you had your car serviced in the last six months?* They repeat the same question until somebody says yes, and then they write that person's name in the box (so if the first person they ask says yes, they only ask that question once).

4 When they find someone, they have to ask a follow-up question based on the prompt below the sentence and note the answer. They will need to construct a grammatically correct question, for example: *Where …? = Where did you have it serviced?* You may wish to check they understand this by doing a couple of examples first.

5 Once they have done this for one sentence, they move on to the next. If the sentence is not true for anybody, the student writes *nobody* instead of a name.

6 When they have one name for each sentence, they can stop asking questions, but they should continue answering other students' questions.

7 After about ten minutes, or when most people have finished, ask each student in turn to tell you one piece of information that he/she discovered, including the answer to the follow-up question. For example: *I discovered that João has had his car serviced in the last six months. He had it serviced at the garage near the station.* As the other students listen, they should write down one other possible follow-up question to ask, for example: *Why did you choose that garage, João?*

8 Finally students can ask their own follow-up questions to the appropriate person. Give them about five minutes.

Sheet A

Find someone who ...   Name

has had his / her car serviced in the last six months.
(Where ...?)   _____

is going to have his / her hair cut soon.
(How ...?)   _____

has his / her passport photographs taken by a
professional photographer.
(Why not ... in a photo booth?)   _____

has never had his / her hair dyed.
(Why not ...?)   _____

Sheet B

Find someone who ...   Name

always washes the dishes himself / herself.
(Why not ... dishwasher?)   _____

has had a tooth extracted.
(When ...?)   _____

had his / her ears pierced when he / she was a child.
(... any other parts of your body?)   _____

has recently had some clothes dry-cleaned.
(What ...?)   _____

Sheet C

Find someone who ...   Name

has had a letter or article published in a newspaper.
(What ... about?)   _____

hasn't had his / her eyes tested in the past three years.
(When ...? – future)   _____

has his / her blood pressure checked regularly.
(Where ...?)   _____

does all the housework himself / herself.
(... like someone to help?)   _____

Sheet D

Find someone who: Name

can sort out computer problems himself / herself.
(How ... learn?)   _____

has had a credit card stolen.
(What ... do?)   _____

has his / her supermarket shopping delivered.
(Why ...?)   _____

has his / her car washed in a car wash.
(Why not ... yourself?)   _____

Vocabulary Describing changes
Grammar Future with *will* and *will have done*
Language to go Predicting future events

By the year 2025 ...

Aim

To give students practice at using the future perfect to talk about the possibility of future predictions, their causes and consequences

Materials

One set of cards per group of three or four students

Time

25 minutes

Preparation

Copy and cut up one worksheet per group

Procedure

1 Put students into groups of three or four. Give each group a set of the cards, face down.

2 Tell students to turn over the cards one at a time and read the prediction. They should discuss whether they think the prediction is certain to happen, probable, possible or impossible, and why (they don't need to agree). They should also talk about the reasons why this prediction might happen, and what its consequences might be. They should not write on the cards.

3 To demonstrate, do the first card on the board as a whole class activity. Write:
By the year 2025, global sea levels will have risen by half a metre.
Elicit students' opinions as to its probability, for example:
I think it's probable that this will have happened.
Elicit possible reasons, for example:
Global warming will have caused the polar ice caps to melt.
and consequences, for example:
People will have to move from coastal areas.

4 Once they've talked about one card, they should turn over the next and talk about that until they have discussed all twelve. Give them about fifteen minutes to work through all the cards.

5 As class feedback, talk about two or three of the predictions that caused most discussion.

By the year 2025 …

Global sea levels will have risen by half a metre.

certain   probable   possible   impossible

reason?
consequences?

By the year 2025 …

People will have stopped eating beef.

certain   probable   possible   impossible

reason?
consequences?

By the year 2025 …

Spanish will have become an official language of the USA.

certain   probable   possible   impossible

reason?
consequences?

By the year 2025 …

The number of people working at home will have increased dramatically.

certain   probable   possible   impossible

reason?
consequences?

By the year 2025 …

China will have become the world's most important economic power.

certain   probable   possible   impossible

reason?
consequences?

By the year 2025 …

The number of immigrants in Europe will have increased to 50% of the total population.

certain   probable   possible   impossible

reason?
consequences?

By the year 2025 …

The hole in the ozone layer will have increased to three times its current size.

certain   probable   possible   impossible

reason?
consequences?

By the year 2025 …

People will have stopped buying books and music in shops.

certain   probable   possible   impossible

reason?
consequences?

By the year 2025 …

State pensions will have been abolished in Western Europe.

certain   probable   possible   impossible

reason?
consequences?

By the year 2025 …

A permanent colony will have been established on the planet Mars.

certain   probable   possible   impossible

reason?
consequences?

By the year 2025 …

The Russian Federation will have joined the European Union.

certain   probable   possible   impossible

reason?
consequences?

By the year 2025 …

You will have become very rich!

certain   probable   possible   impossible

reason?
consequences?

Vocabulary 1   Medical problems and symptoms
Vocabulary 2   Phrasal verbs about illness
Language to go   Describing symptoms of an illness

Healthline

Aim

To read about medical symptoms and discuss causes and treatment

Materials

One worksheet per student

Time

25 minutes

Preparation

Copy the worksheet

Procedure

1 Ask students where they can get advice if they are sick. Ask if they think it is possible to get medical advice over the Internet.
2 Hand out the worksheet and ask students to read the e-mails in Part A.
3 In pairs, they discuss what they think might be wrong with each of the people, and what they think they should do. Allow five to seven minutes.
4 Ask students to read *Healthline's* replies in Part B and match them with the problems in Part A.
5 As class feedback, ask if students had come to the same conclusions about the problems as *Healthline* did. Discuss whether they think *Healthline's* advice is good or not, and why.
6 Finally, divide students into groups of three or four and give them seven to ten minutes to discuss the questions in Part C. Be careful, however, as some of these questions are quite personal. If you have doubts as to whether students will feel comfortable talking about them, leave them out.

ANSWER KEY

Part B
1 e   2 c   3 b   4 f   5 d   6 a

34

Healthline

Part A

Read these e-mails to an Internet medical advice service called *Healthline*. Think about the people's symptoms and decide what you think is wrong with them. What advice would you give them?

1 I've recently come back from a holiday in the Caribbean. Since I've returned my ankles have swollen up. They are red and extremely itchy. They've been like this for three days now.

2 My daughter has come down with something terrible. She has thrown up several times this morning and she says she has a headache. I'm very worried.

3 Yesterday, when I was getting out of the shower, I passed out and banged my head on the side of the bath. This morning I almost passed out again. Why is this happening?

4 I've recently come out in red spots all over my body. My eyes are aching and are very itchy. I've recently got a new cat. Could there be any connection?

5 I was playing football with my friends yesterday and this morning, when I woke up, my foot was hurting a lot and my big toe had swollen to twice its normal size. I can't walk. What should I do?

6 Lately I've been getting very bad headaches and feel tired all the time. Also my chest aches. Do you think I need to go to the doctor?

Part B

These are the replies from *Healthline*. Match each reply with one of the problems in Part 1. Do you think the advice is good?

a) Yes, definitely. Your symptoms could be caused by many things, but I suspect you're suffering from stress. Do you have a difficult job where you have to work long hours? But the fact that you have chest pains means it could be serious. See your doctor immediately.

b) This is more common that you might think. You could be suffering from low blood pressure in the mornings. Try drinking a coffee before you take a shower. If the situation continues, seek medical advice.

c) It's probably food poisoning. Did she eat anything unusual yesterday? She should stay in bed, drink plenty of water and eat boiled rice. If she doesn't feel better tomorrow, take her to the doctor.

d) Oh dear! It sounds as though it was a tough game. Get a friend or family member to take you to the hospital to get an X-ray. Your toe is probably broken.

e) You've probably been bitten by an insect. Put your legs in ice until the swelling goes down. Don't scratch your legs. Go to the chemist and ask for a cream to put on the affected area.

f) Almost certainly. Go to the chemist and ask him for some anti-histamine tablets. If the condition continues, I'm afraid that, much as you may love him, you may have to find a new home for your feline friend.

Part C

Discuss these questions.

1 Do you think it is a good idea to look for medical advice on the Internet, or should you always consult a doctor?

2 Have you or someone you know ever had any of the conditions described in the e-mails? What did you/he/she do? How long did it take you/him/her to get over it?

3 When was the last time you went to the doctor? Were you ill or was it a check-up? What did the doctor do?

Vocabulary   People and groups
Grammar   Past modal verbs of deduction
Language to go   Drawing conclusions about the past

The conclusions game

Aim

To give students practice at using past modals to draw conclusions about the past

Materials

One set of cards per group of four students

Time

25 minutes

Preparation

Copy and cut up one worksheet per group.

Procedure

1 As an introduction, write these two headings on the board: *Sentence* and *Reaction*. In the sentence column, write: *Susan is very tired.* Elicit possible reasons why Susan is tired, for example: *She might have been working too much. She can't (or might not) have slept very well last night.* Write these in the reaction column. Tell students they are going to play a game in which they will have to match sentences with reactions.

2 Put students into groups of four, if possible at a table. Divide the fours into two teams of two.

3 Give each group a set of sentences and a set of reactions. Tell them to put the cards face down on the table so that the backs of all the cards can be seen; on the left, the sentences in three rows of four cards, and on the right, the reactions, also in three rows of four.

4 Explain the rules of the game:
   • There is one reaction that matches each sentence.
   • Team A turns over one sentence and one reaction and places them face up. If they match, the team keeps the cards and has another turn. If not, the cards are placed face down again in the same place and Team B has a turn.
   • The teams try to remember the position of the cards and continue playing until all the cards have been matched and taken. The team with most cards at the end wins.

5 Demonstrate the start of a game for the whole class, then let students play in their groups.

6 When they have finished, one person in the group reads out all the sentences in turn, and the other students in the group have to give the correct reactions. They probably won't be able to remember the exact words, but should have had sufficient exposure to produce similar sentences.

ANSWER KEY
The sentence cards on the worksheet match with the reasons cards in the same position, e.g. *Jack's looking very happy* matches with *He could have had some good news.*

35

The conclusions game

Sentences

When I woke up and looked out of the window, everything was white.	Van Gogh cut off part of his ear!	Jim's one of the best students in the class but he failed his exam.
Jane's got paint on her hands.	Tom arrived late for work yesterday.	Sophie's hair is wet.
Louisa left the cinema crying.	Jack's looking very happy.	Ronnie's got a terrible hangover.
Jessica crashed her car last week, but she's OK.	I went parachuting at the weekend.	I was an hour late for my job interview because the train was delayed.

Reactions

It must have been snowing.	He must have been mad.	The questions can't have been very easy.
She might have been redecorating her bedroom.	His boss can't have been very happy.	She might have been taking a shower.
She might have seen a sad film.	He could have had some good news.	He must have had too much to drink last night.
She was lucky. She could have been seriously injured!	That must have been exciting! Were you scared?	What bad luck! You must have been furious.

Vocabulary Business processes: word building
Grammar Non-defining relative clauses
Language to go Giving extra information

Dear customer

Aim

To give students practice at using non-defining relative clauses, in the context of a letter to persuade customers to use a new product or service

Materials

One worksheet per student

Time

25–30 minutes

Preparation

Copy the worksheet

Procedure

1 Ask students if they ever get mail from companies informing them of new products or services (for example, their bank, their language school). Ask them what kind of information they are sent.
2 Hand out the worksheet and ask students to read the letter.
3 Put students into pairs. Draw their attention to the sentences beneath the letter. They have to decide where these sentences could fit into the body of the letter. They should then transform them into non-defining relative clauses and insert them in the most appropriate place. Do the first one together as an example (see suggested answer key).
4 Give them five to seven minutes to expand the letter in pairs. When they have finished, check the answers with the whole class by asking students to read out the completed letter a sentence at a time.
5 Tell students they are responsible for marketing in one of the companies in the list at the bottom of the worksheet. In pairs, they should choose a company and brainstorm ideas about the new product or service on offer, and any special features that would be attractive to customers. Allow about five minutes.
6 Students write a letter to be sent to customers or potential customers, telling them about the new product or service and persuading them to buy it. This should take about ten minutes.
7 When they have finished, they read another pair's letter and say if they would buy the product or not, and why.

SUGGESTED ANSWER KEY

We are writing to you as one of our most valued customers, to inform you of our latest model of telephone.
Yes, UTS, **which has been one of the leading telecom companies in the country for the last five years**, is pleased to announce the launch of its new UTS 3000.
You probably thought the UTS 2650, **which is the model you currently use**, could not be improved, but our new model will revolutionise your life. Let us tell you about some of the features of the UTS 3000, **which is available now**.
• A display screen, **where you can see the number or name of the person calling**, has been incorporated into this new model.
• A new memory system, **which records and lets you view the calls you receive while you are out**, enables you to keep track of all the people who have tried to contact you, even if you have been away from home for days.
• A recall button, **which automatically calls the last person who called you, without you having to dial**, is another new feature.
For just 20 euros rental a month, **which is a small price to pay**, the most cutting-edge telephone on the market can be yours.

United Telecom Services

UTS

Dear customer,

We are writing to you as one of our most valued customers, to inform you of our latest model of telephone.

Yes, UTS is pleased to announce the launch of its new *UTS 3000*.

You probably thought the *UTS 2650* could not be improved, but our new model will revolutionise your life. Let us tell you about some of the features of the *UTS 3000*.

- A display screen has been incorporated into this new model.
- A new memory system enables you to keep track of all the people who have tried to contact you, even if you have been away from home for days.
- A recall button is another new feature.

For just 20 euros rental a month the most cutting-edge telephone on the market can be yours.

For more information, **phone 1004 now**.

1 UTS has been one of the leading telecom companies in the country for the last five years.
2 It is a small price to pay.
3 It records and lets you view the calls you receive while you are out.
4 It is available now.
5 It is the model you currently use.
6 On the screen you can see the number or name of the person calling.
7 It automatically calls the last person who called you, without you having to dial.

- a restaurant chain which is opening a new restaurant
- a language school which is launching an Internet course
- an airline which is starting to operate a new route
- a toothpaste company which is launching a new brand of toothpaste
- a food company which is launching a new product
- an idea of your own

Vocabulary   Verb expressions about friendship
Grammar   Present perfect with *for* and *since*
Language to go   Describing friendship

Harold's party

Aim

To give students practice at using the present perfect simple and present perfect continuous with *for* and *since*

Materials

One worksheet per student

Time

30 minutes

Preparation

Copy the worksheet

Procedure

1 Ask students to imagine they are meeting an old friend who they haven't seen for a long time. Elicit questions that they might ask, for example: *Where do you live now? Do you still work at ...? What have you been doing recently / since I last saw you?* etc.

2 Hand out the worksheet and ask students to read the letter from Harold, an old friend with whom they have lost contact. They should complete the table below the letter with information about Harold then compare their answers in pairs. Allow five minutes.

3 Tell the students that they are going to Harold's party. There will be a lot of people there that they haven't seen for a long time. Ask them to prepare by completing the information in the second table. They have five minutes to invent information about themselves, being as imaginative as possible.

4 When they've finished completing the second table, elicit the questions they will need to ask to get the information from the other people at the party.
Where do you live now? How long have you lived there? Are you married? How long have you been married/divorced? Where do you work? What do you do? How long have you worked there? Have you got any children? What are their names? Do they go to school? What else do they do? How long have they been doing that? What do you do in your free time? How long have you been doing that? What have you been doing recently? How long have you been doing that?

5 They then go to the party. Students should move around the class and speak to as many people as possible in the time available. Allow ten to fifteen minutes, depending on the size of the class.

6 Finally, put the students into pairs to see if they discovered the answers to the questions at the bottom of the worksheet.

SUGGESTED ANSWER KEY

Name	HAROLD	
Live	Where: Maidenhead	How long: **for two months**
Married	Yes/No: **yes**	How long: **for two years**
Work	Where: **Maidenhead** What: **TV journalist**	How long: **TV journalist since 1993 / Maidenhead for two months**
Children	How many: **one** Names: **Natasha** What they do: **walk / go to nursery school**	How long: **walking for a year / nursery school since November**
Hobbies	What: **photography / tennis**	How long: **photography since school / tennis for one month**
Recent activities	What: **travelling around the world as a foreign correspondent**	How long: **for five years**

Dear Friend,

Do you remember me? I'm sorry I haven't been in touch for so long. The thing is, I've been travelling around the world with my job for the last five years. I've been a TV journalist since 1993. The channel decided I would be a good foreign correspondent and they've sent me everywhere. But I arrived back in the country two months ago and I'm now living and working in Maidenhead!

And you won't believe it, but I'm married. I got married in Moscow two years ago, and we now have a daughter, Natasha. She's been walking for a year now and she's been going to nursery school since November.

Apart from that I haven't changed much. I still like photography – I've been doing that since I was at school. But I started playing tennis last month. I'm terrible, of course.

What about you? Are you still working and living in the same place? Are you married yet? You can tell me everything next month because I'm having a party and I'm inviting all our old friends. You will come, won't you?

Harold

Name	HAROLD	
Live	Where: Maidenhead	How long: for two months
Married	Yes / No:	How long:
Work	Where: What:	How long:
Children	How many: Names: What they do:	How long:
Hobbies	What:	How long:
Recent activities	What:	How long:

Name		
Live	Where:	How long:
Married	Yes / No:	How long:
Work	Where: What:	How long:
Children	How many: Names: What they do:	How long:
Hobbies	What:	How long:
Recent activities	What:	How long:

- Who has lived in the same place for the longest time?
- Who has been married the longest?
- Who has the most children?
- Who has the most interesting job? How long have they had it?
- Who has the strangest hobby? How long have they been doing it?

Vocabulary   Happiness
Function   Polite questions
Language to go   Asking questions about personal issues

I'd rather not say

Aim

To give students practice at using indirect questions to ask for personal information

Materials

One worksheet per group of four students; one dice per group; one counter per student

Time

30 minutes

Preparation

Copy one worksheet per group

Procedure

1 Write on the board:
   How much do you earn?
   How much do you weigh?
   Who did you vote for in the last election?
   Ask the students if they can find a connection between the questions. (Answer: They are very personal questions that many people would prefer not to answer.)

2 Elicit ways of responding if you don't want to answer a question, for example: *I'd prefer not to answer that* or *I'd rather not say*.

3 Ask the students to make the questions on the board less direct, for example: *Could you tell me how much you earn?* Remind them not to use the question form *do you earn* with an indirect question.

4 Tell students they are going to play a game in which they will ask personal questions, but stress that they have no obligation to answer the questions. Put students into groups of four. Each group needs one copy of the worksheet (the gameboard), a dice, and a counter per student (they could use coins).

5 Explain the rules of the game:
   • The players start at the 'Start' square.
   • They take turns to throw the dice. They move the number of squares indicated and ask another student in the group the question in the square on which they land – but as the question is personal, they have to ask it using one of the polite question forms in the centre of the board. They can choose which student to ask, but they have to ask different students during the game.
   • If the question is grammatically correct, they remain on that square. If the question is wrong (for example: *Can I ask you what do you worry about?*), they have to go back to the square they were on before.
   • The person who is asked the question can choose to answer the question or not, in which case he/she has to say:
   I'd prefer not to answer that one or *I'd rather not say*.
   • If they land on an 'Ask the teacher' square, they ask the teacher a personal question using one of the polite question forms in the centre of the board.
   • The winner is the first player to go right round the board and return to the start.

6 At the end, ask students which question(s) most people didn't want to answer, and which questions people didn't mind answering.

Vocabulary	Shopping
Grammar	Third conditional and *I wish / If only*
Language to go	Talking about past regrets

What did I do wrong?

Aim

To give students practice at using the third conditional to talk about past regrets

Materials

One set of cards per two students

Time

30 minutes

Preparation

Copy and cut up one worksheet per two students

Procedure

1 Ask students what advice they would give to somebody going out on a first date. Where should they go? What should they wear? What shouldn't they do?

2 Put students into pairs and give each pair a set of the picture cards in jumbled order. Explain that the pictures tell the story of what happened to Jim on a disastrous first date with a girl named Sandra. Students have to put the pictures in a logical order (there's more than one possibility).

3 The students then have about five minutes to retell the story to each other from the pictures.

4 Ask students: *Do you think it was a good idea for Jim to take his motorbike? What kind of transport should he have used? Why?* Try to elicit a sentence in the third conditional, for example: *If he'd taken a taxi, he wouldn't have been stopped by the police* or *If he'd taken a car, Sandra would have been more impressed.* Write the sentence on the board and focus on the form.

5 In pairs, students should say or write some more third conditional sentences about the story. Allow five to seven minutes.

6 Put students into new pairs. One should take the role of Jim, and the other should take the role of a friend of Jim's. Jim should tell his friend the story of his disastrous evening; the friend should listen and tell him what he did wrong, if possible using the third conditional.

SUGGESTED ANSWER KEY

Third conditional sentences
If he'd taken a taxi, he wouldn't have got into trouble with the police.
If they'd gone to see a more romantic film, Sandra would have enjoyed it.
If they'd eaten in a restaurant, Sandra wouldn't have been so cold.
If Jim had spent more money on a meal, Sandra would have been more impressed.
If Jim hadn't drunk so much, the police wouldn't have stopped him.
Sandra would have liked Jim more if he'd been a better dancer.

Vocabulary   Job applications and interviews
Grammar   Reported questions
Language to go   Reporting a conversation or interview

Guilty or not guilty?

Aim

To give students practice at using reported questions in the context of reporting a police interview

Materials

One copy of Sheet A or Sheet B per student

Time

25 minutes

Preparation

Copy and cut up one worksheet per two students

Procedure

1 Tell students that yesterday at three o'clock a bank was robbed, and the police are interviewing a suspect. Ask them what questions the police will probably ask the suspect, to elicit: *What were you doing yesterday at three o'clock?* Ask students to suggest answers for the suspect, for example: *I was at work. I was driving to Birmingham.* And then ask students to think of a follow-up question the police might ask, for example: *Were you alone? What were you doing?*

2 Give half the class a copy of Sheet A, and the other half a copy of Sheet B. Divide students into pairs, Student As together and Student Bs together.

3 Explain that they are detectives working on the bank robbery case. There are two main suspects and Student As and Student Bs have each interviewed one of them. The interviews were recorded but the recording was not very good and parts of the transcript are missing. In pairs, students have to complete the transcript by working out the questions they asked. Allow five to seven minutes.

4 Check that students have written suitable questions.

5 Divide students into new pairs, (A+B). Give them seven or eight minutes to report their interviews to each other using reported speech. For example:
   A: *I asked Ken Foster where he had had lunch and he told me he had had lunch with Ronnie White at the Red Lion.*
   B: *Really? Ronnie White said they'd had lunch at a Chinese restaurant.*

6 Ask the students if they think Foster and White are guilty or not guilty and why.

SUGGESTED ANSWER KEY

Sheet A
1 what were you doing last Monday at one o'clock?
2 Who did you have lunch with?
3 And where did you have lunch?
4 Which pub?
5 What did you do after lunch?
6 … you were at the cinema?
7 What film did you see?

Sheet B
a what did you do on Monday afternoon?
b So, at one o'clock you were at the cinema?
c What's that?
d Who did you have lunch with?
e So, when did you go to the cinema?
f And what were you doing at three o'clock?
g What film did you see?

Sheet A

Detective:	All right, Foster, [1]_____ ?
Ken Foster:	At one o'clock last Monday? I was having lunch.
Detective:	Who [2]_____ ?
Ken Foster:	With Ronnie White.
Detective:	And [3]_____ ?
Ken Foster:	At the pub.
Detective:	[4]_____ ?
Ken Foster:	The Red Lion.
Detective:	[5]_____ after lunch?
Ken Foster:	We went to the cinema.
Detective:	Really? So at three o'clock, when the bank was robbed, you [6]_____ ?
Ken Foster:	That's right.
Detective:	[7]_____ ?
Ken Foster:	I can't remember. Oh yeah, it was *Die Hard 7*.

INTERVIEW ROOM I

Sheet B

Detective:	All right, Ronnie, [a]_____ _____ on Monday afternoon?
Ronnie White:	I went to the cinema.
Detective:	So, at one o'clock [b]_____ ?
Ronnie White:	No, I was having lunch in the Bamboo Garden.
Detective:	[c]_____ ?
Ronnie White:	It's a Chinese restaurant.
Detective:	Who [d]_____ ?
Ronnie White:	With Ken Foster.
Detective:	[e]_____ ?
Ronnie White:	We went to the cinema after lunch.
Detective:	[f]_____ at three o'clock?
Ronnie White:	I was still at the cinema watching the film. With Ken.
Detective:	Really? [g]_____ ?
Ronnie White:	I can't remember. Oh yeah, it was *Terminator 4*.

INTERVIEW ROOM 2

Test 1

Grammar

1 Choose the correct options to complete the text.

There was a gentle breeze blowing, and the sun was shining when we [1] _____ at the tiny village of Falzano. The road twisted and curled up the mountainside like a corkscrew [2] _____ finally we saw the iron gates.

As we were unloading our cases from the car, a large snake [3] _____ the path in front of us. We stopped and stared, all of us [4] _____ terrified. No one had told us there were snakes!

'[5] _____ a snake before?' my brother said, trying to sound brave. 'A snake [6] _____ hurt you unless you [7] _____ it,' he went on.

We began to explore the villa, each of us trying to forget the snake. 'I [8] _____ for a swim,' said Isabelle excitedly. 'Great,' I said, 'I [9] _____ join you. After all, snakes [10] _____ , can they?'

1 a) are arriving b) arrived c) were arriving
  d) did arrive
2 a) so b) if c) since d) until
3 a) crossed b) was crossing c) has crossed
  d) is crossing
4 a) very b) absolutely c) largely d) great
5 a) Didn't you see b) Aren't you seeing
  c) Haven't you seen d) Don't you see
6 a) won't b) isn't c) does d) would
7 a) will annoy b) are going to annoy c) annoy
  d) annoyed
8 a) will go b) go c) going d) am going
9 a) am going b) will c) can d) am
10 a) aren't swimming b) won't swim c) can't swim
  d) don't swim

                                            | 10 |

2 Underline the correct option in each sentence.

1 When Johnny was only three years old, he *could* / *managed to* swim really well.
2 If *you'll go* / *you're going* out, take an umbrella.
3 I've decided *I'm going to go* / *I'll go* shopping on Saturday.
4 Luke *never went* / *has never been* abroad in his life, but he's going to the US next month.
5 Did you hear that? The flight *will be* / *is going to be* delayed.
6 It took us four hours, but we *could* / *managed to* start the car without a mechanic.
7 We *haven't been* / *didn't go* to Greece last year.
8 What *will* / *would* you do if you don't get the job?
9 When we *were reaching* / *reached* the hotel, it was nearly midnight.
10 *I think John won't* / *I don't think John will* marry Beth.

                                            | 10 |

3 Tick (✓) the correct sentence in each pair.

1 a) Have you ever been to Cairo? ☐
  b) Did you ever been to Cairo? ☐
2 a) If you don't mind to wait, I won't be a moment. ☐
  b) If you don't mind waiting, I won't be a moment. ☐
3 a) What on earth did happen here? It's a mess. ☐
  b) What on earth happened here? It's a mess. ☐
4 a) Revising is more harder than taking the exam. ☐
  b) Revising is harder than taking the exam. ☐
5 a) While I was walking down the High Street,
    I saw an old friend. ☐
  b) While I walked down the High Street,
    I saw an old friend. ☐
6 a) 'I'm going to the cinema.'
    'Great, I'm going to come with you.' ☐
  b) 'I'm going to the cinema.'
    'Great. I'll come with you.' ☐
7 a) Did you manage to fix your computer yesterday? ☐
  b) Could you fix your computer yesterday? ☐
8 a) We must going. It's getting late. ☐
  b) We must go. It's getting late. ☐
9 a) I don't think I'll call my puppy 'Fluff'. ☐
  b) I don't think I won't call my puppy 'Fluff'. ☐
10 a) Trevor was the oldest man at the party. ☐
   b) Trevor was the older man at the party. ☐

                                            | 10 |

4 Correct the errors in each of these sentences.

1 My name is Faith. I think it goes well on my personality.
2 I was called following my great-grandmother.
3 I like summertime best. It reminds me by my childhood.
4 John once accused me to being too romantic and sentimental.
5 I'm really in music. I like jazz and classical best of all.
6 My brother has good taste for clothes.
7 I saw a fantastic job last week, but I was too scared to apply to it.
8 I went to a party and someone introduced me with Karen.
9 Sam congratulated me by my results.
10 Next year, I plan to take on yoga.

                                            | 10 |

Vocabulary

5 Complete the second sentence so that it means the same as the first sentence, using the words given in brackets.

1 John always gets up early. (riser)
John is _____ .
2 Karen has woken up in a bad mood. (wrong side)
Karen has _____ .
3 Let's all go to bed early tonight. (night)
Let's all _____ .
4 I'm going to get up later than usual tomorrow. (lie-in)
I'm going to _____ .
5 I can't stay awake. (eyes)
I can't _____ .
6 Pete's hoping to be promoted. (get)
Pete's hoping to _____ .
7 Is somebody interviewing you next week? (go for)
Are you _____ next week?
8 I like working with other people. (team)
I like working _____ .
9 My uncle can write with both hands. (ambidextrous)
My uncle _____ .
10 That test was really easy. (cake)
That test was _____ .

⌐10

6 Use the appropriate form of the words in the box to complete the memo.

manage   boil   qualify   suggestion   honest

MEMO

TO: All staff
FROM: Michael Jones M.D. _____

There's good news and bad news. The good news is that this year, we've received a record number of applications from graduates with good [1] _____ . The bad news is that the company has discovered a great deal of cheating and [2] _____ among its employees. It isn't easy to find out who the culprits are, but we think that with careful surveillance, the task is [3] _____ .

Many employees have complained that their offices are [4] _____ hot in summer. The comfort of our workers is important to us, and we are looking into the possibility of installing air conditioning. In the meantime, the management [5] _____ that staff keep the windows open and use the fans provided.

⌐5

7 Put sentences A–J in this e-mail in the correct order. Then do the same with sentences K–T.

to: **Kota Kinabalu team members**
subject: **Kota Kinabalu expedition, 4–11 June**

Please note the following important things:

A The climate in Sabah is much
B light T-shirts and rain
C belt; please also carry insect
D clothes are essential. You
E case you forget anything.
F hotter and wetter than our last expedition, so
G aid kit and a money
H repellent: the area is full of
I will each need a first-
J mosquitoes. A checklist is enclosed in

K It is important to carry salt
L as not to get
M fitter by the time we return home!
N dehydrated. Please also bring sun
O sunburn. So, get out those walking
P bottle. Drink two litres a day so
Q tablets, and a large water
R cream, as there is a high risk of
S a lifetime. You will certainly be much
T boots and start preparing for the trip of

1 ___ 2 ___ 3 ___ 4 ___ 5 ___
6 ___ 7 ___ 8 ___ 9 ___ 10 ___
11 ___ 12 ___ 13 ___ 14 ___ 15 ___
16 ___ 17 ___ 18 ___ 19 ___ 20 ___

⌐20

8 Correct the ten mistakes in this e-mail.

Dear Zak

It was great to meet you last week. You asked me to tell you a bit more about myself. So here goes:

[1] I'm really keen sports. I love tennis and squash and I've just taken up judo. [2] I used play a lot of hockey, but when I failed to get into the team, I gave it up. [3] When I was younger, I couldn't swim, but now I swim a lot in order keep fit. If I don't go swimming at least once a week, I feel quite grumpy. [4] Last year, I tried to learn to play icy hockey, [5] but I soon got sickness of being hurt – I kept falling over. I love most sports. [6] The only one I don't stand is rugby. I have never understood the rules.

[7] I like take part in loads of things, [8] especially teaming activities. I took a day off last week just to go abseiling with a group of friends. [9] It was quite hard, but I manage to do it in the end. [10] I was exhausting when I got home, though!

Kim

⌐10
⌐85

Test 2

Grammar

1 <u>Underline</u> the correct verbs.

When I was little, my parents [1] *lived / would live* in France. It was a lovely time in my life because we [2] *were going / used to go* all over Europe on our summer holidays. My dad [3] *would / did* always insist on driving wherever we went, so the four of us [4] *have / would* set off in the car. In those days, it [5] *was / would be* an amazingly long journey to Italy, but I clearly remember going there for a holiday. My brother and I [6] *were loving / used to love* swimming, so we very often went to a seaside town. That year, my parents [7] *would choose / chose* a tiny island called Ponza. It [8] *had / would have* a lovely, long, sandy beach where we played for hours. Every morning, we [9] *would / did* wake our parents up very early and force them to get up and take us out. And of course, every day was the same: we [10] *have built / built* enormous sandcastles and watched as the sea knocked them down.

10

2 Match the sentences to make conversations.

1 You ought to stop smoking.
2 I'm back in the black.
3 What's that noise?
4 Would you mind if I opened the window?
5 Turn that radio down!
6 I've got nowhere to stay tonight.
7 The sea looks beautiful.
8 We'll set off at six.
9 I sent you a postcard.
10 Good luck with the test.

a) Oh, yes, sorry. It's rather loud.
b) But the plane leaves at half past.
c) It hasn't arrived yet.
d) No, not at all.
e) Yes, it's really calm.
f) I'm not sure. It sounds like a drum.
g) Thanks a lot!
h) I can put you up.
i) Great! Well done.
j) Yes, I know I should.

1 _____ 2 _____ 3 _____ 4 _____ 5 _____
6 _____ 7 _____ 8 _____ 9 _____ 10 _____

10

3 Correct the ten mistakes in the dialogue.

Simon: [1] Who was that girl you were putting with last week?
Jim: Oh, that was Lucy. She's a cousin of mine. [2] She lives in the village which I grew up, but she was in Oxford for a rehearsal. [3] She stays at the hotel in Broad Street now.
Simon: [4] Is she the cousin whose with the Shakespeare Acting Company?
Jim: Yes. [5] They're doing a play who hasn't been performed for years. Apparently it's very good. [6] Do you like to go and see it?
Simon: Yes, why not. [7] I must say, if I am an actor, I'd get very nervous before a performance.
Jim: [8] Yes, so could I. [9] It starts at eight, so if we set to

at seven thirty, we'll get there on time. [10] Well, as long as the car doesn't break off, that is.

10

4 Tick (✓) the correct sentence in each pair.

1 a) You shouldn't waste electricity. ☐
   b) You shouldn't to waste electricity. ☐
2 a) I sent to you a letter. Did you get it? ☐
   b) I sent you a letter. Did you get it? ☐
3 a) Katie's seeing the doctor at five. ☐
   b) Katie see the doctor at five. ☐
4 a) Do you think we ought to get ready? ☐
   b) Do you think we ought get ready? ☐
5 a) Jill's one of those people which look calm all the time. ☐
   b) Jill's one of those people who look calm all the time. ☐
6 a) Did Charles her put up last week? ☐
   b) Did Charles put her up last week? ☐
7 a) They've decided going to Paris on honeymoon. ☐
   b) They've decided to go to Paris on honeymoon. ☐
8 a) Rick used to have long hair when he was a teenager. ☐
   b) Rick would have long hair when he was a teenager. ☐
9 a) The bread is smelling delicious! ☐
   b) The bread smells delicious! ☐
10 a) To open the window, please. ☐
    b) Open the window, please. ☐

10

5 Choose the correct option to complete the text.

If you thought life was too busy, you [1] _____ think again. In these days of modern conveniences, fast living, fast food, e-mails and air travel, we can actually cut [2] _____ on work and have much more time to relax. The world is speeding up, but the gadgets [3] _____ come with it make our lives easier. We no longer need [4] _____ time going to the supermarket: we can order our shopping online. If you want to avoid [5] _____ in queues, and if sitting in traffic jams [6] _____ on your nerves, just shop in the comfort of your own home. It's terrific!

If you would [7] _____ to explore other ways of improving your life, why not take a look at Feng Shui? Feng Shui is a phenomenon [8] _____ is relatively new to the western world. Experts are now available to help you arrange your house and furniture. A simple rearrangement could bring you good luck, wealth and happiness. That may [9] _____ strange, but many people [10] _____ the benefits.

1 a) would   b) do   c) should   d) ought
2 a) off   b) down   c) up   d) in
3 a) who   b) whose   c) what   d) which
4 a) using   b) wasting   c) to waste   d) losing
5 a) standing   b) to stand   c) living   d) to live
6 a) is   b) gets   c) becomes   d) makes
7 a) enjoy   b) loving   c) liking   d) like
8 a) where   b) who   c) that   d) whose
9 a) find   b) sound   c) look   d) hit
10 a) discovered   b) found   c) have discovered   d) finding

10

Vocabulary

6 Complete the sentences using the correct form of the words in brackets.

1 Hard work alone does not necessarily make you
_____ . (wealth)
2 To be _____ in business, you need good contacts.
(success)
3 Two of my best friends got _____ last week. (engage)
4 It's horrible being _____ on cigarettes. (depend)
5 _____ is one of the things many people fear. (lonely)

5

7 Match the two halves of these sentences.

1 This soup   a) gets on my nerves.
2 I can't carry on   b) after the baby tonight?
3 This firm wastes   c) interest on your current account.
4 I was very upset, but   d) the red again.
5 We can pay you   e) tastes fabulous.
6 The train   f) so much paper.
7 Doesn't this fabric   g) walking up this mountain.
8 Oh, no. I'm in   h) I've got over it now.
9 Could you look   i) leaves in five minutes.
10 Sometimes he really   j) feel soft?

1 _____ 2 _____ 3 _____ 4 _____ 5 _____
6 _____ 7 _____ 8 _____ 9 _____ 10 _____

10

8 Complete the crossword.

Across
3 I'd like to _____ £200 from my account, please.
5 Can you _____ this cheque for me when you go to
the bank?
6 We should be careful not to waste the world's
_____ . Trees, clean air and water are all being
wasted at the moment.
8 _____ is achieved through hard work and a lot of
luck.
12 Kate is a _____ . She's decided that it isn't healthy
to eat meat.
13 _____ is an important commitment between two
people who love each other.
14 They say Feng Shui will bring you many things,
including money, happiness and _____ .

Down
1 He can't stop smoking. He's _____ to cigarettes.
2 Try not to spend too much _____ thinking about
your bank balance.
4 You need a lot of _____ to quit smoking. How
determined are you?
7 The noun from *happy*.
8 Do you have a _____ account? I save about £50 a
month.
9 Being a TV _____ isn't as glamorous as it looks. It's
very hot in the kitchens.
10 I looked at my bank _____ , but I couldn't see how
much money I had.
11 Did you know that one in three marriages ends in
_____ ?

15

9 Tick (✓) the correct boxes.

1 If you are *in the black*, have you:
  a) got some money? ☐
  b) turned off the lights? ☐
2 If you went to a restaurant and your chicken
was *raw*, would you:
  a) eat it? ☐
  b) send it back? ☐
3 If your alarm *went off*, would you:
  a) get up? ☐
  b) get it repaired? ☐
4 Who *cooks* food:
  a) a cook? ☐
  b) a cooker? ☐
5 If you say you *used to* do something, do you
do it now?
  a) Yes. ☐
  b) No. ☐
6 If you *give up* smoking, do you:
  a) start smoking? ☐
  b) stop smoking? ☐
7 If you *get on* with someone, do you:
  a) dislike them? ☐
  b) like them? ☐
8 If you *cut down* the number of cigarettes you
smoked, would you have quit?
  a) Yes. ☐
  b) No. ☐
9 Would you eat cheese if you were a *vegan*?
  a) Yes. ☐
  b) No. ☐
10 You can say '*fast* food'; can you say '*slow* food'?
  a) Yes. ☐
  b) No. ☐

10
90

Test 3

Grammar

1 Complete the dialogue with the correct form of the verbs in brackets.

Marcus: Jools, where [1] _____ you _____ (be)? I [2] _____ (wait) for you since three, and it's nearly half six now!

Jools: Ah, well, it's a long story. I [3] _____ (arrest) on the way here.

Marcus: Yeah, right. Of course you were. You [4] _____ (waste) my time now, so stop it and tell me the truth.

Jools: OK. I [5] _____ (chat) to this really famous model since about three thirty.

Marcus: Jools! Just tell me what you [6] _____ (do), will you?

Jools: I [7] _____ (kidnap) by aliens and taken to Jupiter. They [8] _____ (photograph) my brain and everything!

Marcus: Oh, dear. By the time you've told me what's going on, I'll be an old man.

Jools: OK, OK. Now, actually I [9] _____ just _____ (fulfil) a lifetime's ambition.

Marcus: And what would that be exactly?

Jools: Well, while you've been waiting for me so patiently, I [10] _____ (queue) for tickets for tonight's match. Now, do you want one or shall I go on my own?

⊂___ 10 ⊃

2 Correct the mistakes.

1 You should think I'm just making excuses, but I'm not.
2 The village was nearly destroyed. Our house was blew down by the wind.
3 Mary went to the park. When she got there, Bill went already.
4 If I was arrested, I'll be scared.
5 You mustn't do that by yourself, I will you help.
6 I doubted if your wallet is here.
7 The machine is invented by an American firm in 1998.
8 Jackie waited for him since early this morning.
9 Let's go out, although the bad weather.
10 Richard said me he wouldn't be long.

⊂___ 10 ⊃

3 Make the sentences passive.

1 Spain beat Italy 3–2 last night.
2 Did the Spanish invent sangria?
3 A dog bit Patrick.
4 They don't sell cigarettes in sweet shops.
5 Someone will find a solution.
6 A friend gave me this book.
7 A firm in Taiwan makes these computers.
8 They opened the hospital last week.
9 They have arrested the mugger.
10 You can recharge this battery.

⊂___ 10 ⊃

4 Match the sentence halves to make complete sentences.

1 Even if I told you,
2 If you pass your driving test,
3 Let's go out
4 If I were you,
5 Paul will invent a gadget
6 He'd marry her
7 If we didn't have e-mail,
8 Of course he'd understand
9 We wouldn't ask you to the party
10 If the sun comes out,

a) if we didn't want you there.
b) they'll have a barbecue.
c) you'd never believe me.
d) tomorrow if he could.
e) we'd use a lot of stamps.
f) if you don't want to cook.
g) if you ask him to.
h) I'd be very careful.
i) we'll get a car.
j) if you explained it to him.

1 ____ 2 ____ 3 ____ 4 ____ 5 ____
6 ____ 7 ____ 8 ____ 9 ____ 10 ____

⊂___ 10 ⊃

5 Choose the correct option to complete the text.

[1] _____ of the [2] _____ rain smashing against the windscreen, we drove on through the night. The journey was only supposed to [3] _____ a few hours, but we thought it [4] _____ be dawn before we arrived at Castle Schlich. We decided to [5] _____ a point of arriving early to surprise the owners. [6] _____ , our plan didn't work as we thought it would. Only two hours after we'd set off, we had a [7] _____ to solve. A huge tree trunk lay in the road in front of us.

[8] _____ the time we found a way round the tree, it was beginning to get light. [9] _____ sun shone down on us as we walked slowly up the stone path to the castle gates. [10] _____ being exhausted, we were delighted to have reached our destination at last.

1 a) Despite   b) However   c) Although   d) In spite
2 a) bright   b) watery   c) heavy   d) thick
3 a) bring   b) take   c) continue   d) carry on
4 a) was   b) should   c) might   d) will
5 a) make   b) do   c) see   d) take
6 a) Because   b) However   c) Although   d) Despite
7 a) reason   b) trick   c) solution   d) problem
8 a) Since   b) To   c) By   d) Until
9 a) Light   b) Bright   c) Slight   d) Tight
10 a) Since   b) Because   c) Although   d) Despite

⊂___ 10 ⊃

Vocabulary

6 Underline the correct options.

Customer: Could I speak to the manager, please?
Receptionist: If you [1] *pass / give* me your name, I'll put you [2] *through / across*.
Customer: It's Jones. Mrs Jones
Receptionist: [3] *Hold / Wait* on, please. I [4] *doubt / believe* if he's in, but I'll try.

Thirty seconds later

Customer: Could [5] I *speak / call* to the manager, please? It's Mrs Jones.
Receptionist: Did you [6] *ring / talk* a minute ago?
Customer: I did, but I got [7] *shut / cut* off.
Receptionist: Oh, sorry. Just a moment. No, sorry the manager's [8] *in / on* the phone. Would you like to [9] *call / come* back?
Customer: Er, can I [10] *take / leave* a message?
Receptionist: Yes, of course.

| 10 |

7 Complete the sentences with the correct form of the words in brackets.

1 You will find details of flight times on the flight _____ screen. (inform)
2 Please proceed immediately to the _____ lounge. (depart)
3 All students will receive a _____ . (certify)
4 Your _____ card tells you which seat you are in. (board)
5 Can you _____ this problem for me? (solution)
6 All _____ must be in their cells by six o'clock. (prison)
7 You'll find the _____ kit in the cupboard with the jigsaws. (construct)
8 To be _____ in the movie industry, you have to be good looking. (success)
9 Marilyn Monroe's films are _____ . (legend)
10 Work really hard and maybe one day you'll be _____ . (fame)

| 10 |

8 Correct the ten mistakes in this text.

[1] My toddler enjoys playing with jigsaw puzzlings [2] but my daughter, who is five, prefers reading and boarding games. [3] Of course, both the teenagers are into compute games and spend hours surfing the Net. It doesn't worry me at all though. [4] I'm just gladly that they're enjoying themselves.

It's funny how things change. [5] I remember at their age we had to use paying phones, whereas now they've all got mobiles.

[6] My son thinks he'll be extremely famously when he's older. He's a very good football player. [7] His father used to play brilliant too.

[8] Both the boys are very fashiony. They're always out buying new clothes. My daughter is just the same, actually. [9] She's quieter, and writes a lot of originally poetry in her spare time. She's not a bad actress, either. [10] Just recently she made an audition for a play in our local theatre and got the part.

| 10 |

9 Tick (✓) the correct options.

1 Do you go on a business:
a) trip? ☐
b) journey? ☐
2 If you make an impression, do people:
a) remember you? ☐
b) forget you? ☐
3 Do you:
a) make your best? ☐
b) do your best? ☐
4 If something is described as a *waste*, it's:
a) good. ☐
b) bad. ☐
5 Are *cabin crew*:
a) people? ☐
b) things? ☐
6 If somebody makes you do something, you can choose whether you do it.
a) True. ☐
b) False. ☐
7 Is taking an exam the same as passing an exam?
a) Yes. ☐
b) No. ☐
8 Do you:
a) win a race? ☐
b) achieve a race? ☐
9 Which two nouns can you use with the verb *spend*?
a) money ☐
b) love ☐
c) time ☐
d) happiness ☐

| 10 |
| 90 |

Test 4

Grammar

1 Rewrite the questions in reported speech.

1 'What are your strengths?'
They asked me _____ .
2 'Do you have any weaknesses?'
She wanted _____ .
3 'Why do you want the job?'
He asked me _____ .
4 'Can you tell me why I should employ you?'
They wanted _____ .
5 'Have you worked in a large office before?'
She wondered _____ .
6 'How much experience of marketing do you have?'
He asked me _____ .
7 'What are your long-term goals?'
They wanted _____ .
8 'Can you give me any references?'
She asked me _____ .
9 'Are you good at working as part of a team?'
He wanted _____ .
10 'Why did you leave your last job?'
They wondered _____ .

(10)

2 Choose the correct option to complete the text.

The famous Cheops pyramid, [1] _____ is also known as the Great Pyramid, at Giza in Egypt is one of the world's most remarkable landmarks. Nowadays, we [2] _____ nothing of building vast structures, but it [3] _____ quite so easy in the days when there were no tractors, no cement mixers and no trucks to carry the stone. Perhaps you think that it [4] _____ centuries to build the Cheops pyramid, but it didn't. It took just 30 years.

King Cheops, [5] _____ was buried alone in the pyramid, [6] _____ great power because he was able to employ thousands of slaves. The work was so hard that the workers' life expectancy was very short. Many men [7] _____ during the construction. It [8] _____ an easy task – each stone weighed 2.5 tonnes. Researchers think that it [9] _____ as many as two million separate blocks of stone for the Ancient Egyptians to build the pyramid. They also believe that the slaves [10] _____ a form of sledge in order to drag them to the site.

1 a) who   b) that   c) which   d) what
2 a) think   b) are thinking   c) can think   d) must think
3 a) must be   b) can't have been   c) can't be
  d) must have been
4 a) must take   b) was taking   c) had taken   d) took
5 a) who   b) that   c) which   d) there
6 a) must have   b) must have had   c) hadn't
  d) can't have had
7 a) died   b) were dying   c) were dead
  d) had been dead
8 a) couldn't be   b) mustn't be   c) can't have been
  d) shouldn't be
9 a) might take   b) might have taken   c) must take
  d) can't take
10 a) must have had   b) can have had   c) must have
  d) can have

(10)

3 Underline the correct option.

1 *I've been ironing / I ironed* for so long that my arm aches.
2 I've *washed / been washing* the car – you should come and look at it.
3 By the time the meeting starts, I will *have written / write* the report.
4 I wish I *didn't buy / hadn't bought* this computer. It's useless.
5 Paddy *must have / could have* been here – the place is a mess!
6 There *won't / wouldn't* be so much to do if you kept your files in order.
7 Don't worry. I *will book / book* the tickets today.
8 Mary *hasn't been cleaning / doesn't clean* the house recently.
9 I discovered that the fridge *doesn't work / hasn't worked*.
10 If only my husband *would / will* do some gardening!

(10)

4 Underline the correct option.

By the time I'm forty, I [1] *understand / will have understood / can understand* how businesses [2] *plan / planned / will be planning* their advertising. Take chips, for example. Perhaps [3] *you've seen / you would see / you're seeing* the advert for 'crinkle-cut' chips. If you [4] *don't / didn't / haven't*, let me explain. A crinkle-cut chip is just the same as an ordinary chip except that a marketing department [5] *has played / was playing / had played* with it. Crinkle-cut chips are a funny shape. Apparently this makes them much more attractive to the consumer, and therefore sales [6] *increased / increase / will have increased*. It's strange, because I always thought that straight chips were pretty tasty. One day in the future, we [7] *are all forgetting / will all forget / all forget* what real chips look like, and that will be a sad day. What I [8] *like / will like / would like* to know is who decides these things? When I [9] *got / was getting / get* home from the supermarket the other day, I [10] *realised / was realising / realise* I'd bought a bag of crinkle-cut chips by mistake. I want a refund!

(10)

5 Tick (✓) the correct sentence in each pair.

1 a) If only I hadn't worn that shirt yesterday, I wouldn't have looked so absurd. ☐
  b) If only I didn't wear that shirt yesterday, I wouldn't look so absurd. ☐
2 a) Pete and Mark repaired the computer themself. ☐
  b) Pete and Mark repaired the computer themselves. ☐
3 a) He was tired because he'd been running all morning. ☐
  b) He was tired because he'd running all morning. ☐
4 a) The marketing strategy which was a great success won the contract. ☐
  b) The marketing strategy, which was a great success, won the contract. ☐
5 a) I'd prefer to go out tonight. ☐
  b) I'd prefer go out tonight. ☐
6 a) Will you have the car service at the garage? ☐
  b) Will you have the car serviced at the garage? ☐
7 a) We've kept in touch since we were children. ☐
  b) We kept in touch since we were children. ☐
8 a) She likes to know what you want for supper tonight. ☐
  b) She'd like to know what you want for supper tonight. ☐
9 a) He asked me what my strengths and weaknesses were. ☐
  b) He asked me what are my strengths and weaknesses. ☐
10 a) I think that weird noise can have been a bird. ☐
  b) I think that weird noise could have been a bird. ☐

☐ 10

Vocabulary

6 Find ten words to do with writers and writing.

B	O	P	N	W	P	U	E	T	N
K	E	O	O	L	K	T	K	P	E
O	K	S	A	E	I	N	U	N	W
O	W	Y	T	S	T	B	I	O	S
B	B	G	B	S	L	R	T	V	P
T	S	E	A	I	E	D	Y	E	A
X	W	W	S	X	W	L	W	L	P
E	L	H	F	B	E	H	L	B	E
T	E	W	R	I	T	E	R	E	R
R	E	N	I	Z	A	G	A	M	R

☐ 10

7 Correct the mistakes.

1 Doctor: What can I do for you?
 Patient: Well, I think I've been swollen by a bee.
2 Patient: I passed off last night and I don't feel well.
 Doctor: Really? How long were you unconscious for?
3 Patient: Doctor, my arm bites. It's horrible.
 Doctor: Well, don't scratch it.
4 Patient: I think I'm coming out in flu.
 Doctor: Let me take your temperature.
5 Patient: My face and back are all red.
 Doctor: Yes, you're coming out in a bite.
6 Doctor: How long have you had this nausea?
 Patient: A week. I feel sick all the time. I keep coming up.
7 Patient: Doctor, I've been stung by a very fierce dog.
 Doctor: Hmm. Did it bleed much?
8 Patient: I've got a dreadful headswell.
 Doctor: Have you taken any aspirin?
9 Doctor: How did you do that to your finger?
 Patient: I bit myself with a kitchen knife.
10 Patient: Doctor, will I turn over this?
 Doctor: Oh, yes. You'll be fine in a day or so.

☐ 10

8 Put these sentences A–H in the correct order. Then do the same with sentences I–O.

While you're in Bruges, why not go to the Sunday flea market?

A You'll find that you can get
B on impulse: when you're satisfied
C be frightened of haggling
D back, because it's a market, so be
E sure before you buy! Try not to buy
F some fantastic bargains. Don't
G for the thing you really want. You can't take things
H with the price, the deal is done.

I Take time to shop
J paintings and even local produce, such
K had enough of the market, why
L around the stalls. There are antiques,
M shopping in the beautiful cobbled streets?
N as lace and chocolate. And when you've
O not do a bit of window

1 ___ 2 ___ 3 ___ 4 ___ 5 ___
6 ___ 7 ___ 8 ___ 9 ___ 10 ___
11 ___ 12 ___ 13 ___ 14 ___ 15 ___

☐ 15

☐ 85

Test answer key

Test 1

1 1 b 2 d 3 a 4 b 5 c 6 a 7 c 8 d 9 b 10 c

2 1 could 2 you're going 3 I'm going to go 4 has never been 5 is going to be 6 managed to 7 didn't go 8 will 9 reached 10 I don't think John will

3 1 a 2 b 3 b 4 b 5 a 6 b 7 a 8 b 9 a 10 a

4 1 My name is Faith. I think it goes well ~~on~~ *with* my personality.
2 I was called ~~following~~ *after* my great-grandmother.
3 I like summertime best. It reminds me ~~by~~ *of* my childhood.
4 John once accused me ~~to~~ *of* being too romantic and sentimental.
5 I'm really ~~in~~ *into* music. I like jazz and classical best of all.
6 My brother has good taste ~~for~~ *in* clothes.
7 I saw a fantastic job last week, but I was too scared to apply ~~to~~ *for* it.
8 I went to a party and someone introduced me ~~with~~ *to* Karen.
9 Sam congratulated me ~~by~~ *on* my results.
10 Next year, I plan to take ~~on~~ *up* yoga.

5 1 an early riser. 2 got out of bed the wrong side.
3 have an early night. 4 have a lie-in. 5 keep my eyes open. 6 get a promotion. 7 going for an interview 8 in a team. 9 is ambidextrous.
10 a piece of cake.

6 1 qualifications 2 dishonesty 3 manageable 4 boiling 5 suggests (suggest)

7 1 A 2 F 3 B 4 D 5 I 6 G 7 C 8 H 9 J
10 E 11 K 12 Q 13 P 14 L 15 N 16 R
17 O 18 T 19 S 20 M

8 1 I'm really keen *on* sports.
2 I used ~~to~~ play a lot of hockey, but when I failed to get into the team I gave it up.
3 When I was younger, I couldn't swim, but now I swim a lot in order ~~to~~ keep fit.
4 Last year, I tried to learn to play ~~icy~~ *ice* hockey,
5 but I soon got ~~sickness~~ *sick* of being hurt – I kept falling over.
6 The only one I ~~don't~~ *can't* stand is rugby.
7 I like ~~take to take~~ */taking* part in loads of things,
8 especially ~~teaming~~ *team* activities.
9 It was quite hard, but I ~~manage~~ *managed* to do it in the end.
10 I was ~~exhausting~~ *exhausted* when I got home, though!

Test 2

1 1 lived 2 used to go 3 would 4 would 5 was
6 used to love 7 chose 8 had 9 would 10 built

2 1 j 2 i 3 f 4 d 5 a 6 h 7 e 8 b 9 c 10 g

3 1 Who was that girl you were putting ~~with~~ *up* last week?
2 She lives in the village ~~which~~ *where* I grew up, but she was in Oxford for a rehearsal.
3 She ~~stays~~ *is staying* at the hotel in Broad Street now.
4 Is she the cousin ~~whose~~ *who's* with the Shakespeare Acting Company?
5 They're doing a play ~~who~~ *which/that* hasn't been performed for years.
6 ~~Do you like~~ *Would you like/Do you want* to go and see it?
7 I must say, if I ~~am~~ *was/were* an actor, I'd get very nervous before a performance.
8 Yes, so ~~could~~ *would* I.
9 It starts at eight, so if we set ~~to~~ *off* at seven thirty, we'll get there on time.
10 Well, as long as the car doesn't break ~~off~~ *down*, that is.

4 1 a 2 b 3 a 4 a 5 b 6 b 7 b 8 a 9 b 10 b

5 1 c 2 b 3 d 4 c 5 a 6 b 7 d 8 c 9 b 10 c

6 1 wealthy 2 successful 3 engaged 4 dependent
5 Loneliness

7 1 e 2 g 3 f 4 h 5 c 6 i 7 j 8 d 9 b 10 a

8 **Across:** 3 withdraw 5 deposit 6 resources
8 success 12 vegetarian 13 marriage 14 health
Down: 1 addicted 2 time 4 determination
7 happiness 8 savings 9 chef 10 statement
11 divorce

9 1 a 2 b 3 a 4 a 5 b 6 b 7 b 8 b 9 b 10 b

Test 3

1 1 have; been   2 have been waiting   3 was arrested
   4 are wasting   5 have been chatting   6 have been
   doing   7 was kidnapped   8 photographed   9 have;
   fulfilled   10 have been queuing

2 1 You ~~should~~ may / might think I'm just making
     excuses, but I'm not.
   2 The village was nearly destroyed. Our house was
     ~~blew~~ blown down by the wind.
   3 Mary went to the park. When she got there, Bill
     ~~went already~~ had already gone.
   4 If I was arrested, ~~I'll~~ I'd be scared.
     If I ~~was~~ am arrested, I'll be scared.
   5 You mustn't do that by yourself, I will ~~you help~~ help
     you.
   6 ~~I doubted~~ doubt if your wallet is here.
   7 The machine ~~is~~ was invented by an American firm in
     1998.
   8 Jackie ~~waited~~ has been waiting for him since early
     this morning.
   9 Let's go out, ~~although~~ despite / in spite of the bad
     weather.
   10 Richard ~~said~~ told me he wouldn't be long.
      Richard said ~~me~~ he wouldn't be long.

3 1 Italy was beaten 3–2 by Spain last night.
   2 Was sangria invented by the Spanish?
   3 Patrick was bitten by a dog.
   4 Cigarettes aren't sold in sweet shops.
   5 A solution will be found.
   6 This book was given to me by a friend.
   7 The computers are made (by a firm) in Taiwan.
   8 The hospital was opened last week.
   9 The mugger has been arrested.
   10 This battery can be recharged.

4 1 c   2 i   3 f   4 h   5 g   6 d   7 e   8 j   9 a   10 b

5 1 d   2 c   3 b   4 c   5 a   6 b   7 d   8 c   9 b   10 d

6 1 give   2 through   3 Hold   4 doubt   5 speak
   6 ring   7 cut   8 on   9 call   10 leave

7 1 information   2 departure   3 certificate   4 boarding
   5 solve   6 prisoners   7 construction   8 successful
   9 legendary   10 famous

8 1 My toddler enjoys playing with jigsaw ~~puzzlings~~
     puzzles
   2 but my daughter, who is five, prefers reading and
     ~~boarding~~ board games.
   3 Of course, both the teenagers are into ~~compute~~
     computer games and spend hours surfing the Net.
   4 I'm just ~~gladly~~ glad that they're enjoying themselves.
   5 I remember at their age we had to use ~~paying~~ pay
     phones, whereas now they've all got mobiles.
   6 My son thinks he'll be extremely ~~famously~~ famous
     when he's older.
   7 His father used to play ~~brilliant~~ brilliantly too.
   8 Both the boys are very ~~fashiony~~ fashionable.
   9 She's quieter, and writes a lot of ~~originally~~ original
     poetry in her spare time.
   10 Just recently she ~~made~~ did / had an audition for a
      play in our local theatre and got the part.

9 1 a   2 a   3 b   4 b   5 a   6 b   7 b   8 a   9 a, c

Test 4

1 1 They asked me what my strengths were.
   2 She wanted to know if / whether I had any
     weaknesses.
   3 He asked my why I wanted the job.
   4 They wanted to know / me to tell them why they
     should employ me.
   5 She wondered if / whether I had worked in a large
     office before.
   6 He asked me how much experience of marketing I
     had.
   7 They wanted to know what my long-term goals
     were.
   8 She asked me if / whether I could give her any
     references.
   9 He wanted to know if / whether I was good at
     working as part of a team.
   10 They wondered why I (had) left my last job.

2 1 c   2 a   3 b   4 d   5 a   6 b   7 a   8 c   9 b   10 a

3 1 I've been ironing   2 washed   3 have written
   4 hadn't bought   5 must have   6 wouldn't
   7 will book   8 hasn't been cleaning   9 doesn't work
   10 would

4 1 will have understood   2 plan   3 you've seen
   4 haven't   5 has played   6 increase   7 will all forget
   8 would like   9 got   10 realised

5 1 a   2 b   3 a   4 b   5 a   6 b   7 a   8 b   9 a   10 b

6 bestseller, magazine, newspaper, novel, play, poetry,
   publisher, textbook, website, writer

7 1 Patient: Well, I think I've been ~~swollen~~ stung by a
                bee.
   2 Patient: I passed ~~off~~ out last night and I don't feel
                well.
   3 Patient: Doctor, my arm ~~bites~~ itches. It's horrible.
   4 Patient: I think I'm coming ~~out in~~ down with flu.
   5 Doctor: Yes, you're coming out in a ~~bite~~ rash.
   6 Patient: A week. I feel sick all the time. I keep
                ~~coming~~ throwing up.
   7 Patient: Doctor, I've been ~~stung~~ bitten by a very
                fierce dog.
   8 Patient: I've got a dreadful ~~headswell~~ headache.
   9 Patient: I ~~bit cut~~ cut myself with a kitchen knife.
   10 Patient: Doctor, will I ~~turn~~ get over this?

8 1 A   2 F   3 C   4 G   5 D   6 E   7 B   8 H   9 I
   10 L   11 J   12 N   13 K   14 O   15 M

THE PASSPORT

Choose a title that sounds interesting and gives some information about the subject of the story.

At the beginning of the story, set the scene. You often say when and where the story happened and you use the past continuous to say what was happening at the time.

Use the past simple to describe the main events of the story.

It was nine o'clock in the morning, and I was sitting in Madrid Charmartín station, waiting for my train to Paris, which was leaving at six in the evening. I was absolutely exhausted, because I had only slept a few hours on the night train from Málaga to Madrid.

I was feeling hungry, so I had breakfast in a café, and <u>then</u> went to the nearest bank to change some money. When I got there, I opened my money belt to get out my passport and traveller's cheques. To my horror, I couldn't find my passport anywhere. <u>Suddenly</u>, I realised what had happened. I had been in a hurry and had left it in my hotel room in Málaga. I immediately asked a bank clerk for directions to the American Embassy.

When I got to the embassy, an official told me I needed an emergency passport, but I would have to wait five to six hours.

Eventually, at five p.m., I got my emergency passport, and fortunately an official gave me a lift back to the station. I got there just in time! I felt very relieved when I got on the train and I knew I was on the way to Paris.

Use linking words like *then* to connect the different events of the story, and 'drama' words like *suddenly* to make the story more interesting.

Use the past perfect to talk about what happened before the time of the story, not to describe the events of the story.

Useful language
- Linking words:
  and then, after that, before -ing, after -ing
- 'Drama' words:
  suddenly, unfortunately, to his / her surprise

Teaching notes

1 Write the word 'stories' on the board. Elicit different types of stories, e.g. 'funny', 'sad', 'news'.

2 Tell students they are going to see some key words from a story entitled 'The Passport'. Write the following on the board:
five p.m. – breakfast – Madrid station – emergency passport – traveller's cheques –
nine a.m. – embassy – five to six hours – couldn't find passport

3 Students work in pairs / groups to try to put the key words in the correct order.

4 If necessary, draw a map of Spain with Madrid and Málaga on it.

5 Give out the model and go through it with students. Ask them to find other examples of 'drama' words in the text and add them to the list. Check meaning and use of linking and 'drama' words.

6 Lessons 1 and 21 in the Students' Book give practice in this type of writing.

Click on:
- the **Get Msg** (= Get message) button to check for new e-mails
- the **New Msg** (= New message) button to compose a new e-mail
- the **Reply** button to answer an e-mail
- the **Reply to All** button if an e-mail was sent to

you and other people, and you want your answer to go to the sender and the other people.
- the **Forward** button if you receive an e-mail and want to send it to another person.

(Note: there may be slight differences between browsers.)

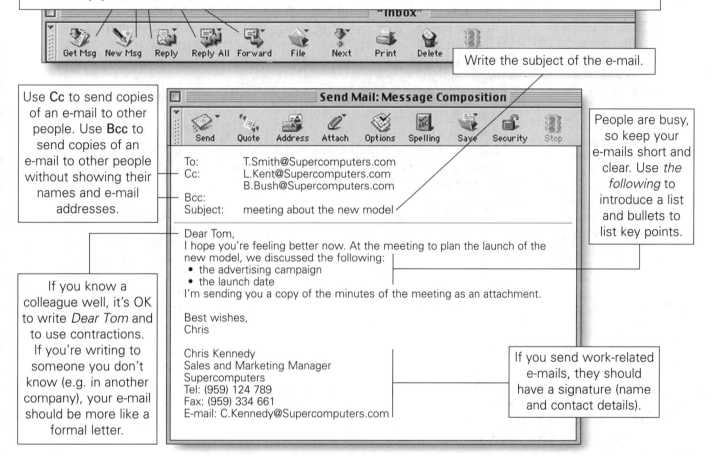

Use **Cc** to send copies of an e-mail to other people. Use **Bcc** to send copies of an e-mail to other people without showing their names and e-mail addresses.

Write the subject of the e-mail.

People are busy, so keep your e-mails short and clear. Use *the following* to introduce a list and bullets to list key points.

If you know a colleague well, it's OK to write *Dear Tom* and to use contractions. If you're writing to someone you don't know (e.g. in another company), your e-mail should be more like a formal letter.

If you send work-related e-mails, they should have a signature (name and contact details).

To: T.Smith@Supercomputers.com
Cc: L.Kent@Supercomputers.com
B.Bush@Supercomputers.com
Bcc:
Subject: meeting about the new model

Dear Tom,
I hope you're feeling better now. At the meeting to plan the launch of the new model, we discussed the following:
- the advertising campaign
- the launch date
I'm sending you a copy of the minutes of the meeting as an attachment.

Best wishes,
Chris

Chris Kennedy
Sales and Marketing Manager
Supercomputers
Tel: (959) 124 789
Fax: (959) 334 661
E-mail: C.Kennedy@Supercomputers.com

Useful language

- You can *send / open an attachment.*
  attach a file / folder.
  compose / reply to / forward an e-mail.
- These are some of the most common abbreviations:

CUL8R	*See you later.*
BTW	*By the way ...*

HAND	*Have a nice day.*
TA	*Thanks again.*
PLS	*Please.*
B4	*before*
RUOK	*Are you OK?*
IMO	*In my opinion ...*
2	*to, too, two*

Teaching notes

1 Write the following comments on the board: *I hate Mondays ... all those e-mails to answer* and *I love checking my e-mails to catch up on all the gossip.*

2 Have students work in pairs / groups to discuss the reasons for the two different attitudes to e-mails, and give feedback.

3 Tell students they are going to read an e-mail. They should answer the questions: *What is the e-mail about? Who is writing to whom?*

4 Give out the model and go through it with students.

5 Lessons 6 and 25 in the Students' Book give practice in this type of writing.

Choose a title that makes the place sound interesting.

First, introduce the place. Say where it is and give some general information.

Use *if* + verb phrase + imperative or just the imperative to give advice about what to do, see etc.

Shanghai – city of the past and the future

Shanghai, China's largest city, is situated on the Huangpu River and is divided into two areas: Pudong (east of the river) and Puxi (west of the river). Pudong is the business centre of the city, but if you are a tourist, you will want to cross the river and visit Puxi. Puxi has a lot to offer, and the best way to get around is the subway system. If you want to go shopping, walk down Nanjing Lu, Shanghai's main shopping area. If you're hungry, try Frenchtown, where you will find a lot of different restaurants. Shanghai also has a very impressive new museum, which is really worth visiting, and there are also parks and gardens where you can relax.

It is easy to get to, and the best times to visit are spring and autumn. Avoid winter, because it can get very cold, and in summer it is hot and humid. So if you want to see the old and the new China, visit Shanghai!

Then give information about the place, for example about sightseeing, the nightlife, transport, the weather etc. Use different paragraphs.

Useful language

*   Tourist attractions:
    It/The museum is worth visiting / seeing.
    You should visit the market.
    The boat trip is a must.
    Don't miss the street carnival.

Teaching notes

1   Elicit/Supply the following areas connected with travel and write them on the board: *location, weather, sightseeing, eating out, shopping, getting there, accommodation, getting around*. Check the meaning.
    Then put students into pairs/groups to discuss what is (not) important when they visit a place.
2   Tell students they are going to read a travel article about Shanghai.

3   Hand out article. As they read, students underline any information about the areas on the board and identify which areas are not mentioned (getting there and accommodation).
4   Ask students to look at the sentences in **Useful language**. Elicit what all the sentences are used for. Elicit/Supply *recommending*.
5   Lesson 9 in the Students' Book gives practice in this type of writing.

Informal letters

Don't put the address you are writing to.

Use *Dear* + name to begin, not ~~*Dear friend*~~.

To introduce and add new information, use these words and phrases.

To end your letter, use:
- *(All my) love* for very good friends and family;
- *Take care* for close friends;
- *Best wishes* for friends and people you know less well.

Angel Acuna 1020
3301 Posadas-Misiones
Argentina

16th December

Dear Suzi,

Thanks for your letter. It was great to hear from you. I'm sorry I haven't written sooner, but I've been very busy.

So what's new? Well, as you can see from the address, I'm not living with my parents any more. I've moved into a flat nearer my job. It's got a spare room, so you can stay with me when you come and visit next summer! I've also just had a pay increase at work. Great isn't it? I was really surprised because I've only been working there for six months.

What else? Well, I went to a party last week where I met this great guy. We spent the whole night chatting and dancing. I'm meeting him again this weekend! Who knows – maybe a new romance!.

Guess what? I got a letter from Toshi yesterday. You won't believe this, but he's getting married!

Well, that's all my news. Let me know how you are doing. I'm really looking forward to hearing from you!

Love,
Andrea

Write your address, but not your name.

Write the date underneath like this:
16th December / December 16th.
Add the year if you want.

An informal letter is like an informal conversation, so use the first and last paragraphs to say 'hello' and 'goodbye', and use contractions.

Useful language

- First lines:
  How are you doing? I'm fine.
  How are you? I hope you're well.
  I'm sorry I haven't written for so long.
- Last lines:
  Hope to hear from you soon.
  It'd (would) be great to hear from you.
  Keep in touch.

- Giving advice:
  If I were you, I'd + verb
  I (don't) think you should + verb
- Requests, invitations and suggestions:
  Could you ... ?
  Would you like to ... ?
  Do you fancy + -ing?
  How / What about + -ing?

Teaching notes

1 Put students into pairs / groups to brainstorm what people write in informal letters. Give feedback. If necessary, elicit / supply the following: *personal news, plans.*

2 Elicit the grammar used to talk about these topics (e.g. present perfect for things that the writer has done since he / she last wrote, present continuous for things he / she is doing at the moment).

3 Tell students they are going to read an informal letter. They should underline any examples of the topics (e.g. personal news: *I'm not living with my parents any more*; plans: *I'm meeting him again this weekend*). Give out the model and go through it with students.

4 Lessons 14 and 15 of the Students' Book give practice in this type of writing. .

Write the name and address of the person you are writing to. If you don't know their name, write their job title (e.g. Sales Manager, Managing Director).

Write your address, but not your name, in the top right corner.

Write the date in full (either *14th January 2002* or *January 14th 2002*) under both addresses, either on the left or on the right.

18 Fleet Street
Dublin 1
Ireland

Ms S. Jones
West Coast Apartments
2000 Neilson Boulevard
Santa Monica
California

14th January 2002

Dear Ms Jones,

I am writing as I would like to rent a holiday apartment. According to *The Five-Star Travel Guide to California*, you specialise in luxurious holiday apartments and that is what I am looking for.

I would like to rent a fully furnished, five-bedroom apartment with private pool in the Long Beach or Santa Monica areas of Los Angeles during the month of July.

Therefore, <u>I would</u> be grateful if you could <u>supply</u> me with the following information:

• First of all, I would like details of all the apartments you have available in July, including information about the facilities which are provided, such as a laundry service, sauna, private tennis courts etc.
• In addition to that, I would like to know if you are able to arrange car hire and if it is included in the price of the apartment.

I look forward to hearing from you in the near future.

Yours sincerely,

Brendan Fitzpatrick

Brendan Fitzpatrick

Use Dear *Ms / Mr Jones* to start. If you don't know the person's name, write *Dear Sir / Madam*.

Don't use contractions (*I would* instead of *I'd*). Try to use formal vocabulary, e.g. *supply* instead of *give*.

Use *the following* to introduce a list and *First of all* and *In addition to* that to list the different information.

If you know the person's name, end with *Yours sincerely*. If you don't know their name, end with *Yours faithfully* (UK) or *Yours truly* (US). Then sign and print your name.

Useful language

• First lines:
I am writing (as I would like) to ...
I am writing in response to your letter of (date).
I am writing (as I would like to) apologise for + noun/-ing
• Last lines:
I hope you will consider my application / look into the matter.
I look forward to hearing from you.

• Requesting:
I would appreciate it if you could / would + verb
• Formal/informal register:
I want to = I would like to / I wish to
give = supply
so = therefore
because = as
• Forms of address:
Mrs and *Miss* can be used instead of *Ms* for women if you know their marital status.

Teaching notes

1 Write these verbs on the board: *complain about, ask for, confirm, apply for* and check meaning.
2 Elicit why people write formal letters. Use these nouns as prompts: *a holiday, a job, a bank loan, a hotel booking, information.*
3 Tell students they are going to read a formal letter. Hand out the letter and have them answer the questions: *Who is the letter to?* (someone who specialises in renting luxury apartments in California) and *Why is the person writing?* (to ask about renting an apartment).
4 Lessons 26 and 36 in the Students' Book give practice in this type of writing.

Letters of application

Write the name and address of the person you are writing to.
If you don't know their name, write their job title (e.g. Sales Manager, Managing Director).

Write your address, but not your name in the top right corner.

Nowy Świat 50
00-472 Warsaw
Poland

The Personnel Manager
Britair
Heathrow Airport
London

15th December 2002

Write the date in full (either *15th December 2002* or *December 15th 2002*) under both addresses, either on the left or on the right.

Dear Sir/Madam,

I am writing in response to the advertisement on your website for flight attendants.
My name is Agnieszka Cezary and I am 23 years old. At present, I am working as a tour guide on sightseeing tours of Warsaw. I have been doing this since I graduated from Warsaw University last year. As you can see from my CV, I have a degree in modern languages and can speak English, French and German fluently. In my job, I mainly accompany tourists on half-day and full-day tours of Warsaw. However, I sometimes have to accompany five-day tours of Poland, when I am responsible for looking after the tourists. When I was a student, I also had a part-time job at the information desk at Warsaw airport.
I believe I would make a good flight attendant as I enjoy meeting people and have good communication skills.
I enclose my CV and look forward to hearing from you.

Use *Dear Sir/Madam* to start if you don't know the person's name. If you do, write *Dear Ms/Mr Jones*.

Don't use contractions (*I am* instead of *I'm*). Try to use formal vocabulary, e.g. *accompany* instead of *go with*.

If you don't know the person's name, end with *Yours faithfully* (UK) or *Yours truly* (US). If you do know their name, end with *Yours sincerely*. Then sign and print your name.

Yours faithfully,

Agnieszka Cezary

Agnieszka Cezary

Useful language

- First lines:
  I am writing in reply to the advertisement in The Times *of 12th December for* (job name).
  I am writing to apply to join the Carlton Club.
- Last lines:
  I hope you will consider my application.

- Describing jobs/skills:
  I am responsible for ...
  I have to ...
  I have good managerial/communication skills.

Teaching notes

1 Elicit the key elements of a job application letter from students, for example *Why you?*, *qualifications*, *present job*, *experience*, and write them on the board. Students work in pairs/groups to decide the order they normally appear in a job application letter. Give feedback.

2 Tell students they are going to read a job application letter. Hand it out and have them read it and compare the order in the letter with their order.
3 Go through it with students to check understanding.
4 Lesson 27 in the Students' Book gives practice in this type of writing.

Write the subject of the essay/discussion.

First, write a general introduction to the subject of the discussion.

Use linking words like *First of all* to present the advantages/disadvantages.

Use words like *However* to introduce a contrast and *In conclusion* to introduce the summary.

Mobile phones – Good or Bad?

Everywhere you go nowadays, you see people using mobile phones. From schoolchildren to retired people, you see them talking in supermarkets, on trains, in the street, everywhere! So what are the advantages of mobile phones? First of all, they are very convenient because you can phone from nearly anywhere. Another advantage is they are really useful in emergency situations. For example, if you are alone in your car and it breaks down, you can get help quickly. In addition, you can also use your mobile to text your friends or connect to the Net.

However, there are also disadvantages, such as the cost. Mobile phone calls cost more than normal calls. Furthermore, it can be annoying if you are on a train or a bus and you have to listen to someone else's boring conversation. Finally, people can contact you anywhere, at any time, unless you switch your phone off!

In conclusion, there are both advantages and disadvantages. Personally, I feel mobile phones are a good thing because they give us more freedom and make communication easier.

In the second and third paragraphs, introduce and present the advantages and disadvantages. Try to give examples.

In the last paragraph, give a short summary, along with your opinion and reasons.

Useful language
- Other linking words:
  Firstly, ...
  Secondly, ...
  Thirdly, ...
  What's more, ...
  Lastly, ...
  On the other hand, ...
- Giving opinions:
  In my opinion, ...
  As far as I'm concerned, ...
- Summarising:
  To sum up, ...

Teaching notes
1 Ask students to suggest things that make communication easier and quicker to elicit *mobile phones*.
2 Students work in pairs/groups to brainstorm the advantages and disadvantages of mobile phones. Encourage them to find at least three advantages and three disadvantages. Feedback and write up ideas on the board.
3 Tell students they are going to read an essay/discussion on mobile phones. Hand out the model and have them read the text to find any pros/cons that aren't on the board.
4 Go through it with students to check understanding.
5 Ask students to identify places in the text where they could substitute linking phrases from the **Useful language** section.